The Boleyn Women

ABOUT THE AUTHOR

Elizabeth Norton gained her first degree from the University of Cambridge and her Masters from the University of Oxford. She is the author of ten books on the Tudors. She lives in London.

PRAISE FOR ELIZABETH NORTON

Catherine Parr

'Scintillating... Norton cuts an admirably clear path through tangled Tudor intrigues'
JENNY UGLOW, *THE FINANCIAL TIMES*

'Eminently readable... Norton's strength is in her use of original sources'
SARAH GRISTWOOD, *BBC HISTORY MAGAZINE*

Bessie Blount

'Secret of the queen that Britain "lost"' *THE SUN*

'A lucid, readable, intelligent account of the life of a woman who might have been queen'
THE GOOD BOOK GUIDE

Anne Boleyn: In Her Own Words & the Words of Those
Who Knew Her

'A very useful compilation of source material on Anne Boleyn... a well produced book'
ALISON WEIR

The Boleyn Women

The Tudor femmes fatales who changed English history

ELIZABETH
NORTON

AMBERLEY

For my son, Barnaby

First published in 2013

This edition first published 2014

Amberley Publishing
The Hill, Stroud
Gloucestershire, GL5 4EP

www.amberley-books.com

Copyright © Elizabeth Norton, 2013, 2014

The right of Elizabeth Norton to be identified
as the Author of this work has been asserted in
accordance with the Copyrights, Designs and
Patents Act 1988.

ISBN 978 1 4456 4047 1 (paperback)
ISBN 978 1 4456 1808 1 (ebook)

British Library Cataloguing in Publication Data.
A catalogue record for this book is available
from the British Library.

Typesetting and Origination by Amberley Publishing

Printed in the UK.

CONTENTS

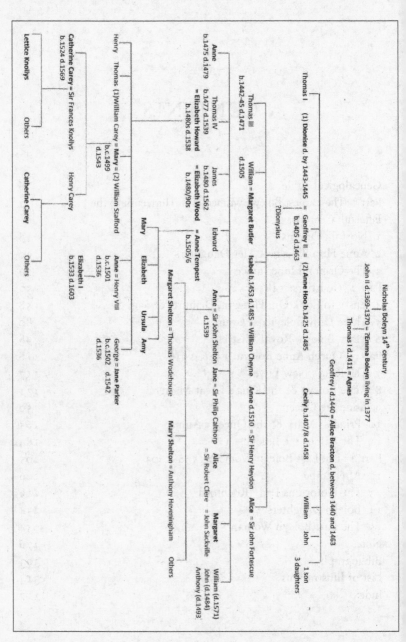

1. The Boleyn women genealogical table.

Part 1
The Earliest Boleyn Women:
The Thirteenth to the Fifteenth
Centuries

I

NORFOLK ORIGINS

The Boleyn family came to international prominence through the marriage of Anne Boleyn to Henry VIII in 1533. This match, which proved so disastrous for the parties involved, produced Elizabeth I, a queen who was arguably one of the greatest rulers England has ever had. Elizabeth I, as the daughter of a Boleyn, must take her place among the other members of a family which produced a large number of remarkable women. From the queens, Elizabeth I and Anne Boleyn, to the royal mistress, Mary Boleyn, to Anne Boleyn, Lady Shelton, who acted as governess of Princess Mary to Elizabeth Howard, Lady Boleyn, the mother of Queen Anne and her sister, Mary, to Lettice Knollys, a Boleyn granddaughter, who won the heart of Elizabeth I's greatest love, the family produced remarkable and active women, who rivalled and, sometimes, surpassed the men of the family in their political ambition. This is the story of the women of the family, both those who joined the family through marriage and those who were born a Boleyn lady. The family rose from the rank of yeoman, or tenant farmer, to the highest position in the land through the agency of its women, before disappearing once again into obscurity with the death of Elizabeth I, the greatest of the Boleyn women.

The family's origins were deeply unpromising and an observer in the thirteenth, fourteenth and even fifteenth century would never have dreamed that the family would produce two queens of England. The name Boleyn and its various spellings (such as its modern form, Bullen) was not an unusual one. It has been suggested that the name, which was often pronounced and spelled in the same way as the name of the city of Boulogne, denoted a French origin for the family.[1] This is not impossible, but it need not be the case. The earliest ancestors who can be identified were firmly rooted in the county of Norfolk.

The first ancestor who can be identified with any certainty was a John Boleyn, who was living in the Norfolk village of Salle in 1283 when he was noted in the Register of Walsingham Abbey.[2] This John was associated with a William Boleyn of Thurning who can presumably be identified as a kinsman. A Simon de Boleyne had previously purchased land at Salle in 1252 and he was perhaps the father of John and William.[3] The next recorded Boleyn of Salle was a Nicholas Boleyn, who was accused of theft in 1318.[4] This Nicholas was a turbulent individual, robbing a man in Lincoln in 1333. That same year Nicholas was ordered by one of the manorial courts in Salle to repair the bank between his land and that of the lord of the manor after he had damaged pastures and trees. At the same time a second John Boleyn makes an appearance in surviving documents relating to Salle, dying soon after his last appearance in 1369. An Emma Boleyn was noted in the Court Rolls for 1377 and it was suggested by W. L. E. Parsons, who carried out a comprehensive review of the early records of the Boleyn family, that she could be identified as John Boleyn II's widow. If so, she is the first known Boleyn lady. Nothing further is known of her.

John Boleyn II can probably be identified as a son of Nicholas Boleyn. A second man, Thomas Boleyn, was identified as a son of Nicholas Boleyn in a later court case brought by his great-grandson in the fifteenth century. However, given that Thomas Boleyn I only begins to appear in the records in 1370, holding much of the same land as the recently deceased John Boleyn II, he is more likely the son of John than of Nicholas. For Nicholas to have committed theft in 1318, he must have been born by at least 1300. Thomas Boleyn I was still active in 1399 and did not die until 1411, suggesting that he would have been too young to be a son of Nicholas. He is more likely his grandson.

Thomas Boleyn I was married to a lady named Agnes in 1398 when the couple secured an indulgence from the pope.[5] Once again, the life of this Boleyn lady is almost entirely obscure. In March 1386 Thomas Boleyn I was associated with one Martin Taverham and a Margaret Anabille in a writ relating to their role as executors for Richard Anabille of Salle.[6] Margaret was the widow of Richard Anabille and it has been suggested that she became Thomas's first wife, something which would also make her the more plausible candidate for the mother of his son Geoffrey Boleyn I, who produced his own children in the early years of the fifteenth century (a daughter, for example, is known to have been born in 1408).[7] However, she was certainly not Thomas's wife in March 1386 and there is no further evidence of a connection between the pair. It therefore seems more probable that Agnes was the only wife of Thomas Boleyn I and the mother of Geoffrey Boleyn I.

Nicholas Boleyn, in spite of his evidently turbulent lifestyle, had been a member of the minor gentry, as is clear from a court case heard in 1463 in which Nicholas's great-great-grandson, Thomas Boleyn II, claimed a manor at Calthorpe, called Hookhall 'as his right and inheritance'.[8] According to Thomas Boleyn II, Nicholas was the rightful holder of this manor following a grant from Edward III. He was dispossessed by Sir Bartholemew Calthorpe and thus unable to pass it on to his descendants. Thomas Boleyn II was successful in his claim for the manor, suggesting that there was indeed substance in his claims. His nephew, William Boleyn, held the manor at his own death in 1505.[9] In 1463, the manor was worth £19, a not insubstantial sum. However, it is perhaps fair to say that, while the family may have had tenuous claims to gentle status they were more appropriately part of the yeoman class – prosperous tenant farmers, with the focus of their activities at Salle. Thomas Boleyn I leased 6½ acres of land at Salle in 1370. Norfolk in the fifteenth century was wealthy, with the wool trade being particularly important. Thomas Boleyn I was wealthy enough by 1399 to pass some of his land at Salle over to his son Geoffrey, a gift which saw him appear before the manorial court for failure to seek the appropriate permission. An eighteenth-century visitor to the church at Salle recorded that there was a window with a fragmentary inscription to a Thomas Boleyn.[10] Given the fact that the church was built in the early fifteenth century, this window would seem likely to have been a gift made by Thomas Boleyn I, as suggested by Parsons in his history of the parish. This gift would accord both with the piety of Thomas and his wife, Agnes, as evidenced by their request for a papal indulgence and of the rapidly rising status of the Boleyn family in the parish. Nothing more is known of Agnes Boleyn. Thomas Boleyn I died in 1411.

It was Geoffrey Boleyn I, in the early years of the fifteenth century, who extended the family's local prominence. In spite of its small size, Salle supported four manors in the medieval period, all of which were established by the time of the Domesday Book.[11] Salle is now a very small settlement and there is no evidence that its size was very much larger in the late medieval period. It has been estimated that the population of the parish has never been more than 400–500.[12] As such, its church, which has been likened to a small cathedral, is very much at odds with the village and was clearly conceived as a monument to the prosperity of the settlement and its citizens. As Eamon Duffy set out in his study of the parish and church, 'this huge building was never full and was never intended to be full; its space was intended as the setting for elaborate liturgy and processions, involving the whole parish, but also for the smaller-scale worship in screened-off side chapels, which housed the daily and occasional activities of the guilds and family chantry-chapels'. The nave of the church bears the arms of Henry V as Prince of Wales over a doorway, something which suggests that at least part of the structure was built between 1405 and 1413 (before Henry V's accession to the throne). As such, Thomas Boleyn I and his wife may well have taken an active interest in the building work, as evidenced by the window inscription. Their son, Geoffrey Boleyn I, was one of the leading builders.

In 1408 Geoffrey Boleyn I found himself before the manorial court with six other men, who were all accused of entering the lord's manor without permission and occupying part of it with the timber that they had prepared for the church.[13] At the same time they had also broken down one small building on the site, as well as despoiled the lord's possessions in the manor house. This was an offence of some seriousness since it represented a direct contravention of the social order in Salle, with tenants actively despoiling the lands of the lord of the manor and, as such, it was deemed too weighty a matter to be dealt with by the manorial court, with the lord and his council to instead consult on a fitting punishment. The reference to the timber for the church makes it clear that Geoffrey was fully involved in the building of Salle's grand new church, a building that was largely completed by the newly rich lower-ranking members of the parish, such as the Boleyns, rather than the more established gentry. Later that same year, Geoffrey was once again before the court, this time with the parson of the church at Salle, with both men accused of occupying a ditch or bank belonging to the lord of the manor without permission so that they could store a great ash tree. The assumption must be that this timber was also required for the church and, this time, Geoffrey was dealt with more leniently, being merely ordered to remove the tree within seven days or face its forfeiture.

Geoffrey often found himself on the wrong side of his lord during the first half of the fifteenth century. In 1412 he was accused of ploughing over a field division in order to extend his own land at the expense of his social betters.[14] He took water belonging to one of the manors in Salle without making any payment, something that resulted in his regular appearances in court between 1419 and

1439 when he finally capitulated and paid a fine. Geoffrey was an ambitious man and acquired a number of pieces of land in Salle and neighbouring parishes, not always paying the specified sums for the land when they fell due.[15] He must have been a substantial man in the town by the time of his death in 1440, but he remained below the rank of a lord. He farmed approximately 30 acres and was prosperous, for example in 1424 selling six loads of barley and oat straw for thatching to the lord of Kirkhall manor in Salle. He, like most of his neighbours, would also have kept sheep.[16] It is the church however which stands as a monument to his prosperity. A memorial brass, commissioned by Geoffrey for both him and his wife, Alice, stands prominently in the middle aisle of the church and testifies to his importance to the building of the church at Salle.

Geoffrey's wife, Alice, is, like her predecessors as Boleyn ladies, a shadowy figure. She was apparently as pious as her husband as the pair are known to have made a gift to the church at Salle of a hearse cloth of tapestry work and two matching cushions.[17] These may well have been decorated with the couple's names and badges and would have further served as a reminder of their important role in the foundation of the new church. Alice was an excellent match for Geoffrey socially, as the daughter and heiress of Sir John Bracton of Bracton.[18] Based on the dates of birth of their children, the couple must have married in the early years of the fifteenth century. The gift of land in Salle that Thomas Boleyn I made to Geoffrey in 1399 would seem to be a probable marriage gift to the couple: an heiress was never acquired cheaply and Alice's father would have insisted on substantial provision being made for her on her marriage. It is a testament to the prosperity of Thomas Boleyn I (and, perhaps, his claims to be a member of the gentry through his grandfather, Nicholas) that he was able to secure a wealthy gentlewoman for his son.

A representation of Alice Bracton Boleyn survives in her funeral brass at Salle. Alice survived her husband, who died in 1440 and she is therefore very likely to have played a role in the commission of the monument and its design. Her representation can therefore be considered an accurate view of how she wished to be presented. The brass shows Geoffrey and Alice standing side by side. Both are dressed fashionably, with Geoffrey wearing a cap and knee-length gown with large hanging sleeves. Alice is depicted wearing a pleated floor-length gown, again with hanging sleeves which are gathered up at the cuff. In keeping with the fashion of the period, she wears a large headdress of cloth which entirely covers her hair and hangs down over her shoulders. The pair stare forward from the brasses. Over their heads, there is a scroll which can be translated as 'God be merciful to us sinners'.[19] Underneath, the inscription reads 'Here lies Geoffrey Boleyn, who died 25 March 1440, and Alice his wife and their children: on whose souls may God have mercy. Amen.' The depictions on the brasses, which are likely to be true likenesses, are conventional for the period and demonstrate that the couple saw themselves as local dignitaries, important in the parish and local area.

A visitor to the church in the late eighteenth century noted that the memorial to Geoffrey and Alice also originally included depictions of their five sons and four daughters. Only three of their children can be identified with any certainty and this, coupled with the fact that the brass inscription referred to their children being buried with them, suggests that a number died before adulthood, as was all too common in the fifteenth century. The names of only two sons are known and, given the fact that both became prominent, it would seem highly likely that their three brothers did not survive to adulthood and to build their own distinguished careers. Certainly, a Simon Boleyn, who served as a priest at Salle and has a memorial in the church there, should not be identified as their son. Simon, who died in 1482, left a will dated 1478 in which he referred to a sister Joan and brothers James and Thomas of Gunthorp.[20] He also mentioned a niece, Joan, who was the daughter of his brother

Thomas. Since Geoffrey and Alice's son Thomas was a priest, it seems highly unlikely that he is the brother referred to (due to the requirement for celibacy). Also, there is no known connection between Geoffrey's son Thomas and Gunthorp. More likely the relationship was considerably more distant. Parsons suggested that Geoffrey Boleyn I could be identified as Simon Boleyn's great-uncle. Heraldic visitations taken of the families of Norfolk in 1563 and 1613 recorded the names of two further brothers of Geoffrey Boleyn II (a son of Geoffrey Boleyn I and Alice): William, who was recorded to have married, and John.[21] However, visitations, which relied on the memories of family members, were often inaccurate. In this case, the parents of the brothers are listed as Thomas Bullen of Salle and his wife Jane, daughter and co-heir of Sir John Bracton. While the visitation appears to have been reasonably accurate with regard to the lineage of Geoffrey Boleyn II's mother (if not her Christian name), it entirely omitted Geoffrey Boleyn I as their father. Given that there are no surviving records relating to William or John, their existence is doubtful. They can, perhaps, also be identified as children of Thomas Boleyn I rather than his grandchildren. The visitations are highly doubtful for the Boleyn family as Anne Boleyn III, who married Sir John Shelton and will be discussed later, was also described as a daughter of her brother, Thomas Boleyn IV, Earl of Wiltshire and Ormond, something that would have made her a sister of her namesake, Queen Anne Boleyn, rather than her aunt.

Given the fact that women married and changed their names (and often led less prominent lives) it is probable that more of the daughters of Geoffrey and Alice survived infancy. An Alice Boleyn married a gentleman, Henry Aucher of Otterden in Kent, a marriage which would place her birth date at around 1410.[22] This Alice bore her husband two sons, John and Henry. It is not at all impossible that she can be identified as a daughter of Geoffrey Boleyn I and Alice Bracton Boleyn. However, there is no further evidence of her parentage and the name Boleyn was not uncommon – any identification must therefore be tenuous. The only daughter of Geoffrey and Alice who can be certainly identified is Cecily. Geoffrey Boleyn II, who was by far the most prosperous early member of the family, purchased the fine manor of Blickling in Norfolk, moving the centre of the family's interests there from Salle. He evidently took his unmarried sister, Cecily, there with him as a fine brass survives to her in the church next to the manor, recording that 'Here lieth Cecily Boleyn, sister to Geoffrey Boleyn, lord of the manor of Blickling, which Cecily deceased in her maidenhood, of the age of L [50] years, the xxvi [26] day of June the year of our lord MCCCClviij [1458], whose soul God pardon Amen'.

Cecily was born between 27 June 1407 and 26 June 1408, making her the youngest of the three known children of Geoffrey Boleyn I and Alice Bracton Boleyn (with Thomas as the eldest son and Geoffrey II born in 1405). Her memorial brass, which was commissioned by her brother Geoffrey, shows a woman with her hands at prayer and downcast eyes. She is bare-headed, with a large (and very likely plucked) forehead, which was the height of fashion in the late fifteenth century. Cecily is depicted simply dressed in a pleated high-necked gown drawn in beneath her breasts. Her sleeves are full and hanging with plain under-sleeves glimpsed at the wrists. The simplicity of Cecily's pose and dress can be contrasted sharply with that of her niece, Isabel Boleyn Cheyne, who is also commemorated on a brass at Blickling and appears in a furred gown with jewellery and an elaborate headdress. Given the emphasis on the fact that Cecily died a maid, coupled with the fact that she described herself as the spiritual daughter of Thomas Drew, the chaplain at Salle, who died in 1443 and bequeathed her a rosary, it does appear that there was a pious motive to Cecily remaining unmarried.[23] This did not extend as far as taking holy vows and she evidently remained at Salle with her parents until at least 1443. Alice survived her husband, who died in 1440, and her daughter presumably remained with her until her death at an unknown date. After that, Cecily lived with her brother, Geoffrey. The siblings were close enough for Geoffrey Boleyn II to commission the fine memorial to his sister after her death in middle age.

The close relationship between Cecily and Geoffrey Boleyn II was echoed in the relationship between Geoffrey Boleyn II and his brother, Thomas Boleyn II, something which suggests that Geoffrey Boleyn I and Alice Bracton Boleyn enjoyed a contented family life as parents. It was Thomas who claimed to be the son and heir of Geoffrey Boleyn I in a court case in 1463 in which he claimed the manor of Calthorpe and he can therefore with certainty be identified as the eldest surviving son. Since Geoffrey II was born in 1405, this would place Thomas II's birth in the early years of the fifteenth century and he lived to a venerable age, dying in 1472. The fact that he became a priest, something which was unusual for an heir, suggests that he may originally have had an elder brother who predeceased him. Thomas was ordained as a deacon in March 1421 and then as a priest later in the year.[24] He was already a fellow of Trinity Hall at Cambridge at that time, something that suggests that he had studied at the university. He retained a connection with Cambridge for most of his life, becoming the seventh master of Gonville Hall (which later became Gonville and Caius College) in 1454. He was fond of the college and donated a window in the old dining hall there. Thomas was relatively well known in court circles and, in 1434, was chosen by the king to attend the Council of Basle – a singular honour. He was also selected by Henry VI to be one of six men to draft the statutes for Queen's College, Cambridge, in 1446 at the college's foundation.[25]

Thomas Boleyn II's career took him far from his family's agricultural origins in Salle and he was to have a career as prominent as that of his younger brother. There is strong evidence for affection between the two brothers in Geoffrey II's will, where he asked that '£20 sterling of my goods be dispended upon the work of the body of the church of Blickling aforesaid, or upon ornaments for the same church or on both, as shalbe thought most necessary by the discretion of my brother Master Thomas Boleyn, and of my executors'.[26] Geoffrey specifically asked that Thomas should attend a dinner held in his memory and that he should be one of the people asked to compose the guest list. Thomas, along with Geoffrey's wife and executors, was further given discretion over the distribution of bequests to Geoffrey's daughters, as well as being named as one of the people who were required to assent to the daughters' marriages. Thomas was finally paid the complement of being the overseer of Geoffrey's will.

The surviving evidence suggests strongly that Geoffrey Boleyn I and Alice Bracton Boleyn were able to build a contented family life, as well as launching their sons into prominent positions. Further testament to the family's close relationship can be seen in the will of Geoffrey Boleyn II, in which he left 200 marks to fund an 'honest and virtuous priest' to pray for Geoffrey II's soul 'and the soul of Dionise sometime my wife, and for the souls of Geoffrey and Alice my father and mother, and of Adam Book, and for the souls of all them that I am bounden unto'. Geoffrey II's parents were evidently still remembered fondly by him and he took steps to ensure the safety of their souls. Geoffrey's will, which is dated 1463, makes it clear that Alice Bracton Boleyn had already died although there is no further evidence for her date of death, save that it occurred between 1440 and 1463.

Geoffrey Boleyn II's first wife, Dionise, or Denise, is an even more shadowy figure. The mention of her in her husband's will is the only surviving evidence for the marriage. The recent suggestion that Dionise may have been the mother of Geoffrey's eldest surviving son, Thomas Boleyn III,[27] is highly likely to be false as Thomas referred to Geoffrey's second wife, Anne Hoo Boleyn, as his mother repeatedly in his own will and placed a good deal of trust in her in the document, including making her his executor, something that does suggest that she was more likely to have been his mother than her predecessor.[28] In all probability, the marriage to Dionise was a short one and she was soon supplanted by her more prominent successor, Anne Hoo. There is a tantalising hint in the records that she may have borne a child, and, in a list of early benefactors to Queen's College, Cambridge, which was founded in 1446 and with which Thomas Boleyn II was strongly associated, a Dionysius Boleyn appears alongside Geoffrey Boleyn II and Anne his wife, as well as Thomas Boleyn II.[29] The name Dionysius is so unusual that a comparison with the name Dionise must be made. It is perhaps not too romantic an interpretation to suggest that Dionysius was the son of Geoffrey Boleyn II and Dionise, with the child named in memory of a mother who died in childbirth – a common enough end for young married women in the medieval period. Dionysius was presumably an adult when he made his gift to the college at some point before his father's death in 1463. This also suggests the possibility that he was the child of Dionise as Geoffrey's remaining children, who were born to his second wife, were all minors at the time of his death. Dionysius, if he can be identified as the son of Geoffrey Boleyn II, died within his father's lifetime, presumably still as a young man as he merited no further mention in surviving documents, including his father's will.

The lives of the earliest Boleyn ladies were, to a large extent, obscure. The women, many of whose names no longer even survive, lived lives centred on Salle. They would have kept their houses and been involved in agriculture. The family was always reasonably prosperous, although their claims to gentry status were tenuous. This all changed with the career of Geoffrey Boleyn II and his marriage to his second wife, Anne Hoo, who laid claim to being a member of the nobility.

2

ANNE HOO BOLEYN & HER DAUGHTERS

The marriage of Geoffrey Boleyn II to his first wife Dionise would have been entirely forgotten if it were not for its brief mention in Geoffrey's will. Geoffrey's second wife, Anne Hoo, the mother of all his surviving children, was considerably more prominent and brought the Boleyns to the fringes of the nobility for the first time.

Until the time of his great-granddaughter, Queen Anne Boleyn, Geoffrey Boleyn II was the most prominent and illustrious member of the Boleyn family. One historian has posited that Geoffrey's father might also have been engaged in business in London.[1] It is not impossible that Geoffrey Boleyn I did indeed have some business connections, as evidenced by the fact that his son was set up in trade in the capital. However, in the main Geoffrey Boleyn I's interests were based in Salle, where he was a prosperous farmer. By the 1430s Geoffrey Boleyn II had been set up in London as a hatter.[2] This was a respectable trade but one in which he was not destined to remain for long, instead becoming, in 1435, a member of the prestigious Mercer's Company in London, indicating that, by that stage, his affairs had taken on a more general trading nature. He was already somewhat established as the entry in the wardens' account book for 1435 for the Mercer's Company also refers to his apprentices, of whom Robert Hastings and William Brampston are known for the period.[3] He was able to pay the significant fee of over 5 pounds for his entry. Geoffrey quickly became an active member of the Mercer's Company, with his name regularly featuring in company accounts, including a number of fines for defaulting on summons made on him to court in 1437–8, 1438–9 and 1440–1.[4] Geoffrey evidently had a dislike of such appointments, as can be seen in the fact that, in October 1458 and again in July 1461, he received an exemption for life from the king for his good service to the king's father:

> From being put on assizes, juries, inquisitions, attaints or recognisances and from being made trier of them, taxer, collector or assessor of customs, taxes, tallages, fifteenths, tenths or other subsidies, knight, mayor, sheriff, escheator, commissioner, constable, bailiff or other officer or minister of the king against his Will.[5]

Geoffrey's wife, Anne Hoo Boleyn, also benefited from the first of these grants, ensuring that she would not be forced into any official capacity against her will. The fines that Geoffrey received from the Mercer's Company did nothing to hinder his rise in the company and by 1443 he had been appointed as one of its wardens. During his term of office Geoffrey had five apprentices admitted to the company, the highest number among the company members.[6] In 1449 he was appointed as a Member of Parliament for London.[7] In 1451 he was also one of five men who lent the king the combined sum of £1,246, a huge sum, to pay for the war in France, something which stands as a testament to his financial prosperity.[8] He may have been less than committed to Henry VI's Lancastrian cause, however, as in 1461, when the members of the Mercer's Company agreed to together lend £100 to the prominent

Yorkist the Earl of Warwick, Geoffrey supplied the highest sum.[9] That same year the company also granted 1,000 marks to the new king, Edward IV, 'for the speed of the earl of Warwick in to the North' with Geoffrey this time supplying the joint-highest sum at over 13 pounds.[10] In June 1453 he hosted the officers of the Mercer's Company in his own house while elections were held for wardens of the company, another indication that he was one of the most prominent, and wealthy, of his fellows in the city.[11]

In 1457 Geoffrey reached the pinnacle of his career when he was elected as Lord Mayor of London.[12] This role allowed him to mix with barons, abbots and chief justices in ceremonial processions and banquets and, in addition, provided him with a seat on the royal council.[13] Although Geoffrey only served for a year, it was far from being a merely ceremonial appointment, with Geoffrey and his aldermen and sheriffs receiving a royal commission in November 1457 to raise 1,137 archers in London and its suburbs.[14] The following August he was given a commission with others to enter the dwellings, houses, warehouses and cellars of any Genoese merchants in London in order to make inventories and confiscate their goods and merchandise.[15] As a merchant himself, this was not entirely to Geoffrey's taste and the commission was later vacated because no action had actually been taken to carry out its commands.

Geoffrey Boleyn II, through his prosperity, mixed in higher social circles. His increasing prominence in the City of London brought about his marriage to Anne Hoo, the daughter of Lord Hoo and Hastings. This was the first time that the Boleyn family, which had only recently had aspirations to gentry status, had attempted to forge links with the nobility, although it must be pointed out that Anne's father, Thomas Hoo, was only the first member of his family to hold a peerage and that his barony was a new creation. Anne was certainly not a member of an ancient noble family as later Boleyn wives would be. Her father had also not been ennobled at the time of her marriage. Lord Hoo and Hastings obtained his title when Anne was already twenty-three. Since Anne and Geoffrey's eldest son, Thomas, reached his majority at some point between 1463 and 1466, he was evidently born between 1442 and 1445 when Anne was aged between seventeen and twenty. As discussed in the previous chapter, Thomas is most likely Anne's son rather than that of her predecessor, Dionise, particularly given the fact that the name Thomas was a favourite in the Hoo family, with both Anne's father and his half-brother confusingly bearing the name. The marriage of Anne and Geoffrey, who was twenty years older than his bride, took place before her father's ennoblement and before Geoffrey became Lord Mayor of London in around 1442–44. It may even have occurred earlier as two of Anne's younger half-sisters are known to have been married in their early teens, with one, another Anne, being widowed before she turned fifteen and a second, Eleanor, recorded as a wife when she was aged thirteen or fourteen.[16] Anne Hoo Boleyn's marriage could therefore conceivably have occurred as early as 1437 or 1438, particularly as she was then potentially a very great heiress. In the fifteenth century it was not that uncommon for gentlewomen to marry into the merchant classes and Geoffrey's wealth more than made up for the fact that the match was beneath Anne socially. For Geoffrey, the marriage firmly cemented his status as a gentleman and provided links to Anne's father, an important royal servant. He had hopes that Anne would prove to be her father's sole surviving child, with Hoo's third marriage only producing its first child in 1448, some years after Geoffrey and Anne's marriage.[17]

Anne's father, Thomas Hoo, was created Lord Hoo and Hastings by Henry VI in 1448 and had been elected as a Knight of the Garter a few years before. He had a somewhat complicated personal life, being married three times. His first marriage produced one son who died in his father's lifetime, while his second, to Elizabeth, the daughter and heiress of Sir Nicholas Wychingham, produced one daughter, Anne Hoo, who was born in 1425.[18] His third marriage allowed Hoo to ally himself with a more established noble family, when he took Eleanor, the daughter of Leo, Lord Welles, as his bride. This marriage produced a further three daughters: a second Anne, who married Sir Roger Copley; Eleanor, who married into the Carews of Beddington; and Elizabeth, the wife of Sir Thomas Massingberd and then Sir John Devenish.

Family members came to prominence as royal servants in the reigns of Edward III and his two successors. Anne's own father, Thomas Hoo, served Henry VI in France for some years, spending thirteen years as Chancellor of France for the English king. The family had lived in Sussex since at least the reign of Edward II in the early fourteenth century.[19] With the death of her elder half-brother, Anne Hoo Boleyn and her much younger half-sisters found themselves to be their father's heirs on his death in 1455. The sisters had a rival in their uncle, another Thomas Hoo, who was his brother's heir male. However Anne, as the eldest, was able to negotiate a beneficial settlement, with her own son, William Boleyn, being named as his uncle's heir on his death in 1486 as a result of a settlement agreed between Thomas Hoo and Anne in 1474.[20] Lord Hoo's probate was a lengthy and disputed business and Anne was lucky to come out of it with anything from her father's estate. Lord Hoo died so in debt that his chosen executors, his widow and his brother, 'expressly refused to act', with the Archbishop of Canterbury instead appointing a professional executor.[21] Shortly after the death that executor complained that Hoo's widow had carried away jewels, goods, chattels and anything else that was moveable and had refused to return them, leading to the deceased's debts remaining unpaid. Anne Hoo Boleyn's young half-sister, Eleanor, also found herself without the bequest that she received in the will when her first, unconsummated, marriage was followed by a second match without her family's permission, providing her mother and uncle with a pretext for withholding her funds.[22]

The evidence of Geoffrey Boleyn's will, which is discussed below and in which he displayed a great deal of affection and trust in his wife, suggests that the marriage immediately became close, as does the fact that at least five children were born to the couple: Thomas, William, Isabel, Anne and Alice. In addition to this, Geoffrey evidently forged bonds with members of Anne Hoo Boleyn's family, making a bequest in his will of an annuity to 'Dame Joanne Hoo my cousin, nun of the house of Barking', who can be identified as a kinswoman of his wife.[23] In return, he asked specifically that Joanne pray for his soul.

With his success in trade, Geoffrey was determined to fully cement his position as a member of the gentry and, as such, he required a family seat. In 1452 Geoffrey opened negotiations with Sir John Falstolf, a wealthy landowner and a member of the king's council, for the purchase of the manor of Blickling in Norfolk.[24] A letter survives among the famous Paston letters, which was sent by Geoffrey to John Paston in 1460, detailing some of his business dealings with Paston's patron and friend, Sir John Falstolf.[25] In the letter, which is written in the hand of a scribe but signed personally by Geoffrey, he pointed out that he had purchased the manor of Blickling from Falstolf both for a 'great payment' and for an additional yearly annuity, which was, as Geoffrey explained, 'to me great charge'. The negotiations for the purchase had taken place at Falstolf's house at Southwark and, at the same time, due to the great sums that Geoffrey committed to pay for Blickling, Falstolf made an oath on his primer that he would also allow him first refusal to purchase a second manor, that of Guton in Norfolk, 'for a reasonable price'. With Falstolf's death, Geoffrey had trouble in securing this manor, writing to Paston as Falstolf's executor 'to pray you to show me your good will and favour in this behalf, wherein ye shall discharge my said master's soul of

his oath and promise, and I shall do you service in that I can or
may to my power'. The manor meant enough to Geoffrey that he
was prepared to 'wait on you at any time and place where ye will
assign'. However it was perhaps convenient for Geoffrey that he
was the only surviving witness to Falstolf's alleged oath, which
he used to his advantage to push his claims to a desirable manor.
Paston may well not have been favourably disposed to Geoffrey
since it appears that he had not readily paid the purchase price for
Blickling, with Falstolf petitioning the king's chancellor in 1452
to complain that he had only received half of the sums agreed.[26]
Blickling became the Boleyn family's primary seat, with Geoffrey
commissioning a chapel, dedicated to St Thomas, on the north side
of the chancel in Blickling church, which stood beside the manor.[27]
In his will, Geoffrey also left sums to pay for improvements to the
church.

Geoffrey was well known to John Paston and his family by
1460 and there is some indication that the two families were not
on entirely favourable terms. In 1452, for example, while Geoffrey
was busy with his negotiations with Sir John Falstolf, Agnes Paston
wrote from Norwich to her son, John Paston, to report that

Sir John Fastolf hath sold Heylysdon to Boleyn of London; and
if it be so, it seemeth he will sell more. Wherefore I pray you, as
ye will have my love and my blessing that ye will help and do
your devoir that something were purchased for your ij brethren.
I suppose Sir John Falstolf, and he were spake to, would be
gladder to let his kinsmen have part than strange men.[28]

There was some jealousy between the families over Geoffrey's land
acquisitions. In November 1454 Thomas Howes, an agent of Sir
John Falstolf, wrote to John Paston to say that he had raised the
possibility of a marriage between Paston's daughter and a young
ward of Falstolf's. Matters had moved so far that Howes had

'enquired after the said child, and no doubt of but he is likely and of great wit, as I hear be reported of sundry persons'.[29] However, Howes also had a warning for Paston that, while this promising child would evidently be perfect for a Paston daughter, 'I am credibly informed, that Geoffrey Boleyn maketh great labour for marriage of the said child to one of his daughters'. Howes assured Paston of his own personal support, declaring that while he wished well to Geoffrey, he wished better to Paston.

Both the famous Paston family and the Boleyns had strong Norfolk interests and, with their similar backgrounds, it is perhaps not surprising that they regularly came within each other's spheres of influence. The Pastons originated from the village of Paston, only 20 miles from Norwich and, thus, not far from Salle. The John Paston who was executor to Sir John Falstolf was a lawyer although, like the Boleyns, the family had some less than illustrious ancestry, with one fifteenth-century description of the family claiming that they were descended from one Clement Paston, a husbandman, who ploughed his land and 'rode to mill on bare horseback with his corn under him and brought home meal again under him, and also drove his cart with diverse corn to Wynterton to sell'.[30] The family farmed a few acres at Paston and, on the basis of this description, does not sound very far removed from Geoffrey's own grandfather, the builder of the church at Salle, Thomas Boleyn I.

While there was evidently some rivalry between the two families, it was the Boleyns who outstripped their Norfolk rivals. Sir John Falstolf's executor, John Paston, left two sons: Sir John Paston, the elder, and his younger brother, another John. Sir John Paston soon established himself as a leading member of Norfolk society while his brother, the younger John, attempted to build on his own social position and career by making a prestigious marriage. Interestingly, the first object of the younger John's affections was Alice Boleyn, the youngest daughter of the by then deceased Geoffrey and his widow, Anne.

John Paston, as a younger son, had little to recommend him when he first approached Anne to suggest a match with her daughter. As a result, the younger John went to his brother for advice and Sir John in turn went in person to speak with Anne in March 1467. He found her unmoved at his pleas, writing to give his brother the disappointing news that

> as for my Lady Boleyn's disposition to you-wards, I cannot in no wise find her agreeable that ye should have her daughter, for all the privy means that I could make, insomuch I had so little comfort by all the means that I could make, that I disdained in mine own person to common [i.e. speak] with her therein.[31]

The best that Sir John could obtain from Anne, who was seeking a more prestigious husband for her daughter, was that she assured him that 'what if he [younger John] and she [Alice] can agree I will not let it, but I will never advise her thereto wise'. This was hardly approval from the prospective mother-in-law, although it does show some degree of indulgence in Anne as a mother that she was prepared to allow her daughter to make her own choice with regard to the match. Anne was indeed an indulgent mother, who was close to all her children, with her eldest son, William, later requesting to be buried close to her.[32] Her second daughter, Anne Boleyn Heydon, inherited a silver-and-gilt bowl with a cover which bore the arms of the Hoo family from her mother, something which she treasured all her life, eventually passing it on to her own granddaughter in her will: a testament to the close relationship between Anne Hoo Boleyn and her daughter and namesake.[33] It may well be that Anne was concerned about her daughter's suitor's motives: it is perhaps telling that the Paston family held the manor of Kirkhall in Salle at the time and that young John, after his pursuit of Alice came to nothing, later married Margery Brewes, the daughter of Sir Thomas Brewes, who held the manor of Stinton in Salle.[34] It seems improbable that he just happened to fall in love with two young ladies with close landed connections to Salle, an area in which he wished to extend his interests.

Anne's words did not dissuade the young man, in spite of the fact that she was negotiating another marriage for her daughter at that time with a man named Crosseby. Soon after her meeting with Sir John Paston, Anne returned home to Norfolk with her daughter. She was overtaken on the road by Sir John's letter to his brother in which he advised him to continue in his pursuit of Alice, both by seeking out and charming the mother, as well as taking more immediate steps to win the daughter herself. According to Sir John, who had fully weighed up his brother's advantages:

Ye be personable, and peradventure your being once in the sight of the maid, and a little discovering of your good will to her, binding her to keep it secret, and that ye can find in your heart, with some comfort to her, to find the mean to bring such matter about as shall be her pleasure and yours, but that this ye cannot do without some comfort of her in no wise.

Both brothers had high hopes that the younger John would win Alice's affections, although Sir John finished by counselling his brother that 'bear yourself as lowly to the mother as ye list, but to the maid not too lowly'.

The younger John was not as forthcoming as his brother wished and, instead, the following month wrote to complain that he could not possibly speak to the formidable Lady Boleyn unless his brother came home and was with him.[35] His timidity cost him a meeting with Anne, who, on her return to Norfolk, travelled to Norwich for the week after Easter, accompanied by both her married daughter, Anne Boleyn Heydon, and her youngest daughter, the desirable Alice. This was a missed opportunity for John, who was then at Caistor and claimed not to have been aware of the visit until it was too late. According to reports of Anne's servants that reached the younger John, 'she had none other errand to the town but for to sport her; but so God help me, I suppose that she wend I would have been in Norwich for to have seen her daughter'. Given Anne's earlier response to young John's suit, this seems unlikely. He did not receive another opportunity and Anne took no steps to promote the match.

Alice's father, Geoffrey Boleyn II, had died in 1463. He had divided his time between London, the centre of his business interests, and his Norfolk estates, decreeing in his will, which was made only shortly before his death, that he hoped to be buried in the church of St Lawrence in the capital 'if it happen me to decease in London or elsewhere within the Realm of England, saving always that if I decease within the shire of Norfolk, I will that then my body be buried in the Church of Blickling'.[36] Geoffrey went into considerable detail in his will as to how he was to be buried, with his specifications indicating that he was a man of fairly austere tastes. He asked that his body be buried with black candlesticks and that thirteen torches be carried aloft by the same number of poor and needy people. These torchbearers, who Geoffrey specified should be poor householders rather than beggars, were to each be given a rosary, a gown lined with russet or black and a hood of black, as well as 12 pence. At the same time, Geoffrey specified that there was to be little other ceremony for him, stating that:

> I will not that any hearse or gilt candlesticks be ordained or set about me not any great feast made, but a dinner to my wife and to my brother Master Thomas and to my executors and such other friends and neighbours as my said wife, my brother and executors will call unto them.

Evidently Geoffrey trusted his wife and brother's judgement in this regard and it can be inferred that his relationship with Anne was a close one. He left her a wealthy widow, bequeathing her a significant share of his goods and chattels, including one half of his silver plate. In an age where married women were not permitted to hold any property personally he significantly left Anne all her own clothes, ornaments and jewels, a bequest which, while it seems natural to modern eyes, was not something that all fifteenth-century husbands would have condescended to do. Geoffrey's own clothes and other personal goods were to be sold to pay for bedding, clothes, linen and woollens for poor people. Geoffrey left extensive sums to charity, something that both attests to his charitable disposition and his wealth at his death.

His children were also not forgotten, with his sons, Thomas and William, each receiving the sum of 300 marks. Geoffrey's daughters, Isabel, Anne and Alice, each received the substantial sum of 1,000 marks. In addition to this, Anne Hoo Boleyn and her brother-in-law, Thomas Boleyn, were given the discretion as to how the remaining half of Geoffrey's silver was to be divided between his sons and daughters. The bequests to Geoffrey's children were all conditional on them either reaching the age of twenty-five or marrying, a common enough provision where large sums were involved, with Isabel's to be held by Geoffrey Randolf, a merchant and friend of Geoffrey Boleyn's. Two apprentices of Geoffrey's took on the role of trustee for the younger daughters' legacies. Significantly, although Anne Hoo Boleyn was not appointed to act as trustee for any of her children, she was given considerable control over the futures of all her offspring, with Geoffrey declaring that:

> I will and ordain by this my testament that none of my foresaid children be married within his age of twenty-five years without the will and assent of Anne my wife, her mother, and of my brother Master Thomas and of my

executors or of the more part of them, so that the same Anne my wife while she standeth sole [i.e. unmarried] and my said brother be of the same more part. And if any of my said children be married against the form aforesaid, or be governed in otherwise than by the will and assent of her said mother while she standeth soul, and of my said brother and of my executors or of the more part of them in form aforesaid, I will and ordain that then the bequests by me abovemade to such of my said children as happen to be married or governed contrary to my Will aforesaid rehearsed be utterly void and of none effect.

To hammer home the point, Geoffrey declared that such forfeited sums should be used charitably for the good of his soul. It is clear from this part of the will why the consent of Anne Hoo Boleyn was so crucial to John Paston: it was an extraordinary concession on her part that she was prepared to allow her daughter to potentially marry for love, even if she could not recommend the match, given the power that the will gave her to control her youngest daughter's choice so effectively. As a final proof of Geoffrey's affection for his wife, she was the first named executor to his will, which was proved on 2 July 1463, only eight days after the will was drafted. The claim in an eighteenth-century work on the history of Norfolk that Anne Hoo Boleyn remarried in 1501, taking a Thomas Fenys as her second husband, is groundless, with Fenys actually taking another member of the Hoo family as his wife.[37] Instead, Anne remained a widow until her own death.

Alice Boleyn, as the youngest daughter of Geoffrey and Anne, was the last to marry, eventually taking Sir John Fortescue as her husband.[38] The second daughter, Anne, married Sir Henry Heydon, who had been associated with her father at least as early as 1452 when it was falsely rumoured that he had asked Geoffrey to purchase Blickling on his behalf.[39] Heydon enjoyed prominence as the steward of Cecily, Duchess of York, the mother of Edward IV and Richard III. He was also a Norfolk landowner. He owned a house at West Wickham in Kent and was knighted in 1485. Sir Henry died in 1503, requesting that he be buried in Norwich Cathedral, and leaving Anne Boleyn Heydon a widow at a fairly advanced age.

Anne Boleyn Heydon's will survives and demonstrates something of the wealthy and comfortable life that she led as a widow. She lived to a good age, dying in May 1510 in the second year of Henry VIII's reign. In her will, which was dated less than six months before her death, Anne declared that she was in full and whole mind, before requesting that 'my sinful body to be buried in the chapel of Saint Luke in the Cathedral church of the Holy Trinity of Norwich if I die in Norwich or in Norfolk'.[40] Anne Boleyn Heydon obviously had an affinity with Norwich which had, of course, been the town closest to her childhood home at Blickling and which she visited with her mother during the early years of her marriage. She also left a bequest for the repair of the cathedral, on the condition that she was indeed granted a burial there as she wished and that a solemn dirge and requiem Mass were said for her soul. Gifts were given to the prior, sub-prior and to each of the monks in order for them to pray for her. Anne was living in Norwich at the time of her death and had evidently involved herself with the poor of the city, further requesting that her executors should give alms to poor householders there, especially those 'that be dwelling within the parish that I dwell in'. There were gifts to the black friars, white friars, grey friars and Austin friars of the city for the good of her soul – a pious gift but, given the fact that each order was to receive the same amount, suggests that she had no particular interest in any over the other.

She was clearly pious, as can be seen by the religious apparatus listed in her will. One bequest, for example, involved a gift to Thomas Landons in recompense for a primer that she had received from his father. She possessed a number of rosaries, including one made of amber beads. While she lived, Anne Boleyn Heydon presented herself as a great lady and she was determined that this continued after her death. Like her father, she took a great interest in preparations for her own funeral, declaring in her will that

> there be provided xij beadmen of the poorest persons to hold light about mine hearse and each of the to have a black gown of frieze and 5*d* in money, and each of them to say a dirge and mass at my burying our Lady's psalter and 5 pater noster 5 avas and a creed.

Her grave was to be marked with a slab of marble displaying her image and her arms. Anne made a great deal of charitable donations to the church in her will, as well as arranging for an 'honest and virtuous' priest to be found who would sing and pray for her at Cambridge while also attending to his learning there. During her lifetime she had already been responsible for funding the studies of one scholar, Master English, who was a priest and she specifically requested that he be appointed to sing and pray for her after her death, a reasonable request by a patron. During her lifetime, Anne was wealthy enough to employ her own chaplain, a Sir John Caley, and she also had a household of servants and attendants. These household servants were to receive black gowns from her executors, providing that they attended her funeral. Charitably, Anne ordered that her household be kept in place for three months after her death, a period calculated to give her servants sufficient time to find new employment for themselves although some way below the usual one year's wages that servants in a royal household could expect.

While Anne Boleyn Heydon's charitable gifts give an insight into her character, it is the bequests that she was able to make that demonstrate the wealthy lifestyle that she led. As well as living mainly in Norwich, Anne kept a house in Kent, leaving her household goods there to her eldest son, John. Her daughter, Dorothy Cobham, received

> three goblets of silver and gilt with one cover to the same, a psalter covered with blue velvet, one pair beads of gold, my chain of gold, one seler [i.e. a bed canopy] and tester with the covering of blue damask, iii curtains of blue sarcenet, one cushion of tawny and purple velvet, one pair fustions, vi pair sheets, mine hanging of cloth of arras.

Her daughter, Bridget Paston, received rich household furnishings, as well as a feather bed and two of the best sheets. She received two salts of silver and gilt, as well as a silver gilt cover and two pillows. Bridget's husband, who was favoured by his mother-in-law, received two silver pots. For a third daughter, Anne Dymoke, there was a standing cup with a cover and a cross of gold while her husband received a silver-and-gilt bowl. A younger son, Henry, gained a silver basin and ewer, as well as two feather beds and bedding. He also received hangings of yellow and red which had decorated his mother's own great chamber. An unmarried daughter, Margaret, received blankets, as well as a tapestry coverlet and fine cushions. Margaret may have had a pious reason for the fact that she remained unmarried, as her mother also passed her some of her religious paraphernalia, including two silver chalices and a vestment made of fine cloth of Baudkin, which was a particularly rich fabric interwoven with threads of gold. She received a specific bequest of all other goods 'that pertaineth to the altar except that is bequest before and after'. Anne Boleyn Heydon remained on good terms with all her children, also remembering her grandchildren in her will. A grandson, George Cobham, for example, was to receive two salts of silver and gilt with a cover, to be delivered to him when he reached the age of twenty-one, with his father keeping the items safe for him in the meantime. Anne took steps to provide for George's upbringing, leaving him an annuity of 10 shillings per year for five years to be delivered to his mother. George's sister, Anne Cobham, received 66 shillings for her marriage, which was to be paid to her mother in the meantime, while another granddaughter, Frances Gurney, received an annual sum for her living expenses until she married. Frances also received a number of rich bequests and a sum to be paid on her marriage. She was a particular favourite of her grandmother, who bequeathed her all her gowns and furs, save those that had otherwise been disposed of in her will.

Anne Boleyn Heydon evidently delighted in her family in her old age, spending time with her children and grandchildren. Her will notes that she acted as godmother to a number of her grandchildren, something that suggests a particular closeness towards them and their parents. Furthermore, she made a gift of 20 shillings to one Elizabeth Thomas, a servant of her daughter, Dorothy Cobham: clearly, mother and daughter were frequently enough in each other's company for them to be familiar, and even friendly, with each other's servants.

Anne Hoo Boleyn's eldest daughter, Isabel, who was born in 1453, married William Cheyne, esquire, of the Isle of Sheppey. Cheyne was the second son of Sir John Cheyne and his elder brother, who was also knighted, became a knight of the Garter.[41] William was a member of the gentry and it was a solid, but far from spectacular, match. Isabel bore her husband two sons, Francis and William. She died in 1485, while still only in her early thirties, and significantly chose to be buried at Blickling, demonstrating her continuing attachment to her birth family. In her funeral brass she is depicted in fashionable clothes, with her dress and headdress resembling the Yorkist queen Elizabeth Woodville in style, something that is indicative of the fact that she aspired to the nobility and also that she was a fashionable woman.

The sleeves and collar of Isabel's gown are furred, with a decorative veiled cap and ornate belt. Her low-cut dress, with a pleated skirt, shows a darker under-dress at the chest and she also wears an elaborate necklace with five dangling jewelled pendants visible. Isabel was depicted with a stylishly high forehead, with her hair largely hidden by her cap: such an effect would have been achieved through the plucking of her hair on her forehead. Interestingly, unlike the other memorial brasses at Blickling, of Isabel's aunt, Cecily, and niece, Anne, Isabel's facial expression appears striking and proud, rather than pious with downcast eyes. Her hands display an open gesture as opposed to the praying posture of the two other ladies depicted. From the evidence of the brass it would appear that Isabel had no wish to be depicted as a particularly pious woman, instead choosing to be portrayed to display her beauty, wealth and status.

Isabel's husband survived her and both he and his brother proved to be staunch supporters of Henry VII, with her husband receiving a number of grants from the king after his accession in August 1485.[42] He also served as sheriff of Kent in 1477 and was again carrying out this office in 1485 at the time of Isabel's death.[43] Given that the role of sheriff required a personal presence in the county it would seem probable that Isabel was also resident in Kent at the time of her death and that her death may have happened unexpectedly while she was visiting her family at Blickling.

All indications suggest that Anne Hoo Boleyn busied herself with her children, as well as managing the family estates, after the death of Geoffrey Boleyn II. Her eldest son, Thomas, succeeded his father while still legally a minor. He had reached his majority by 1466, suggesting that he was at least eighteen at the time of his father's death.[44] This Thomas Boleyn III was short-lived, dying in April 1471. His death was not unexpected. He was able to make a will, something which suggests ill health. In his will he asked to be buried with his father in London, leaving his mother as his executor and asking her to use his funds to provide for his soul's health.

Anne Hoo Boleyn died in Norfolk in 1485.[45] She was buried in Norwich Cathedral with her grave marked by a memorial brass. Sadly, her memorial has been moved since the sixteenth century and all that survives is the outline of a woman on the re-positioned stone. As the daughter of a nobleman, she brought an added level of prestige to the rising Boleyn family. This was followed by the even more spectacular marriage made by her eldest surviving son, William Boleyn, to Margaret Butler, whose father became Earl of Ormond.

3

THE ORMOND INHERITANCE

While the Boleyn fortune, which had been built on trade, was substantial by the mid-fifteenth century, it was William Boleyn's marriage which cemented the family's links to the nobility and led to them becoming great landowners.

In around 1475 William Boleyn, who, following the death of his elder brother, Thomas, had succeeded to the Boleyn estates, married Margaret Butler.[1] Margaret, whose parents are known to have been married by 1445 when her mother was only fourteen and her father a few years older, was probably of a similar age to her husband – in her early twenties.[2] There appears to be some dispute over Margaret's parentage, with one recent writer on the Boleyn family declaring, confusingly, both that she was the daughter of Thomas Butler, 7th Earl of Ormond, and of Thomas's elder brother, John Butler, 6th Earl of Ormond.[3] Clearly, Margaret was not the product of two different fathers! An earlier writer also believed that she was a daughter of the sixth earl.[4] There is in fact no doubt that both Margaret and her sister, Anne, were the daughters of the 7th Earl of Ormond. In the earl's will he specifically referred both to 'my daughter Dame Anne St Leger' and 'my daughter Dame Margaret Boleyn late the wife of Sir William Boleyn'.[5] Both daughters received personal bequests from their father which he specifically noted as having belonged to their mother, with Margaret, for example, receiving a bed of tapestry work and an old great carpet. Anne, the elder sister, did rather better in the will, receiving, among other items, a little mass book covered with russet velvet.

The Butler family was an Irish one, with its earliest known member, Theobald Butler, recorded as having died in Ireland during the reign of Edward I.[6] Theobald's great-grandson was created Earl of Ormond by Edward III in the early fourteenth century, with the title passing smoothly from father to son up to the time of the fifth earl. Margaret Butler Boleyn's father had been only the third son of the 4th Earl of Ormond. His eldest brother, James, had attained the family earldom in 1452 on the death of their father, having previously also been granted the English earldom of Wiltshire in 1449 due to his loyalty to the Lancastrian king, Henry VI.[7] Henry VI relied heavily on James Butler, appointing him first as Lieutenant of Ireland and later as Lord Treasurer of England. The earl fought with the king at the first Battle of St Albans during the Wars of the Roses, finding himself forced to flee the field when it ended in defeat. He again fought for the Lancastrians in 1460 when they won a great victory at the Battle of Wakefield, leading to the capture and execution of Richard, Duke of York, the rival claimant to the crown. York's death did not prove the end of the Civil War: early the following year his eldest son entered London and was declared king as Edward IV. James Butler, along with his two younger brothers, John and Thomas, remained loyal to the Lancastrian king. After defeat at the Battle of Mortimer's Cross, James was captured, before being executed at Newcastle on 1 May 1461. Disastrously for the Butler family, this was followed in November by the earl's attainder by Parliament, leading to him (and his heirs) being stripped of his earldoms and lands.

James Butler, in spite of making three marriages, died childless, with his younger brother, John, eventually acquiring the earldom of Ormond after making his peace with Edward IV. The earldom of Wiltshire was not however returned, instead being bestowed on a follower of the new king. At the time of Margaret's marriage to Thomas, her uncle, the sixth earl, was still living, although his failure to marry meant she had reasonable prospects of eventually being the daughter of an Earl of Ormond. This occurred in 1478 when the sixth earl died unexpectedly during a pilgrimage to the Holy Land, with his brother, Thomas Butler, inheriting the earldom in his place.

In 1475 Margaret was already a potential heiress to her father's estates, a factor that must have been considered by William Boleyn and his mother when they negotiated the marriage. Margaret's father had married Anne, the daughter and co-heiress of Sir Richard Hankford.[8] This marriage produced only two daughters: Anne, who married Sir James Saint Leger, and Margaret, the younger daughter. Anne Hankford, who was past childbearing age by the time of her youngest daughter's marriage, died in 1485.[9] The seventh earl desired a male heir of his own and he took a second wife, Lora Berkley, who was the widow both of Lord Mountjoy and Sir Thomas Montgomery, at some point between January 1495 and November 1496.[10] This marriage only produced a further daughter, Elizabeth, who died in childhood in February 1510, before her father's death.[11]

Even without certain hopes of inheriting the lands connected with the earldom through his marriage, William's choice of Margaret was helped by her impeccable pedigree. While her mother's father was a mere knight, her maternal grandmother was a daughter of the Earl of Shrewsbury. Thomas Butler, as well as being the son of an earl, was also the maternal grandson of Lord Bergavenny. This family connection was a close and important one, with Butler's grandmother, Joanne, Lady Bergavenny, leaving substantial bequests to her three Ormond grandsons and her Ormond granddaughter in her will of 1434.[12] Margaret's father, as the youngest son, received the least from his grandmother, although he was still granted the very personal bequest of bed of white and black velvet, with cushions and other furnishings to match. He evidently remembered his grandmother fondly and, in his will written nearly eighty years after her death, he left funds so that she, along with himself, his wife and parents, should be prayed for.[13] In addition to this connection, Butler's sister, Elizabeth, married the Earl of Shrewsbury, providing links to the highest levels of the English peerage. Butler remained close to his sister and his youngest daughter, Elizabeth, who was named after her, was buried in Sheffield church, a building strongly associated with the Shrewsbury family and suggesting that she may have been staying with her aunt at her death.

It is not at all impossible that the match between William and Margaret came about due to both family's connections with London trade. William had been a younger son and, at the time of his father's death in 1463, was still a child. It seems highly likely that his father would have contemplated a career as a merchant for him, something which he had himself of course undertaken as a younger son. There does not however seem to be surviving evidence to support the recent claim that William was admitted to the Mercer's Company in 1472, however, or that he was also admitted as a lawyer to Lincoln's Inn the following year.[14]

Margaret's father had a connection with the church of St Thomas Acon in London, where he was buried.[15] His mother, Elizabeth Beauchamp, had already been buried there and it is clear that the Butler family felt a strong affinity to the church, with Margaret's father bequeathing a Psalter bound in white leather and signed in his own hand to the church, to be attached by a chain of iron to his tomb 'for the service of God better to be had' and so that anyone who wished could make use of it.[16] The church of St Thomas Acon had reputedly been built on the birthplace of St Thomas Becket, and was founded by one of the martyred archbishop's sisters in the late twelfth century. Interestingly, the Butler family claimed descent from Agnes, another of the archbishop's sisters, who had married an Irish gentleman. It is this connection, which was referred to in a petition to Parliament in the mid-fifteenth century made by Thomas Butler's brother, James, the fifth earl, which brought about the family's interest in the church. The seventh earl was devoted to the saint, specifically bequeathing his soul to the 'glorious martyr Saint Thomas' in his will. In addition to this, the church, which was the chapel of the Hospital of St Thomas, had strong connections with the Mercer's Company, which was based at the site and acted as its patron. The Mercer's had begun to make use of the hospital's hall by at least 1391 and, early the following century, they built their own hall adjoining the hospital church.[17] When the hospital was dissolved during the reign of Henry VIII, the company took over the remains of the foundation, making use of the church as its own chapel. Thomas Butler and his family, through their own patronage of the hospital church, would have come into contact with the Mercer's Company and, in all probability, Sir Geoffrey Boleyn and, later, his eldest surviving son.

The marriage of William and Margaret proved fruitful, with a number of children surviving to adulthood. William was evidently a fond father, making bequests to his eldest son, Thomas, who was born in 1477, as well as younger sons James (born 1480), William and Edward in his will.[18] Young William became a priest and later served as Archdeacon of Winchester, dying in 1571.[19] He was educated at Gonville Hall in Cambridge, where his great-uncle had been master and was later promoted by his niece, Queen Anne Boleyn.[20] Sir William Boleyn also remembered his daughters, Alice and Margaret, who were then unmarried, as well as the eldest surviving daughter, Anne, who had by them married Sir John Shelton, in his will. Alice and Anne came to prominence in middle age under their niece, Queen Anne Boleyn.

William and Margaret's youngest daughter, Margaret, married John Sackville of Buckhurst in Sussex and had a family. A further daughter, Jane, predeceased her father. She was presumably the second daughter to survive to adulthood as she died married, as the wife of Sir Philip Calthorp of Norwich.[21] The will of her sister, Alice Boleyn Clere, includes a bequest to her niece, Elizabeth Calthorp, of a pomander of gold, something which demonstrates that Jane bore at least one child who was still living and unmarried in 1539, over thirty years after her mother's death.

As well as losing their daughter Jane in her early adulthood, William and Margaret had the misfortune to lose at least three children in childhood. A daughter, Anne, received a fine memorial brass in Blickling church, showing her as a grown woman with hair pulled back tightly from her face and a furred and pleated gown. This depiction of Anne as an adult was wistful and the inscription on the brass makes it clear that she died as a very young child in 1479, aged only three years, eleven months and thirteen days. It appears from the fact that her age was so specifically noted that her fourth birthday had been anticipated in the family and her death was sudden. Certainly, she was a much-loved child as can be seen from the expense incurred in providing her with such a fine memorial brass: given her early birth in 1475, coupled with the choice of the name Anne, after both her grandmothers, she was probably their eldest daughter. She is also likely to have been the couple's eldest child, with their eldest known son only being born in 1477. She was certainly not forgotten and a later daughter, who survived to adulthood, was named after her. A son, Anthony, died on 30 September 1493 at the age of around ten, and was buried close to the altar at Blickling.[22] Another son, John, who appears to have been an infant, had already died in 1484 and is also reported to have been buried at Blickling.[23]

Regardless of his father's original plan for him to go into trade, William Boleyn quickly began to take steps to build a solid court career, being created a knight of the Bath at the Coronation of Richard III in 1483.[24] In 1498 William and Margaret hosted a visit of the king to Blickling: a significant honour.[25] The visit went well and a few years later William was appointed to the post of Third Baron of the Exchequer. He moved his family's primary landed interests away from Norfolk and, by 1489, he was described as being a gentleman of Kent, where his residence of Hever Castle was situated.[26] William maintained his close links to Norfolk, being appointed to commissions of the peace in the county in 1483 and 1485, for example.[27] He served as sheriff of both Kent and Norfolk on occasion. In 1482 he was commissioned alongside Edward IV's brother-in-law, Anthony, Earl Rivers, and a small number of other gentlemen to arbitrate in a dispute among other members of the local Norfolk gentry which had led to murder, trespass and other offences, with the commissioners being required to report directly to the king and his council.[28] His increasing prominence was helped by the favour which Henry VII showed to Margaret's father, appointing him as ambassador to Burgundy in 1497, for example. He was also a member of the king's Privy Council and had earlier acted as ambassador to France, as well as serving as chamberlain to Queen Elizabeth of York.[29] With the death of their stepmother in around 1501, Margaret and her elder sister must have begun to consider their eventual succession as their father's heiresses a certainty, with their prospective shares being increased with the death of their younger half-sister in 1510.

There is little evidence for the relationship between William and Margaret. In his will, which was written shortly before his death in October 1505, William requested that his heir, Thomas, pay Margaret 200 marks a year out of the revenues of some of the principal Boleyn manors.[30] There is no real evidence of affection and it was close to his mother, Anne Hoo Boleyn, that William asked to be buried, rather than requesting burial beside his wife when she died. Given the high number of children born to the couple they obviously spent a considerable amount of time together although Margaret, like her mother-in-law before her, ploughed her energies into supporting and advancing her children, in particular her eldest son.

Margaret had been a widow for nearly ten years when her father died, at the advanced age of around ninety, in August 1515. She was herself already well into her sixties – elderly for the time. The 7th Earl of Ormond was extremely wealthy, possessing seventy-two manors in England alone, as well as his extensive Irish estates.[31] He was described by an eighteenth-century biographer as 'the richest subject the king had, and left £40,000 in money besides jewels, and as much land to his two daughters in England, as at this day would yield £30,000 per annum'.[32] This was an astronomical sum and, even if considerably exaggerated, the sheer extensiveness of the earl's lands in both England and Ireland demonstrate vast wealth.

Margaret had a very close relationship with her eldest son, Sir Thomas Boleyn, who identified strongly with her prestigious family background. It is significant that when he was first ennobled by the king in 1525, he took the title of Viscount Rochford. Rochford, in Kent, had been one of his grandfather's leading English manors and was also the location of the old earl's only English peerage, that of Baron Rochford, which was the title the earl used when summoned to attend Parliament.[33] Although Thomas was a Boleyn family name, it seems likely that Thomas Boleyn was named for his grandfather, who treated him as something of a favourite. In his will, drawn up shortly before his death, the seventh earl paid his younger daughter's eldest son the compliment of leaving him a precious family heirloom: a white ivory horn, garnished with gold which, according to the earl 'was mine ancestors at first time they were called to honour, and hath since continually remained in the same blood; for which cause my lord and father commanded me upon his blessing, that I should do my devoir to cause it to continue still in my blood'. The horn, quite apart from its obvious monetary value, was of great sentimental importance to the old earl, and was also rumoured to have been the cup from which St

Thomas Becket drank.[34] In the event that Thomas Boleyn did not leave male heirs of his own, the seventh earl asked that the horn be passed to another grandson, Sir George St Leger. In the event that this male line also failed, it was to pass first to any other male heirs of his two daughters, before being bequeathed to the male heirs of his father, the fourth earl, which were represented in the person of Piers Butler, a descendant of the fourth earl's younger brother, 'so that it may continue still in my blood hereafter as long as it shall please God'.[35] In later life, Margaret continued to enjoy a happy relationship with her son, with Thomas paying 9s 8d to fur one of her gowns as a gift in late 1526, for example.[36]

At his death, the seventh earl's two daughters were his heirs-general and co-heiresses to any property that was not entailed upon his heir male. It was necessary to look back several generations to the younger brother of the earl's father, whose great-grandson in the male line was an Irish landowner named Sir Piers Butler, to find the heir male.[37] With the earl's death leaving separate heirs general and heirs male, there was an immediate dispute over just how the inheritance should be divided, with the two sisters, who were English resident, obtaining possession of the English estates, while Piers immediately took possession of the Irish lands, as well as declaring himself to be Earl of Ormond. To further complicate matters, Sir James Ormond, an illegitimate son of John Butler, 6th Earl of Ormond, who had acted as his uncle's steward in Ireland, laid claim to the inheritance, retaining some of the Irish manors for his own use.[38]

It has been suggested that the attempts of the sisters, Margaret Butler Boleyn and Anne Butler St Leger, to obtain their inheritance were wrongful and this appears largely to be based on the prominence of Piers Butler's branch of the family at court from the early sixteenth century onwards. An earlier biographer of the family accused the daughters of obtaining the English lands through trickery, acting with their father to suppress deeds which demonstrated that the lands should pass to his heir male.[39] He also claimed that 'this earl's daughters endeavoured to dispossess Piers Earl of Ormond of all the Irish estates', only being prevented when the king himself intervened and passed them to Piers. The Butlers were popular with Elizabeth I during her reign due to their kinship connection with her mother and the Boleyns, with it being considered by the early seventeenth century that the court was the 'natural habitat' of the family.[40] In addition to this, Piers's grandson, Thomas Butler, 10th Earl of Ormond, was educated with the future Edward VI at court and would have been known personally to the children of Henry VIII.[41] In the early seventeenth century the Piers Butler branch of the family were ennobled as Dukes of Ormond and later writers were unwilling to offend the powerful family when discussing their dispute with the daughters of the seventh earl. The facts however do not support either Margaret, or her sister, acting in such an underhand way. They had a very strong claim to all the Ormond possessions, and the title itself, if they were strong enough to claim it.

In the late nineteenth century the historian J. H. Round carried out a study into the dispute over the earldom of Ormond, coming to the conclusion that it was indeed Margaret and her sister who were the rightful holders of the family estates and titles. Round pointed out that the original earldom had been one of six created in Ireland before 1330 and that it then passed from father to son or brother to brother without interruption until 1515, something which served to obscure the true inheritance rights attached to the earldom.[42] The seventh earl's English barony of Rochford lapsed at his death without a son. However, the earldom of Ormond had never been limited to only the male line and, as such, should rightly have passed to the heirs general rather than the heir male, as Margaret and her sister claimed. While the sisters had legal right on their side, it was a different matter for them to actually claim their Irish inheritance. As Round pointed out 'the two co-heiresses were widows, widows moreover of Englishmen and of commoners. The heir male, "the Red Piers", in addition to all his local prestige, had, to support him, the anti-feudal feeling of the natives in favour of the heir male, the preference for an Irishman-born over unknown absentees, and the undoubted, but misleading fact, that, from the accidental circumstance of none of the earls having till then left female heirs, the earldom had never passed from the male line'.[43] In 1515 Margaret Butler Boleyn and Anne St Leger had very little chance of winning in their battle for the Irish estates and title, particularly as Piers had already proved himself to be a prominent, and useful, supporter of English rule in Ireland.

In spite of the near impossibility of their claim, and the fact they were both, by 1515, advanced in age, Margaret and Anne laid claim to the Irish portion of their inheritance, assisted by Margaret's eldest son, who was a prominent courtier. A surviving letter by Margaret to her son, makes clear the affection between them and the fact that she relied on him with regard to her claims to her inheritance:

And whereas I understand to my great heaviness, that my lord my father is departed this world to Almighty God, on whose soul I beseech Jesu to have mercy, wherefore I pray and heartily desire you that you will do for me in everything as you shall think most best and expedient. And in everything that you shall do for me after as you think best, I will, on my part, affirm and rate it in as like manner as though it were mine own deed.[44]

Margaret was evidently feeling her age by the time of her father's death and was anxious to allow her eldest son to take as much of the strain as possible, further commenting that 'and if hereafter you shall think it necessary for me to come up to London to you,

I pray you send hereof to me your mind, and I shall pain myself to come; howbeit if you may do well enough without my coming in my behalf, then I were loath to labour so far'. Margaret's sister, Anne St Leger, was also happy to hand matters to Thomas Boleyn. The sisters remained on good terms with Anne applying for a licence in April 1520 to found a perpetual chantry in Devon to pray for the souls of a number of family members, including her husband, parents and sister.[45] Margaret's health may also have been in decline by the time of her father's death as, by at least 1519, she was considered to be a lunatic.[46] The evidence for her condition is contained in an inquisition held into her lands in Cambridgeshire and perhaps accounts for her apparent willingness to hand over control of her matters and lands to her eldest son. Given her advanced age for the period in 1519, it seems not impossible that her 'lunacy' was some form of dementia, meaning that she may have retained some limited control over her own affairs.

Thomas Boleyn, like his father and grandfather, had made a prestigious match to Elizabeth Howard, the daughter of the 2nd Duke of Norfolk. In 1520 Thomas's brother-in-law, the Earl of Surrey, was sent to Ireland to act as the king's deputy there. Before he went, Thomas pressed his brother-in-law for his assistance in resolving the dispute over the Irish inheritance. Privately, Henry VIII was prepared to recognise the legal right of Margaret and Anne's claim, writing in a personal letter to Surrey of 'Sir Pierce Butler, pretending himself to be Earl of Ormond'.[47] However he was certainly not prepared to offend the prominent Irishman, something to which Surrey, aware of the difficulty in maintaining English control over Ireland, concurred. Surrey found Piers to be a useful ally, writing to the king's chief minister, Cardinal Wolsey, on 3 November 1520:

Beseeching your Grace to cause thankful letters to be sent from the King's Grace to the Earl of Ormond [i.e. Piers

Butler], as well for his diligence showed unto me, at all times, as also for that he showeth himself ever, with his good advice and strength, to bring the king's intended purposes to good effect. Undoubtedly he is not only a wise man, and hath a true English heart, but also he is the man of most experience of the feats of war in this country, of whom I have, at all times, the best counsel of any of this land.[48]

Surrey had no intention of alienating Piers, regardless of his family loyalty to his brother-in-law. Even before this letter was written, however, Surrey had put his mind to ways in which the dispute could be brought to an end, writing to Cardinal Wolsey on 6 October of that year to suggest that a marriage should be arranged between Piers Butler's eldest son, James, who was conveniently then resident in England and a member of Wolsey's household, and Thomas Boleyn's remaining unmarried daughter, the future Queen Anne Boleyn.[49] Surrey hoped that this would cause 'a final end to be made' between Thomas Boleyn and his Irish cousin. This solution was, to the English government, an excellent one, with the king writing back to his deputy to confirm that:

And like as ye desire Us to endeavour ourself, that a marriage may be had and made betwixt the Earl of Ormond's son, and the daughter of Sir Thomas Boleyn, knight, Comptroller of our Household; so we will ye be mean to the said Earl for his agreeable consent and mind thereunto, and to advertise Us, by your next letters, of what towardness ye shall find the said Earl in that behalf. Signifying unto you, that, in the meantime, We shall advance the said matter with our Comptroller, and certify you, how We shall find him inclined thereunto accordingly.[50]

Faced with the king's own personal interest in the matter, Thomas Boleyn could do very little but acquiesce, and he recalled his daughter from France where she had spent some years serving in the household of the Queen of France. On the face of it, the match had much to recommend it and James Butler, who was born in around 1496, was only approximately five years older than his French-educated cousin.[51] He was highly educated himself and later evidence suggests that he was a well-liked and personable young man.

The future Queen Anne Boleyn had arrived in England by early 1522, joining the household of Queen Catherine of Aragon. She had little interest in her Irish suitor, quickly beginning her own relationship with a more prestigious potential husband. It is not impossible that she played a role in the stalling of the marriage negotiations: as her sixteenth-century biographer, the favourable George Wyatt pointed out, 'she was indeed a very wilful woman'.

The fact that the marriage negotiations came to nothing strongly suggests that the Boleyn family, headed by Thomas and his mother, were not favourable to the proposed solution, offering, as it did, only the possibility that one of Thomas's daughters would be Countess of Ormond, rather than actually securing the title and lands for the family. This position must have looked hopeless however when, in March 1522, Piers Butler was appointed to act as Deputy in Ireland following Surrey's return to England.[52] Although apparently initially favourable to the Boleyn marriage, by May 1523, Piers had come to understand that it was unlikely to occur, with the Earl of Kildare writing to the king that he had heard that he intended to defend his claim to the earldom by force if necessary.[53] This was something that the king could not sanction and it may have been an attempt to compensate the Boleyn family, as much as the king's then romantic interest in Thomas's eldest daughter, Mary Boleyn, that he created Thomas Viscount Rochford at a lavish ceremony in June 1525, at the same time that the king's own illegitimate son, Henry Fitzroy, was given two dukedoms and an earldom.

The Butler family's old English barony, upgraded to a viscounty, was no compensation for an earldom and the family continued to push for the restitution of the title. It was only with the relationship between Henry VIII and Thomas's daughter, Anne Boleyn, which led to the couple becoming betrothed in 1527, which resolved the matter. In 1527 Cardinal Wolsey was instructed to draw up articles of an agreement to be entered into by Margaret and her sister and Piers Butler.[54] The three parties signed in February 1528, agreeing that the earldom of Ormond would be placed entirely at the king's disposal. The family estates were divided equally between the two sisters, save where it could be demonstrated that their deeds required them to pass to the heir male. At the same time, the sisters agreed that the bulk of the Irish lands would be leased to Piers and his family: a compromise which saved the face of all involved given that Piers had no intention of giving them up. Six days later the king created Piers Butler, Earl of Ossory, in compensation for the loss of his hopes of the Ormond title and in recognition of his efforts in Ireland. That this settlement was legally fair can be seen in the fact that the two sisters were treated equally, with the elder, Anne St Leger, being given precedence in the document. However, the settlement cost Henry VIII financially with the need to bestow and endow a new earldom and it seems highly unlikely that he would have brokered its terms if it was not for the influence of his fiancée: rather, he would probably have allowed the status quo to continue, regardless of the Boleyn family's protests. At the end of the following year, after a decent interval, Henry VIII created Thomas Boleyn as Earl of Ormond, as well as resurrecting the old Butler title of Earl of Wiltshire. This was the culmination of all Margaret Butler Boleyn's hopes, particularly as her own son was granted the family titles in preference to her nephew. It also suitably aggrandised the king's fiancée.

Thomas Boleyn's acquisition of the Ormond title had obviously been assisted by the prominence of his daughter. With the fall of Queen Anne Boleyn in May 1536 and the execution of her only surviving (and childless) brother, George, at the same time, Thomas Boleyn quite understandably retreated from court for a time. Although it was never suggested that he should lose his titles of Earl of Wiltshire and Ormond, he had lost the king's favour. Piers Butler and his son, James, on the other hand, had continued to grown in esteem and had proved themselves great allies to the English in Ireland. James Butler, who was recorded in a grant of land in October 1537 to have 'shed his blood in the wars against the Geraldines and other rebels', also proved to be a successful treasurer of Ireland.[55] After being disappointed in his marriage to Anne Boleyn, he had married the heiress of the Earl of Desmond and proved to be a loyal and useful ally to the English.

In 1537 a further agreement was finally reached in which it was agreed that, since Piers had been found to be the seventh earl's heir male and that he had been reputed and accepted as the Earl of Ormond for some time, he should be allowed to make use of the title again, receiving a new creation of the earldom of Ormond.[56] In recognition of the undoubted rights of Margaret and her son, this creation did not in fact strip Thomas of his own Irish earldom, with it instead being noted that 'the Earl of Wiltshire is contented he [Piers] be so named Earl of Ormond in Ireland, semblably as the two Lords Dacres be named the one of the South and the other of the North'. That it was intended that there were to be two independent earls of Ormond – one in England who was also Earl of Wiltshire and one in Ireland who was also Earl of Ossory – is clear from the fact that Thomas Boleyn's grandson, Lord Hunsdon, felt confident enough to appeal for the return of the Boleyn earldom of Ormond during the reign of his cousin, Elizabeth I, on the basis that the title could pass to heirs general and that he was the eldest son of Thomas's eldest daughter, Mary Boleyn.[57] That Hunsdon was prepared to do this in spite of the prominence and favour shown to the Butler Earl of Ormond at the time is testament to the fact that it was envisaged that there were to be two earls bearing the same title.

Thomas Boleyn and his mother, if she was well enough, were aware of the practical difficulties of remaining in control of their Irish estates and, shortly before Piers acquired the earldom of Ormond in 1537, it was also agreed between the two earls that Piers would lease certain lands in Ireland which nominally belonged to the original earldom, but which Piers had taken back from squatters who had apparently occupied the lands for over 200 years.[58] Such lands were never reasonably going to yield any profit to Margaret and Thomas without Piers's aid and they accepted his tenancy without demure. In any event, the coincidence of Thomas's return to court in October 1537, when he played a role in the christening of the king's son, Edward, Prince of Wales, which occurred at a similar time as his agreement with Piers, may have been used to persuade him of the wisdom of agreeing to the king's demands – with the prospect of a return to his role of courtier being offered if he acquiesced. His hopes were indeed met, with there even being rumours that he would be allowed to marry the king's niece, Lady Margaret Douglas, after the death of his wife in April 1538.[59]

Margaret Butler Boleyn inherited her father's longevity and lived to see a number of great-grandchildren, as well as outliving many of her children and grandchildren. She continued to be involved in relation to her own estates up until the end of her life, for example joining her son Thomas and granddaughter-in-law Jane Parker Boleyn, Viscountess Rochford, as a party to a sale of land in Buckinghamshire in October 1538, which had made up part of her inheritance.[60] The extent of her actual involvement must however be questionable, given the evidence of the precarious state of her mental health. Her eldest, and apparently favourite, son, Thomas, died in 1539, something that must have caused Margaret considerable grief if she was well enough to understand. She was living with her son at Hever when he died, remaining at the castle until her own death.[61] Thomas had also shown enough concern for his mother that only a year before his own death, he made a grant to her of 400 marks a year from the Ormond lands, ensuring that she remained comfortable in her old age.[62] She died in March 1540, aged around ninety.

Margaret Butler Boleyn was one of the most important women to marry into the Boleyn family and she brought the family considerable wealth. She was not the most prestigious Boleyn bride, however, and that honour must go to her daughter-in-law, Elizabeth Howard, who married Thomas Boleyn in the last years of the fifteenth century.

Part 2
Courtiers: 1485–1526

4

LUSTY TO LOOK ON, PLEASANT, DEMURE, & SAGE

While Sir Thomas Boleyn was frequently associated with his mother during his lifetime, his wife, Elizabeth Howard Boleyn, also played a major role in increasing the family's prominence at court. Elizabeth, unlike her mother-in-law, brought little financial benefit to her marriage, but socially she was a member of one of the highest noble families in England: surprisingly, the Howards had first been ennobled only a few brief decades before her birth, a fact that accounts for her marriage to a mere knight.

The Howards, who although by the early years of Henry VIII's reign were one of the most prominent families in England, had obscure origins. By the late seventeenth century they were claiming Anglo-Saxon forebears, with one account suggesting that 'William the Conqueror found them in a great condition of estate and quality here, according to the mode and method of those times, bearing distinctions proper of barons: they continued most eminent in their country, and linked themselves to the greatest families in the kingdom'.[1] Another claim, which was based on the similarity of names, stated that the family were descended from the Anglo-Saxon Hereward the Wake.[2] It has been pointed out by a recent historian that 'this was wishful thinking on their part and the fabrication of clever heralds'.[3] In fact, the Howard family line cannot be traced back that far, with the first certain ancestor, a Sir William Howard, appearing depicted in stained glass in the church of Long Melford in Suffolk. Sir William was a lawyer of some standing who had come to the attention of Edward I in the fourteenth century, being appointed as one of the chief justices of Common Pleas.[4] The family continued to prosper over the following century, increasing their lands through marriages to East Anglian heiresses on a number of occasions.[5] In 1410 the head of the family, John Howard, died leaving an infant daughter as heiress to the bulk of the Howard family lands. This left John's half-brother Robert Howard with only the small estates of his own mother. It was Robert who eventually brought his branch of the family to the highest levels of the English nobility through his own very unlikely marriage.

The second surviving son of Edward I, Thomas of Brotherton, Earl of Norfolk, left a daughter whose husband was created Duke of Norfolk.[6] This couple were also survived by only one daughter, Elizabeth Seagrave, who married John, Lord Mowbray, and was the mother of Thomas Mowbray, who was created Duke of Norfolk in 1397. The first duke was followed by his son, grandson and great-grandson before the title passed to another heiress, Anne Mowbray, who died young. Robert Howard joined the household of the second Duke of Norfolk early in the fifteenth century, a position which brought him to the attention of his patron's youngest sister, Margaret, when she returned from serving Queen Catherine of Valois in France.[7] The match was highly unequal and was arranged between the couple themselves without recourse to the bride's family. Margaret's elder sisters made much better matches and the fact that they received manors as part of their dowries, while Margaret received none, does suggest that her family were not entirely happy with the marriage. They accepted the *fait accompli* with which they were presented, with Robert remaining in his brother-in-law's employ. The marriage proved to be brief, with Robert's early death in 1436 although it produced three surviving children.

Elizabeth's grandfather, John Howard, was the son of Margaret Mowbray and Sir Robert Howard and was born in around 1421. He remained associated with his Mowbray kin throughout much of his life, to his great advantage. Early in his career he was appointed to act as chamberlain to his cousin, John Mowbray, 3rd Duke of Norfolk. It was this appointment which led to him becoming an esquire in the royal household in 1449 and a Member of Parliament. He fought in France in 1453, although was unfortunately taken prisoner by the French.[8] As his cousin's chamberlain, John played a very personal role, with his accounts from the 1460s making it clear that he was responsible for paying many of the duke's personal expenses, sums for which he would later be reimbursed. For example, in 1462 he paid for the making of a jacket of crimson cloth for the duke, as well as incurring an additional 12 pence cost for lining the jacket.[9] The duke particularly entrusted John with his wardrobe, with John Howard also purchasing a short gown of russet velvet as well as a tawny cloak lined with velvet and a jacket of the king's own livery.

In 1464 John's accounts show that he was even responsible for paying a ferryman to transport the Duchess of Norfolk and her household, as well as expending sums to buy sheets for the children of Norfolk's chapel.[10] He was entrusted with taking delivery of 17 yards of crimson cloth to be given as gifts by Norfolk to a number of gentlemen in 1465, including the Yorkist supporter Humphrey Blount of Kinlet in Shropshire, something which suggests a political motive to the generosity.[11] Towards the end of 1467 Howard incurred expenses 'riding in my lord's need to Framlingham unto York and from thence unto Holt, with 15 servants and 16 horses by 12 days'.[12] This loyalty was consistently rewarded by John's prosperous kinsman, although at no little cost to Howard: in January 1467 John Howard was given the honour of acting as deputy to the Duke of Norfolk as Earl Marshall in a court tournament, a role which cost him more than 300 marks.

John Howard naturally adopted his kinsman's Yorkist sympathies and fought at the Battle of Towton before attending Edward IV's Coronation in June 1461. Edward appointed Howard as his carver, a prestigious post that can only have come about through Mowbray influence. He remained in favour throughout the reign, with Edward IV's wardrobe accounts of 1480, for example, recording that a royal gift was made to John Howard of 9 yards of black velvet.[13] Edward's queen, Elizabeth Woodville, had earlier given 7 yards of green velvet to be made into a gown for him.[14] He was ennobled by Edward IV as Lord Howard and his surviving accounts demonstrate that he was wealthy and able to live in some style during the reign. In his accounts from the early 1480s, for example, John made payments to a goldsmith, as well as purchasing cushions of red worsted for his home.[15]

John entertained lavishly, purchasing delicacies such as venison and cygnets, as well as sugar, pepper, cloves, grains, raisins and almonds.[16] He enjoyed music and the arts, making payments to a bagpiper, as well as to a company of players who performed before him in December 1481.[17] John enjoyed playing chess in his spare time.[18] In 1463 John paid a servant 16 pence for riding to Framlingham to fetch a book that had evidently been left there on an earlier visit.[19] The following year he purchased two books: one in French and the other a copy of the political treatise *Dives et Pauper*, further evidence of an interest in reading and education.[20] John Howard cut a fine figure when he visited court or his estates, with records of his clothes including a long gown of black satin lined with purple velvet, a doublet of crimson satin, a short gown of tawny velvet and a long gown of russet, decorated with fur.[21] The

head of Elizabeth's family liked comfort, possessing several pairs
of slippers. When he sailed, he also took a number of rich goods
with him for his personal needs, including religious paraphernalia,
sheets, a silver basin, a case containing four goblets, a candlestick,
his own cutlery and even a silver chamber pot.[22] John Howard
has been described as 'conspicuously loyal' to the royal house of
York, something that ensured that the king showed him favour
and promoted him in return for his services.[23] In addition to the
profits that he achieved through royal favour, he was also active
in business as a prominent ship owner and was well connected
among the merchants of England, something that is very likely to
have brought him to the attention of Sir Geoffrey Boleyn.

Elizabeth's father, Thomas (the future Earl of Surrey and second
Duke of Norfolk), was as loyal to the Yorkist kings as his father. He
fought, and was injured, at the Battle of Barnet, fighting to restore
Edward IV to the throne in 1471 after the temporary reinstatement
of the Lancastrian Henry VI.[24] On a personal level the battle had
a fortunate consequence for Thomas, whose comrade Humphrey
Bourchier, the heir to Lord Berners, was killed in the fighting.
Soon afterwards Thomas married Bourchier's widow, Elizabeth
Tylney. While Elizabeth Tylney was her father's heiress, she was
not a particularly good match for Thomas and there may have
been more to the match than financial gain, with one commentator
suggesting that the couple are likely to have known each other, with
Thomas being aware of his wife's attractions.[25] It is possible that
the couple made a love match, although the fact that Elizabeth, as
the daughter of a Norfolk knight, Sir Frederick Tylney, also had
territorial interests in Norfolk must have been a consideration.
The Howards were certainly interested in Elizabeth Tylney's lands
and those of her first husband, with her son, John Bourchier, Lord
Berners marrying Catherine Howard, his stepfather's half-sister.
The couple settled at Elizabeth's principal manor of Ashwellthorpe
in Norfolk, suggesting that the match was indeed considered to

be of sound financial advantage to Howard, even if the existence of Elizabeth's son by her first marriage meant that all Thomas Howard could hope for was a life interest in his wife's estates, rather than their inheritance by his own children.

It is likely that there was affection in the marriage. Certainly, Elizabeth's children by her first marriage seem to have been assimilated easily into the family. Elizabeth Howard Boleyn was close enough to her half-brother, Lord Berners, in later life to receive the gift of a sapphire ring from him.[26] In addition to this, the couple's first child, Thomas Howard, who would later become the third Duke of Norfolk, was born in 1473, relatively soon after the wedding. The marriage was well received by the Howard family, with Thomas's father's accounts making regular references to both his daughter-in-law and to his grandchildren and step-grandchildren. For example, in January 1482 he paid for a girdle of gold that was sent to Elizabeth Tylney, presumably as a New Year's gift.[27] At the same time a little horn was sent to 'my young Master Howard' who can be identified as Elizabeth Howard Boleyn's eldest brother, Thomas. Later in the year John Howard paid from his own pocket for his son-in-law and step-grandson, Lord Berner's medicines.[28] It is clear that family was important to Elizabeth's grandfather, with payments in his accounts regularly made for his children's clothing, such as a payment for fine green cloth for a livery gown for his third daughter, Jane.[29] In February 1465 his second daughter, Margaret, received a gift of 'a devise of gold' and also a pair of shoes from her devoted father.[30]

Elizabeth Tylney quickly proved her fecundity to her second husband. Young Thomas's birth was followed in 1477 by Edward and then Edmund in around 1479. The three sons were followed by two daughters, Elizabeth and Muriel, with four sons and one daughter also dying young.[31] Elizabeth's date of birth is nowhere recorded. However she had married by the last years of the fifteenth century, suggesting a date of birth early in the 1480s. Her mother died in 1497 and her father quickly remarried, producing a family of seven further surviving children, including another daughter called Elizabeth who eventually married the Earl of Sussex.[32]

Elizabeth Howard Boleyn's father and grandfather remained devoted to the Yorkist dynasty during the years after Barnet, with both being steadily rewarded by Edward IV. They came to particular prominence in 1483 with the controversial accession of Richard III, to whom they were conspicuously loyal. John Mowbray, Duke of Norfolk, died suddenly in 1476, leaving a daughter, Anne Mowbray, as his heiress. She was married in childhood to Edward IV's second son, Richard, Duke of York, but did not long survive, ensuring that John Howard and his cousin, William, Lord Berkeley, stood as potential co-heirs to the Mowbray estates. Shortly after Richard came to the throne, he repaid the Howards' loyalty by creating John Howard first Duke of Norfolk. At the same time his son, Elizabeth's father, was created Earl of Surrey and given an annuity of £1,100, in recognition of the fact that the earldom had little endowment. He was appointed Lord Steward of the Household at the same time.[33]

The following year, after he had made his peace with his brother's widow, Queen Elizabeth Woodville, Richard III gave the Howards an even greater honour by betrothing his niece, Anne of York, who was the daughter of Edward IV, to Elizabeth's eldest brother, young Thomas. It is therefore no surprise that both were prominent among the king's supporters at the Battle of Bosworth Field in August 1485 when he faced the Lancastrian claimant, Henry Tudor. The first Duke of Norfolk paid for this loyalty with his life, dying on the battlefield alongside his king. Elizabeth's father survived but was injured, finding himself a prisoner of the victor and new king, Henry VII. He was incarcerated in the Tower and was unable to succeed to his father's dukedom, with both being attainted by Parliament on 7 November 1485, with the loss of their lands and honours which this entailed.

As he sat in the Tower awaiting his fate, Surrey had time to reflect on the unfairness of it all. Given that two of Henry VII's three 'titles' to the crown had only come into existence after the Battle of Bosworth Field – title by conquest and title by marriage to Elizabeth of York (which did not in fact occur until 1486), dating his reign to the day before Bosworth based only on his dubious title as heir to the house of Lancaster was highly ambitious. Surrey could hardly have been expected to recognise that a descendant of the legitimised Beaufort family, who were produced in a long-running affair between John of Gaunt, third surviving son of Edward III, and his Hainault mistress who later became his third wife, was in fact the true hereditary king before Bosworth, particularly since the first Tudor claimed through his mother, the then-living Margaret Beaufort, whose husband, Lord Stanley, could have made an equally good attempt at claiming the crown matrimonial. Surrey was no traitor to have fought for his crowned king, and a man who certainly had a better claim to the throne than Henry Tudor, regardless of the rights and wrongs of Richard III's own position regarding the bastardisation of his brother's children. Unfortunately for Surrey, such legal niceties carried little weight in the years after Bosworth as Henry VII sought to cement his claim to the throne. Henry VII was always aware that there were rival claimants to the crown and he required absolute loyalty from his nobility, ensuring that, until Surrey had been able to prove his loyalty to the new king, he was going nowhere.

For Elizabeth Tylney and her children, news of the outcome of the Battle of Bosworth was a disaster and she immediately moved with her family to the Isle of Sheppey, a location that was calculated to afford easy access to the Continent if required.[34] She found herself in particular difficulty, with records from October 1485 recording that Lord Fitzwalter, a supporter of the new king, had broken up her household at Ashwellthorpe and dismissed her servants. She appealed to her husband's kinsman, the Earl of Oxford, who took both her eldest son, the eighteen-year-old Lord Berners, and her third son, Edward Howard, into his household.[35] The eldest Howard brother, young Thomas, may perhaps have entered royal service at this time, an indication that the family were not considered to be fully in disgrace, although Elizabeth Tylney's younger children, including young Elizabeth, remained with their mother while they waited to see whether their fortunes would be revived.[36]

Signs of royal favour came relatively quickly with a limited pardon granted to Surrey in March 1486, although he remained in prison. He was finally released in January 1489 and the attainders against him reversed, although he was still not permitted to take up his father's title of Duke of Norfolk. For Surrey, this release was intended as a test of his loyalty to his new master and he immediately headed north with a royal army to take up a position as Lieutenant of the North.[37] Surrey performed well at this task and quickly obtained the return of his lands. In 1495 the king even allowed his sister-in-law, Anne of York, to marry Surrey's son in fulfilment of the couple's long-standing betrothal. This was clear evidence of royal favour and Elizabeth, who by 1495 was of marriageable age herself, also saw her own prospects rise.

Few details survive of Elizabeth Howard's early life. She appears to have remained with her mother throughout her childhood and in the 1490s travelled with her parents and siblings to Sheriff Hutton Castle in Yorkshire.[38] Elizabeth's half-brother, Lord Berners, and eldest full brother, Thomas, had a very similar handwriting style which suggests that they were educated together. In addition to this, her half-sister, Margaret Bourchier, was known for her own learning, while Thomas was fluent in French, as well as knowledgeable in Latin and Italian. In later life he enjoyed reading every night before he went to bed, something which strongly suggests that education was valued by Elizabeth's parents and that she too would have received a good education. This would have fitted her for her marriage to Thomas Boleyn, who was reputed to be the best French speaker at Henry VIII's court and who promoted the education of his children. If Elizabeth was still unmarried in 1495 when her own brother married, she gained a new companion with the arrival of her sister-in-law, Princess Anne of York, who, under the terms of the marriage contract, was to live with her parents-in-law while her sister, the queen, paid an annual sum for her clothes and expenses. This may have been Elizabeth Howard's first exposure to royalty and would have assisted her in her later role as a lady-in-waiting to Queen Catherine of Aragon. Certainly, Elizabeth of York maintained an interest in her sister throughout her life, with a payment of £120 'to my Lord Howard for the diets of my Lady Anne for a year ended at Michaelmas last passed' appearing in her accounts for March 1503.[39] The queen took an active interest in the dress of Anne of York, suggesting her close involvement in her life after marriage, something which would have benefited the Howards. In May 1502, for example, she made a payment for 7 yards of green satin from Bruges for a kirtle 'for my Lady Anne'.[40] She paid her sister pocket money, with two references in her surviving accounts mentioning sums of money paid to Anne personally, one of which was noted to be 'for her purse'.[41]

Elizabeth, like all female members of her class, was raised for marriage. While her oldest half-brother, Lord Berners, had been married to her aunt to secure his inheritance for the Howards, Surrey cast his net further when arranging marriages for his two stepdaughters, with Margaret Bourchier marrying John Sandys of the Vyne in Hampshire as a child in 1478: a solid, but unspectacular match.[42] This match proved to be short-lived with Margaret, who would later become the lady governess to her own great-niece, Princess Elizabeth, later marrying Sir Thomas Bryan. Elizabeth's other elder half-sister, Anne Bourchier, married Thomas

Fiennes, Lord Dacre, while Surrey was able to provide an heiress for his second son, Edward, with his marriage in around 1500 to Elizabeth, daughter of Miles Stapleton.

It has been suggested that Elizabeth, as the eldest Howard daughter, had been intended for Henry Bourchier, Earl of Essex, following the grant of his wardship to her grandfather by Richard III.[43] This is certainly possible and it was common for the guardian of a ward, who also possessed the rights to their young charge's marriage, to arrange a match with a member of their own family. If Elizabeth was engaged to Essex, however, this came to nothing after Bosworth and her father was instead left to negotiate a new match for her at some point after his release from the Tower in 1489. Given the fact that Surrey's lands lay predominantly in East Anglia, it is no surprise that he came to look at Thomas Boleyn, whose father he knew. As one commentator has pointed out, 'from Surrey's point of view the connection was also highly advantageous, for not only was Sir William very active in local government in Norfolk, but he brought several other powerful Norfolk families closer to the Howards, such as the Sheltons, Heydons and Cleres'.[44] Elizabeth's father was still only Earl of Surrey rather than Duke of Norfolk and coupled with his very recent release from imprisonment, the match was not particularly unequal, especially given the wealth of the Boleyn family. The marriage occurred in the last years of the fifteenth century and certainly before 1499 when Surrey acquired the wardship of John Grey, Viscount Lisle, who was a significantly higher-status individual and to whom he chose to marry his second (and presumably only unmarried) daughter, Muriel. This marriage proved to be short-lived, with Lisle dying in 1504, leaving an infant daughter, Elizabeth. Muriel herself quickly remarried, taking Thomas Knyvet as her second husband.

The surviving evidence suggests that Elizabeth Howard was an attractive woman. She was certainly highly praised by the poet John Skelton, who knew Elizabeth and the female members of her family personally. In his early career, Skelton has been described as a protégé of Elizabeth's mother, the Countess of Surrey, who took a personal interest in his work.[45] *The Garland of Laurel*, which has been described as Skelton's most biographical poem, was published in October 1523, but set at Sheriff Hutton Castle when Elizabeth's family were present there at some point between 1489 and 1499. Astronomical references in the poem itself suggest a date of 8 May 1495, something which is possible given the fact that Elizabeth's parents are both known to have been in the North at this time. However, it is clear that the poem, which refers to the countess and her ten ladies weaving a crown of laurel for him to wear, does not relate to any one date or event as not all the ladies referenced can have been in attendance at the time. Instead, it appears that Skelton was familiar with the ladies of the countess's household and that his work was the result of a number of visits and meetings with ladies, including Elizabeth Howard herself before her marriage. Notwithstanding the fact that not all the ladies can be assembled at the same time, a date of the 1490s would suit Elizabeth very well, when she was then a young woman and still the maiden described by Skelton.[46]

In his work, Skelton provides a picture of domestic contentment, with the Countess of Surrey surrounded by female members of her family. As well as Elizabeth and her younger sister, Muriel, the countess was also attended by her elder daughter, Lady Anne Dacre of the South, who was a child of her first marriage. In addition to her daughters, the countess's niece, Margery Wentworth, who would later become the mother of Henry VIII's third wife, Jane Seymour, was present. Other kinswomen included Margaret Tylney, whose sister-in-law later became Elizabeth Howard Boleyn's stepmother, suggesting close family links. The other ladies also had family connections. The poet suggests a happy family circle at Sheriff Hutton while Elizabeth and her siblings were growing up and before the death of her mother in 1497, her own marriage towards the end of the century and the marriage of her sister, Muriel, in 1500.[47] Given that he wanted to honour his patroness in his work, it is no surprise that Skelton was flattering in his depictions of the countess and her attendants. In spite of this, his description of Elizabeth is likely to have been largely accurate, if allowances are made for a certain amount of flattery. There is also no indication in the work that it had been substantially rewritten before publication, particularly as the Howards were by 1523 even more politically prominent.

For Skelton, in *The Garland of Laurel*, Elizabeth's mother was of 'noble estate', chaste and bountiful and 'of gentle courage and perfect memory'.[48] His more fulsome praise was however left for some of the younger ladies, including Elizabeth herself, who was described as:

To be your remembrance, madam, I am bound,
Like to Irene, maidenly of port,
Of virtue and conning the well and perfect ground;
Whom Dame Nature, as well I may report,
Hath freshly embeautied with many a goodly sort
Of womanly features, whose flourishing tender age
Is lusty to look on, pleasant, demure and sage.

Good Criseyde, fairer than Polexene,
For to enliven Pandarus' appetite;
Troilus, I trow, if that he had you seen,
In you he would have set his whole delight:
Of all your beauty I suffice not to write!
But, as I said, your flourishing tender age
Is lusty to look on, pleasant, demure, and sage.[49]

For Skelton, Elizabeth was one of the most attractive of the ladies described, with only her half-sister, Anne Dacre, coming close, being described as a beauty and 'princess of youth, and flower of goodly port'. Skelton took pains to describe each of the ladies' virtues as he saw them, with Margery Wentworth, for example, praised for her gentleness and Gertrude Statham, who rejected Skelton's advances, grudgingly praised for her chaste virtue. For Elizabeth, her chief virtue described was her beauty, strongly suggesting that she was indeed a striking woman. This was evidently a family trait, with Skelton also referring to Elizabeth's sister, who was then still a child and called 'my little lady' in the poem, as a child within whom:

> The embedded blossoms of roses red of hue,
> With lilies white your beauty doth renew.[50]

The evidence strongly suggests that Elizabeth Howard was considered to be a contemporary beauty, which praised fair hair, pale skin and blue eyes. A surviving portrait which is commonly attributed to Elizabeth's daughter, Mary Boleyn, suggests this colouring and she may have taken after her mother. The second daughter, Anne Boleyn, on the other hand, was famously dark, although this recalls the surviving portrait of her father, Thomas Boleyn.

Other than Skelton's depiction of her in his poem, little evidence survives of Elizabeth's character. Like her husband, she was a courtier, being considered an expert on court protocol in later life. For example, in 1537 Lady Lisle, who was the wife of Edward IV's illegitimate son, Arthur Plantagenet, Lord Lisle, became troubled by the correct status of her stepdaughter, Frances Plantagenet, due to the illegitimate birth of her father. In a letter to Lady Lisle in Calais from her agent at court, John Husee, she was reassured that this shall be signifying the same that ij days since I moved my Lady Rutland again concerning Mrs Frances, and her ladyship standeth in doubt of that matter. But madam, I have been in hand with the Heralds of Arms, and they saith plainly that the woman shall never lose no part of her degree, but shall always be taken as her father's daughter. And if need be, to this I can have both their seals and hands, which is sufficient, for they hath the perfect knowledge.[51]

This assurance was not enough for the cautious Lady Lisle, and only six days later Husee again wrote to her on the matter:

And touching Mrs Frances, the heralds saith planly that she shall lose no degree, but use the same according the dignity of her father. Howbeit, if I might speak with my Lady Wiltshire [Elizabeth], I will not fail to have her advice in it.[52]

Sadly Elizabeth's response does not survive, although it is clear that she was considered something of an authority on the matter, presumably due both to knowledge gained due to her long years at court and, perhaps, due to her known pride in her own status as a daughter of the Duke of Norfolk, rather than as the wife of Sir Thomas Boleyn. Elizabeth was friendly with Lady Lisle, perhaps due to the fact that her sister, Muriel, had been married to John Grey, who was the brother of Lord Lisle's previous wife. In April 1536, when her daughter was still Queen of England, Lady Lisle received a letter from a Thomas Warley which provides one of the only first-hand accounts of Elizabeth, in which he stated from court that also, this day my lady the Countess of Wiltshire [Elizabeth] asked me when I heard from your ladyship, and how you fared, and heartily thanks your ladyship for the hosen; and said you could not have devised to send her a thing that might be to her a greater pleasure than they were considering how she was then diseased; and further desired me that I would not depart over to Calais until I should speak with her, which, God willing, I will not fail. And I ensure your ladyship she is sore diseased with the cough, which grieves her sore.[53]

Given that Elizabeth died just under two years later it seems not impossible that her cough represented the early stages of tuberculosis which was all too common in the Tudor period. In this brief anecdote she appears friendly and approachable, recalling fondly the gift that her friend had sent her, something which shows her character in a favourable light.

The date of Elizabeth's marriage to Thomas Boleyn is not recorded. It has been estimated to have been as early as 1495 and it was certainly by 1499, given her father's acquisition of the wardship of John Grey, who was instead assigned as a husband to her younger sister.[54] Elizabeth's dower, which was settled upon her by her father-in-law in July 1501, survives, in which she was given a life interest in Boleyn lands in Sussex and Norfolk, as well as a life interest after William Boleyn's death in Hever and other manors in Kent.[55] While these documents do prove that Elizabeth was married by July 1501, they do not provide the date of the marriage, particularly as it was frequently a term of contemporary marriage agreements that a financial settlement would only be made to the bride within a specified period following the birth of a first child. Thomas had joined the court by around 1500, something which may well have been motivated by poverty since he later lamented that, at the time of his marriage, he had had only £50 per year to live on, in spite of Elizabeth's fecundity, something which also suggests that he and Elizabeth lived as man and wife for some years before she received her financial settlement from his father.[56]

Thomas was known to be a proficient jouster, which brought him to the attention of the future King Henry VIII. Certainly, he was knighted at the young king's Coronation in 1509 and took part in court ceremonials during the early years of the reign. He has been described as a courtier and this description is apt. Elizabeth and Thomas spent much time at court during the years of their marriage, although the couple were frequently apart, with Thomas serving as ambassador abroad during Henry VIII's reign. For example, in May 1512 he was sent as English ambassador to Margaret of Austria, Regent of the Netherlands, an appointment which lasted nearly a year.[57] Thomas could be very charming and became a particular favourite of the regent's, with her making a friendly wager with him, on which they shook hands, over the likely outcome of the negotiations.[58] As a reward for his services, Thomas and Elizabeth jointly received the royal grant of a Norfolk manor in September 1512 while Thomas was still in Brussels.[59]

Even after his return to England, he did not remain in the country for long, joining the king's army in France in the summer of 1513 with a retinue of 100 men under his command.[60] Before Henry VIII's accession, Thomas Boleyn, his father-in-law, Surrey, Elizabeth's three brothers and her brother-in-law, Thomas Knyvet, were often at court. Elizabeth's eldest brother, Thomas Howard, and his wife, Anne of York, buried their four young children in Lambeth during the last years of Henry VII's reign, suggesting that they spent much time at the Howards' London residence in the parish, while Muriel and Knyvet are also known to have spent time there. Given that Elizabeth later chose to be buried at Lambeth, it is likely that she and Thomas Boleyn also stayed at the residence for long periods when they were in London, a location that would have given them very easy access to the court.[61] Thomas Boleyn was a regular participant in court tournaments during the early years of the reign.[62] In addition to this, he and Elizabeth were in high enough favour with the king to receive a visit by him to their residence at Newhall in Essex in 1515, with the property apparently so impressive that the king later acquired it for himself. Thomas had already been appointed as an Esquire of the Body by 1509 and he had become a Knight of the Body by 1515. His court career progressed steadily, with his appointment as Comptroller of the Royal Household in 1520 and Treasurer of the Household in 1521.

There is no evidence to suggest that Elizabeth had her own court position during the reign of Henry VII, something which would, in any event, have been unlikely following the death of Queen Elizabeth of York in 1503. The presence of small memorials to two of Elizabeth's minor children, Henry and Thomas, at Hever and Penshurst respectively suggests that the family were most likely resident in Kent. There is little evidence of Elizabeth's personal relationship with her husband. The fact that she bore at least five children in the early years of her marriage suggests that they were close. Although Thomas was also close to his mother, Margaret Butler, there is no evidence that Elizabeth was overshadowed by the older woman. In a royal pardon granted in 1520–21, for example, concerning the Boleyn manor of Fretwell in Oxfordshire, Elizabeth was named as a party along with her husband and mother-in-law, suggesting that she had an equal standing.[63]

Most of Elizabeth's early married life was taken up with childbearing: her husband later commented in a letter that, after their marriage, his wife brought him a child every year up until at least his father's death in 1505 – something which must have been rather expensive for a young man who had not yet attained his inheritance and may hint at why Thomas was so keen to pursue a court career.[64] The names of five of Elizabeth's children are known: Mary, Anne, George, Thomas and Henry. It is possible that there may have been others, particularly as the two children who are known to have died young, Thomas and Henry, bore the names of their father and the king and may well each have been the oldest son during their brief lives. It is therefore no surprise that both received some form of commemoration following their deaths in the form of small brass crosses in Penshurst church and Hever church. These memorials, in spite of one recent author's assertion that the younger Thomas Boleyn lived until adulthood, are clearly memorials to children.[65] They are the only records of the two boys' brief lives. It is not at all impossible that further children, in particular young daughters, may have escaped any commemoration or notice in contemporary sources. Elizabeth's daughter, Anne, for example, left no record in surviving contemporary documents until she was approaching her teenage years.

There is some uncertainty about the dates and order of the births of Elizabeth's three surviving children: Mary, Anne and George. A contemporary of the siblings, George Cavendish, later claimed of George that 'years thrice nine my life had passed away' when he became a member of the king's Privy Council in 1529, suggesting a date of birth of 1502.[66] Anne's date of birth is usually claimed as either 1507 or earlier, perhaps 1501. The Elizabethan historian William Camden, in his history of Anne's daughter, Elizabeth, claimed that Anne had been born in 1507, a date which was also given in the early seventeenth-century *Life of Jane Dormer*, an account of the life of an attendant of Anne's stepdaughter, Mary I. However, it is clear that the author of the *Life of Jane Dormer* was familiar with Camden's work and the authority for Anne's birth being in 1507 must therefore rest with Camden alone. If Camden is correct with this birth date then Anne would have been only six years old when she first left home to serve Margaret of Austria in the Netherlands. While princesses were, on occasion, sent abroad at young ages, this was unheard of for lower members of society and twelve was the commonly accepted earliest age for which a girl could take up service in another noble household. An earlier birth date of 1501 therefore seems more plausible for Anne, particularly due to the fact that a letter survives from Anne to her father from her time in Brussels in which she declared that 'I beg you to excuse me if my letter is badly written, for I assure you that the orthography is from my own understanding alone, while the others were only written by my hand'.[67] While the letter is written in the eccentric French of a beginner, it is certainly not the work of a six-year-old. This is also supported by the fact that Anne would later bemoan her lost youth to Henry VIII while she waited to become his bride, and the fact that she was considered to be rapidly ageing and losing her looks during her time as queen: something more likely in a woman approaching her late thirties than a woman still in her twenties, regardless of the stresses of her position. Although Anne Boleyn's birth date is by no means universally agreed upon, 1501 is very likely, making her the senior of her only surviving brother.

The seniority of the two Boleyn sisters has been highly debated. It was Anne who was sent to Brussels in 1513, while Mary remained at home, something which would suggest that Anne was the elder. However, Mary was sent to France the following year and it is possible that Thomas Boleyn merely decided to send his more promising daughter to Brussels. It was Mary who married first, in 1520, suggesting seniority, although it is not impossible that a younger daughter could have married first, especially as it was then only Mary who was resident in England. Better evidence of Mary's seniority is provided in a letter written by her grandson, Lord Hunsdon, in which he claimed the earldom of Ormond. In order to substantiate his claim, he set out his position to Elizabeth

I, who was, of course, the heir to the other daughter, pointing out that Thomas Boleyn's heir was 'his eldest daughter Mary' and that even if the attainder over the younger daughter, Anne Boleyn, was overlooked, it could be considered 'whether my Grandmother being the eldest daughter ought not to have the whole dignity as in the earldom of Chester'. To confuse matters further, a monument to Hunsdon's daughter later referred to Mary Boleyn as the second daughter, although it does appear that Hunsdon, who was, after all, seeking to claim a title in preference to the queen herself, did his research thoroughly. It is most likely that Mary was the eldest surviving child of Thomas and Elizabeth, with a date of birth of around 1499.

Blickling is the most likely birthplace of all of Elizabeth's children. Given her near-constant pregnancies, Elizabeth must have been an accessible presence in her children's early childhoods, spending much of her time at home with them at Blickling either awaiting the birth of a child or recovering from the birth. Elizabeth was responsible for teaching her daughters traditional feminine accomplishments such as singing, music, dancing and needlework, although the evidence suggests that Anne was not an enthusiastic seamstress, later sending Henry VIII's shirts to be embroidered by paid needlewomen once she had succeeded in wresting the duty of making his shirts from Catherine of Aragon. Elizabeth may have taught her children their letters, although, since both George and Anne are known to have been highly educated, tutors must have been employed. George is believed to have studied at Oxford University and was also renowned as a poet by contemporaries, although no examples of his work survive. Following the move to Hever in 1505 and the end of her childbearing years, Elizabeth spent more time at court, culminating in her appointment to the queen's household in 1509. However, her absence from royal records for much of the time does suggest that she was not at court particularly regularly, ensuring that she remained available to her children.

There is clear evidence from later in her children's lives that Elizabeth was close to them. Following the arrests of her two children, Anne and George, in 1536, there were rumours that Elizabeth and her husband had joined them in the Tower, suggesting close links.[68] The fact that Lady Lisle's agent found Elizabeth at court in April 1536 and considered her worth cultivating due to her connection with her daughter is also significant. Earlier, in February 1533, within a few weeks of Anne Boleyn's marriage to the king the Imperial ambassador, Eustace Chapuys, was reporting that the king had been married in secret in the presence only of Anne's parents, brother, two of her friends and one of his priests.[69] Whether Elizabeth was indeed present at her daughter's secret wedding is not known, but the fact that she was believed to have been there speaks volumes for her close relationship with her daughter. Elizabeth was also prominent at Anne's coronation later in 1533 when she rode in the first chariot with her stepmother, the Dowager Duchess of Norfolk, in procession after the queen.[70] Further, rather surprising evidence of Elizabeth's closeness with her younger daughter can be seen in the records of the interrogation of Elizabeth Barton, the nun of Kent, who famously prophesied the king's doom if he married Anne Boleyn.[71] According to Barton, the king offered to make her an abbess if she would desist with her prophecies, which were given widespread credence in England. At the same time, apparently, 'my lord of Wiltshire [Thomas Boleyn] sent to the Emperor, how the queen [Anne Boleyn] would have had her to remain in the court, and my lady, her mother, did desire her to wait upon her daughter'. Clearly Elizabeth was able to wield some influence over her daughter Anne and was often present with her at court. The roots of this closeness probably lie in Anne's early childhood.

In spite of her domestic duties, Elizabeth also had responsibilities at court during the reign of Henry VIII. She was very much a presence there in the early years of the reign.

5

THREE LADY BOLEYNS AT COURT

There was at least one Lady Boleyn present at court from early in the reign of Henry VIII. The identity of this lady or ladies is disputed, with three sisters-in-law – Elizabeth Howard Boleyn, Elizabeth Wood Boleyn and Anne Tempest Boleyn – all potential candidates.

Elizabeth Howard Boleyn's high birth made her perfectly suited to take up a position in the household of Queen Catherine of Aragon in 1509, which lasted until the mid-1520s.[1] There is however some confusion over whether Elizabeth ever held any official position in the queen's household. One recent biographer of Elizabeth's daughter, Mary Boleyn, has suggested that there is no evidence that Elizabeth was a lady-in-waiting to the queen and that, instead, she has been confused with her sister-in-law, Anne Tempest Boleyn.[2] That writer claims that there is no evidence for Elizabeth's presence at court before the reference to her as in attendance on the queen at the Field of the Cloth of Gold in 1520, the grand meeting between Henry VIII and Francis I of France held at Calais. This is, however, a rather circular argument since there is evidence of at least one Lady Boleyn at court during the early years of the reign; it is simply that if a writer chooses to identify these sources as solely referring to Anne Tempest Boleyn then it would obviously appear that there is no evidence of Elizabeth Howard Boleyn in the queen's household. There is no doubt that there was at least one other Lady Boleyn active at court during Henry VIII's reign: after Anne Boleyn's fall she was placed under observation by an aunt named Lady Boleyn, and the same Lady Boleyn, or another, was also named in connection with the discovery of the covert relationship between the king's niece, Lady Margaret Douglas, and Elizabeth's half-brother, Lord Thomas Howard, which came to light in the summer of 1536.[3] The Lady (or Ladies) Boleyn from 1536 are obviously not Elizabeth Howard as she would, by that stage, always have been referred to as the Countess of Wiltshire. In addition to this, sources for Catherine of Aragon's household early in the reign are fairly incomplete, something which hinders an identification of Elizabeth Howard Boleyn's activities.

There are two possible alternative candidates for references to Lady Boleyn at court. The first is Elizabeth Wood, the wife of Thomas Boleyn's younger brother, Sir James Boleyn. Elizabeth Wood was one of the four daughters of John Wood and his wife, Margaret, of East Barsham in Norfolk.[4] The Wood family had occupied the manor since the reign of Henry VI in the mid-fifteenth century with the arrival of John Wood of Briston. This John died in 1470, leaving his brother Robert as heir, who was, in his turn, succeeded by Elizabeth's father, John. John Wood died in 1496, leaving a son, Roger, who was then a minor, as his heir. Roger was not confirmed in his inheritance until 6 November 1513, something that would have occurred when he was aged around twenty-one, suggesting a date of birth of late 1492. Roger's sister, Anne, was of childbearing age in 1512, which suggests that she would have been born around the same time. In addition to this, his mother, Margaret, took a second husband, Sir Henry Fermor, and bore him at least one child, something which supports the view that her children were young at the time of her first husband's death. Elizabeth Wood was therefore probably born in the late 1480s or early 1490s.

Elizabeth was one of four sisters, with a sister, Alice, marrying a Michael Mackerel, a tradesman of London before 1518. A further sister, Dorothy, had married a gentleman, William Whayte, by the same date. Following her marriage to James Boleyn, Elizabeth settled with her husband at Blickling. In 1512 her sister, Anne, who was the wife of Thomas Astley, another Norfolk gentleman, visited her at Blickling, sadly dying during the visit. Given that the sisters were close enough to receive visits from each other, this must have been a traumatic experience for Elizabeth. Anne Astley's funeral brass from Blickling church shows her holding her infant twins and wearing a dress with the open lacing characteristic of pregnancy.[5] This strongly suggests that she arrived at the visit pregnant and, perhaps unaware that she was expecting twins, went into labour prematurely and unexpectedly. Given that she was depicted as pregnant with memorials to her two children, it appears that all three died at Blickling during the birth, something which must have deeply affected her sister who, in all likelihood, would have attended the birth. The evidence of Anne Wood's grave at Blickling makes it clear that Elizabeth had married James by 1512 at the latest, although the couple had no surviving children of their own.

She is almost certainly not the Lady Boleyn present at court early in Henry VIII's reign due to the fact that her husband was not then knighted, making her 'Mistress Boleyn' rather than 'Lady Boleyn'.[6] Surviving records of James suggest that he was largely based in Norfolk during the early years of the reign, with his presence regularly recorded on commission of the peace and array for the county. While Thomas Boleyn was also often present on the same commissions and he is known to have been regularly absent from the county on royal business, he was at least a major landowner there, something which James was not, suggesting that his inclusion was due more to personal presence. It is usually assumed that James was not knighted until 1520, although this is in fact not the case.[7] James had not been knighted by 27 November 1515 when a document refers to him still in Norfolk as simply James Boleyn.[8] By December of the following year he had both been knighted and established himself in the royal household as one of the knights of the Body, a role that did require some personal attendance on the king.[9] His court presence increased with the position of his niece, Anne Boleyn, as queen, with 'Sir James Boleyn' recorded as owing her £50 at the time of her death.[10]

Elizabeth Wood Boleyn's brother, Roger, went on a pilgrimage to Jerusalem in 1518, where he died. There was some contention over the inheritance of his estates, with it being agreed on 14 September 1519 that his stepfather, Sir Henry Fermoys, would receive the family lands, in return for a payment of £35 to each of his three surviving stepdaughters. This was a substantial sum but it would not have increased Elizabeth's status as the wife of a younger brother living at Blickling only with the permission of the head of her husband's family. She was certainly no great heiress. Elizabeth Wood Boleyn may well be the Lady Boleyn present at court in the 1530s, but the relatively low status of her husband and the fact that she had not yet attained her own inheritance makes it highly unlikely that she was the Lady Boleyn who stood in for the queen as godmother at the christening of Henry VIII's niece, Frances Brandon, in July 1517.[11] For similar reasons, she is also unlikely to be one of the ladies listed in a record of daily liveries in the king's household compiled in October 1519, which recorded that a 'Lady Bullayn' was entitled to a breakfast at court, while a 'Lady Bolayn' was a member of the queen's chamber.[12] This record may refer to the same lady or, equally, it may refer to the two sisters-in-law, Elizabeth Howard Boleyn and Anne Tempest Boleyn.

Anne Tempest was some years younger than her sisters-in-law and was the wife of Thomas Boleyn's youngest brother, Sir Edward Boleyn. The Tempest family were an old one, tracing their descent to at least Sir Richard Tempest, who was Lord of Bracewell and

Waddington in Yorkshire in the late fourteenth and early fifteenth centuries.[13] This Sir Richard's wife, Margaret, had the unfortunate distinction of being abducted by the Scots from Roxburgh Castle in 1385 while her husband was warden there. The couple were survived by a son, Sir Piers, who fought at Agincourt with Henry V and whose son, Sir John, assisted Henry VI during his time as a fugitive in the north of England in the 1460s following his deposition from the throne. Sir John Tempest's fifth son married as her second husband Catherine, daughter of Leo, Lord Welles, who became one of her father's heiresses following the death of her half-brother John, Viscount Welles, during the reign of Henry VII.[14] John Welles was wealthy with strong royal connections as the maternal half-brother of Lady Margaret Beaufort, the king's mother. In addition to this, he had been permitted to marry Cecily of York, daughter of Edward IV, although the couple had no surviving children. Robert Tempest's fortunate marriage to Catherine Welles provided him with lands far in advance of what a fifth son could usually expect and he died relatively wealthy in 1509. The couple's eldest son, Sir John, died in the same year, having married Joan Roos on 15 April 1501.[15]

John Tempest's marriage produced two daughters: Margaret, who was aged four in 1509, and Anne, who was aged seven at the time of an inquisition post mortem held for her father on 4 February 1513, and later went on to marry Sir Edward Boleyn.[16] The youth of the two girls is further attested by the fact that Anne's wardship was granted in June 1510 to William Tyler and confirmed on 31 July 1517.[17] Margaret's was granted in July 1517 to Sir William Compton and Sir John Sharpe. Both girls were minors in July 1517 and unmarried; it appears that Margaret died unmarried, presumably not long after the grant of her wardship. The date of Anne's marriage is not recorded although it is highly unlikely to have taken place before she was at least twelve, a birthday that would have occurred at some point between 5 February 1517 and

3 February 1518. As set out above, it was also not before 31 July 1517, meaning that she was not the Lady Boleyn who attended the christening of Frances Brandon. The earliest reference to Anne as Sir Edward Boleyn's wife is her presence at the Field of the Cloth of Gold in the summer of 1520. On 19 November 1520 she and her husband were granted livery of her lands, demonstrating that she had finally come into her inheritance.[18] Given that she was still aged well below the usual age of inheritance of twenty-one, it would seem likely that this concession was made in the light of her recent marriage.

Twelve was also recognised as the earliest date at which a girl could take up an appointment in the queen's household. While Anne had royal connections thanks to her association with the Welles family, she was hardly a great heiress and it may have taken her longer to establish herself at court, with appointments with the queen highly sought after – certainly, the better-connected Lady Lisle, who was the wife of an illegitimate son of Edward IV, later struggled to obtain a post for her daughter with Queen Jane Seymour.[19] She cannot therefore be the Lady Boleyn recorded at court any earlier than 1517 and the lady in question should be identified with Elizabeth Howard Boleyn, particularly as Margaret Butler Boleyn, the only other potential candidate, made it clear in her letter to her son, Thomas Boleyn, which was written in 1515, that she came up to London only very rarely and only when necessity required it.

From 1525 Elizabeth Howard Boleyn would have been referred to as Lady Rochford, and later Lady Wiltshire. Between at least 1520, when Anne Tempest was referred to as the wife of Sir Edward Boleyn in attendance on the queen at the Field of the Cloth of Gold, and 1525, there is some confusion between her and her sister-in-law. However any reference earlier than at least 1517 must be Elizabeth Howard. Since Anne Tempest is known to have been married by 1520, it is clear that she did indeed marry young, something that would have been expected of an heiress. Sir Edward

Boleyn was almost certainly helped in his pursuit of the heiress by the Welles connection, with the elder sister of Anne's paternal grandmother, Eleanor Welles, being the stepmother of Sir Edward's own grandmother, Anne Hoo Boleyn.[20] The Hoo and Boleyn families had remained closely connected and this relationship may well have secured the match for Sir Edward. Sir Edward Boleyn and Anne Tempest Boleyn had four daughters: Mary, Elizabeth, Ursula and Amy, all of whom survived to adulthood.[21] These daughters were born early in the marriage, suggesting that Anne Tempest Boleyn spent much of her time in that period occupied in childbearing rather than attending the queen on a regular basis, unlike Elizabeth Howard Boleyn, who had, by then, long since completed her family.

Elizabeth Howard Boleyn attended the Coronation of Henry VIII and Catherine of Aragon in 1509 as a member of the new queen's retinue, a post for which she received material for a new gown from the royal stores.[22] In the same royal document, which detailed arrangements for the Coronation, Elizabeth was listed among the baronesses in the queen's chamber, along with her sister Muriel, a household which was headed by Elizabeth's grandfather-in-law, Queen Catherine's chamberlain, the Earl of Ormond. While it is possible that temporary appointments were made to the queen's household for the Coronation, it is unlikely and Elizabeth can therefore be considered to have received a court appointment with the queen soon after the royal marriage, a date that is far too early for either Elizabeth Wood Boleyn or Anne Tempest Boleyn to have been alternative candidates. It has also long been considered by historians that Elizabeth Howard Boleyn had a post in the queen's household from early in the reign, with considerable reason.[23] A 'Lady Bulleyn' received a New Year's gift from the king in 1513, receiving a cup with a gilt cover weighing 16½ ounces.[24] The recipient of this gift again cannot have been either of Elizabeth's sisters-in-law, as set out above. The only other candidate, Margaret

Butler Boleyn, is rather implausible given that, at that stage, she was merely the elderly daughter of the Earl of Ormond and the widow of a knight living away from court: certainly, her sister, Anne St Leger, was not similarly honoured. While a New Year's gift does not necessarily mean that the recipient held a court position, it is strongly suggestive of the fact that they were at least often at court and in the king's remembrance, especially where the recipient was not of particularly high status (with Elizabeth only the daughter of an earl and the wife of a knight). Also, Lady Boleyn's gift was one of the heaviest presents given to non-royal ladies, a mark of considerable esteem, with it being only smaller than those received by Lady Hastings (a sister of the Duke of Buckingham and former mistress of the king's), the elder Lady Guildford, Lady Lucy and Lady Mountjoy. Lady Guildford held a position with the king's sister, Mary Tudor, as her governess, while Lady Mountjoy was the wife of an important officer in the queen's household and one of the attendants whom she had brought with her from Spain. The fact that Elizabeth received a gift among this company either demonstrates considerable court presence or a position in the queen's household.

Although Elizabeth's court duties and those of her husband would have taken her regularly to court, some evidence of her social circle when she was at home survives. She spent time with her husband's niece, Anne Shelton, who was the daughter of her sister-in-law, Anne Boleyn Shelton.[25] Anne Shelton was friendly with Anne Lestrange, who lived in Hunstanton. In 1519 Lady Lestrange's accounts show that Anne Shelton stayed with her for seven days, with additional visits being made in 1526, following her marriage.[26] Interestingly, Elizabeth visited Lady Lestrange with her niece in 1526, something that suggests that she was also friendly with her hostess. The association with Anne Shelton shows that Elizabeth took steps to befriend her husband's family. The fact that Anne had by then married Elizabeth's nephew, Sir

Edmund Knyvet, who was the son of her sister Muriel, strongly suggests that she, as the couple's common aunt, played a role in arranging the match, something which again suggests a friendship with both parties. Knyvet attended the visit with his wife and aunt.[27] It was certainly not unnatural for Elizabeth to socialise with the Lestranges or her Shelton kin when she was resident at Blickling. All three lived within 40 miles of each other.[28] She was well entertained at her visit, with the Lestrange household accounts recording that seven rabbits were taken out of store for the company to eat.

Elizabeth benefited from the increasing prominence of her own family during the years of her marriage. During Henry VII's reign Elizabeth's father continued to prosper, something which increased her own status as his eldest daughter. In 1501 Henry, who had become convinced of the elder Howard's loyalty, appointed him as High Treasurer of England.[29] The family were finally restored to their full social position in 1513 following Elizabeth's father's great victory over the Scots at Flodden Field when Surrey led an English army against the Scots while Henry VIII was absent in France. The victory was both brutal and complete, with James IV of Scotland and much of his nobility killed, something which persuaded Henry VIII to finally restore his loyal general to the dukedom of Norfolk in February 1514, with his son, Elizabeth's eldest brother, promoted to the earldom of Surrey. The grateful king also granted the new duke twenty-six manors, vastly increasing his wealth, as well as allowing him to add part of the royal arms of Scotland to his heraldic shield as a reminder of his victory.[30]

The acquisition of the duchy of Norfolk by her father served to increase Elizabeth's prestige substantially. When Elizabeth was chosen to attend the queen at the meeting between Henry VIII and Francis I of France at Calais in 1520, which is known as the Field of the Cloth of Gold, she was listed among the baronesses due to her status as a duke's daughter, something which entitled her to take two female servants, three male servants and six horses to the meeting.[31] Her sister-in-law, Anne Tempest Boleyn, was merely listed among the knights' wives, something which allowed her only one female servant, two male servants and four horses. Elizabeth's own daughter, Mary Boleyn, was only allowed to take one woman, two male servants and three horses, with the status gap between Elizabeth and other female members of the Boleyn family obvious at the meeting. Elizabeth's father did not die until 1524 when he was nearly eighty years old.

For much of her marriage, Elizabeth had access to the court. It appears that she did not necessarily have an entirely spotless reputation. In 1533 a Mistress Amadas, whose own name had earlier been linked with the king, declared scandalously that 'my lady Anne [Boleyn] should be burned, for she is a harlot; that Master Norris was bawd between the king and her; that the king kept both the mother and daughter, and that my lord of Wiltshire [Thomas Boleyn] was bawd both to his wife and his two daughters'.[32] Elizabeth Amadas had a family connection to another of the king's former mistresses, Bessie Blount, through the marriage of Bessie's sister, Isabel, to William Reed of Oatlands, a goldsmith like Amadas's husband and the nephew and heir of her father's prominent friend and her brother's godfather, Sir Bartholomew Reed.[33] She may therefore have had a political point to her claims: there was a party in England at the time who hoped that the king would marry Bessie and legitimise their son, rather than taking Anne Boleyn as his bride.[34] Her claims should be treated with caution, perhaps as an outburst due to her disappointment in the king's marriage.

Mistress Amadas was not the only individual to scandalously repeat this rumour during Elizabeth's own lifetime, with Henry VIII's opponent, Friar Peto, also making a similar claim in 1532. Other early evidence of this is included in a letter written by Sir George Throckmorton in the late 1530s when he recounted a meeting with

Henry VIII during the parliament of 1529 when he had been in opposition to the government. According to Throckmorton's later recollection, during this interview he attempted to dissuade the king from marrying Anne Boleyn by pointing out that 'it is thought you have meddled both with the mother and sister'.[35] Henry VIII, apparently caught off guard, immediately responded, 'Never with the mother,' and it was left to his chief minister, Thomas Cromwell, to quickly add, untruthfully, that the king had never meddled with the sister either.

The gossip surrounding Henry VIII and Elizabeth was later used and developed by the Jesuit writer, Nicholas Sander, who was writing in the reign of Elizabeth's granddaughter, Elizabeth I. Sander, who was strongly opposed to Elizabeth I, wrote a scurrilous account of her mother, Anne Boleyn, something which was embellished by the following passage:

Anne Boleyn was the daughter of Sir Thomas Boleyn's wife; I say of his wife, because she could not have been the daughter of Sir Thomas, for she was born during his absence of two years in France on the king's affairs. Henry VIII sent him apparently on an honourable mission in order to conceal his own criminal conduct; but when Thomas Boleyn, on his return at the end of two years, saw that a child had been born in his house, he resolved, eager to punish the sin, to prosecute his wife before the delegates of the archbishop of Canterbury, and obtain a separation from her. His wife informs the king, who sends the marquis of Dorset with an order to Thomas Boleyn to refrain from prosecuting his wife, to forgive her, and be reconciled with her.

Sir Thomas saw that he must not provoke the king's wrath, nevertheless he did not yield obedience to his orders before he learned from his wife that it was the king who had tempted her to sin, and that the child Anne was the daughter of no other than Henry VIII. His wife then entreated him on her knees to forgive her, promising better behaviour in the future. The marquis of Dorset and other personages, in their own and in the king's name, made the same request, and then Sir Thomas Boleyn became reconciled to his wife, and had Anne brought up as his own child.[36]

Sander's work is not so wholly inaccurate that it should be dismissed out of hand: he correctly recorded that the king did indeed enjoy a relationship with Elizabeth's elder daughter, Mary Boleyn, with the claim that 'he had her brought to the court, and ruined her', although the claim that she had first come to his attention through his visits to her mother are likely to be false given that Mary was in France for some months before returning to England to take up a court position when she first caught the king's eye.

The idea that Henry VIII could possibly have been the father of Anne Boleyn is entirely false. In his account, Sander claims that Anne was born after Henry VIII became king during an absence of Thomas Boleyn from England of at least two years. Henry VIII came to the throne in 1509 at the age of seventeen. Thomas Boleyn, who attended the king's Coronation, took part in a court masque in January 1510, as well as jousts in May 1510 and February 1511.[37] He further appeared in a court masque in December 1514. The earliest period in which his two-year absence could have taken place is therefore some point between February 1511 and December 1514. It is true that he served as ambassador to Brussels for nearly a year during this period, an appointment that could, perhaps, have been misidentified by Sander as in France. However, although there is some uncertainty over Anne Boleyn's birth date, it is certain that she was not born between 1512 and 1514. Thomas Boleyn used his friendship with Margaret of Austria, Regent of the Netherlands, which developed during his mission to Brussels, to secure a place in his household for his younger daughter, with a letter written by Anne to her father surviving from this period: clearly, this letter was not the work of a two-year-old. In addition to this, both Boleyn sisters served in the household of Mary Tudor, Queen of France in 1514, with Anne then transferring to the household of Francis I's wife, Queen Claude: this was hardly the career of an infant. Quite apart from the fact that Henry VIII was highly unlikely to want to marry his own child, his taste in wives and mistresses tended towards women in their twenties and even thirties, making it unlikely that he would seek to marry a girl in her early teens when he first began to attempt to make Anne Boleyn his queen in 1527. Sander was clearly intent upon slander in his work when he declared that Thomas Boleyn warned the king off Anne, telling him that he knew her to be Henry's own child, something to which Sander claims that the king replied, 'Hold your tongue, you fool, hundreds are compromised; and be her father who he may, she shall be my wife.'

Sander's story, the central point of which was to highlight a scandalous paternity for Anne Boleyn rather than to focus on a supposed royal affair for her mother, is therefore entirely improbable. However, the evidence of Throckmorton's letter, other contemporary rumours and the fact that Sander later developed the tale does suggest that there was some substance to the claims and that there may have been some kind of relationship between them, even if it was not one that produced a child. The evidence that Elizabeth was a mistress of Henry VIII must therefore be considered. In *The Garland of Laurel*, Skelton very pointedly compared Elizabeth to Criseyde and commented that Criseyde's legendary lover, Troilus, Prince of Troy, would have loved her if he had seen her, presumably in preference to Criseyde herself. It is just possible to posit a deliberate comparison between Troilus, Prince of Troy, and Henry, Prince of England, falling in love with the charms of the beautiful Elizabeth Howard in their youths, an allusion which, given the fact that the poem was not published until 1523, Skelton could have added to an earlier draft of his work after witnessing a relationship between Elizabeth and Henry VIII. However, given the fact that it is Troilus, Criseyde's princely lover, who is betrayed by her, rather than any husband, it is probably stretching the source too far to posit from this that Elizabeth had a reputation for faithlessness in her lifetime as one recent writer has suggested.[38] If anything, Skelton's poem positively highlights Elizabeth's character, calling her both demure and sage in her conduct.

Another point which must count against Elizabeth being Henry VIII's mistress in the period before he became king is quite how over-protected the young prince was known to be by his father, whose hopes of founding a dynasty rested on the shoulders of his only living son. A surviving poem, *The Justes of the Moneths of May and June*, describes jousts held in the late spring of 1507 when the future Henry VIII was sixteen. In his description of the June jousts, the poet recorded that Prince Henry was a prominent spectator, a prince 'most comely of stature' who was eager to engage the combatants in talk of the jousts and clearly displayed an ambition to take part himself, something that would never have been allowed by his over-protective father.[39] The poet recorded of the future king that:

> And though a prince
> And a king's son he be
> It pleaseth him of his benignity
> To suffer gentlemen of low degree
> In his presence
>
> To speak of arms and of other defence
> Without doing unto his grace offence.

Henry VII was simply not prepared to hazard the person of his only son in any way, and, given the generally held belief that sexual activity could be dangerous to an adolescent, it would seem highly improbable that such a cloistered young man could have taken a mistress, particularly after the premature death of his elder brother, Prince Arthur, within a few months of his own marriage when a youth of fifteen.

If there was any relationship between Henry VIII and Elizabeth it must have taken place after 1509 when Henry came to the throne and when Elizabeth had secured a court appointment as one of his wife's ladies. Henry tended to draw his mistresses from the households of his wives and this is therefore not impossible in relation to Elizabeth: both Mary Boleyn and her predecessor, Bessie Blount, were members of the queen's household. Skelton's description suggests that Elizabeth Howard was a beautiful woman with an extrovert personality and she may therefore have captured the king's attention.

In 1509 she was in her mid-thirties and still attractive. Henry VIII's taste in women, although fairly eclectic, does suggest an interest in more mature women: his first wife, Catherine of Aragon, with whom he believed himself to be in love, was twenty-four at the time of their marriage, while Henry was seventeen. Anne Boleyn was probably already aged twenty-six at the time that she first caught the king's eye, eventually marrying him when she was in her early thirties. Jane Seymour was aged around twenty-seven or twenty-eight at the time of her marriage, while Henry's sixth wife, Catherine Parr, was thirty-one. Admittedly, one of the criticisms levelled at the appearance of Henry's fourth wife, Anne of Cleves, was that when she arrived in England for the first time she was found to look older than expected. However, there is no evidence that Henry himself voiced this complaint, instead directing his criticism to her figure, manner and personal hygiene. Even Henry's mistresses tended not to be young girls: he is believed to have been involved with the married Anne Hastings early in his reign, as well as the mature Jane Poppincourt. The exceptions to this are Henry's fifth wife, Catherine Howard, who may have been as young as fifteen at the time of her marriage and was certainly under twenty, and his mistresses Bessie Blount and Mary Boleyn, who were in their late teens and early twenties respectively.

The idea that Elizabeth Boleyn might have been Henry VIII's mistress early in his reign cannot be entirely dismissed. However, Throckmorton's letter, which has the king himself denying an affair with Elizabeth while failing to deny one with her eldest daughter, is probably conclusive. Henry had no reason to lie about an affair with his future mother-in-law while tacitly admitting to having one with his future sister-in-law, since both relationships would have made the validity of his marriage to Anne Boleyn suspect. The evidence suggests that Elizabeth and Henry were not lovers, with the first member of Elizabeth's immediate family to consummate her relationship with the king being instead her niece, Elizabeth Carew, who was the daughter of her half-sister, Margaret Bryan, and had been suggested as a royal mistress early in the reign.[40] That said, the obvious rumours that something had occurred between Elizabeth and the king hint at a flirtation and it is likely that Henry made his attraction to her known at court, even if it was not actually acted upon. He certainly found the women of her family attractive: marrying her daughter, Anne, her niece, Catherine Howard, and the daughter of her first cousin, Jane Seymour. The king also had an affair with Elizabeth's daughter, Mary, her niece, Elizabeth Carew, and was rumoured to be attracted to another niece, Mary Howard, Duchess of Richmond. It would not have harmed Thomas Boleyn's career, or the court prospects of Elizabeth's kin, if the king had indeed been attracted to her early in the reign.

One final issue concerning Elizabeth Howard that is worthy of investigation concerns the statement, first posited by Agnes Strickland in the nineteenth century and later followed by other historians, that Elizabeth died in 1512 in childbirth.[41] Strickland then claimed that Thomas Boleyn took a second wife of humble origin, something which allowed Elizabeth I to have a connection with some of her poorer subjects in Norfolk. The source from which Strickland took her statement on Elizabeth's death appears to have confused her with her sister, Muriel, who did indeed die in 1512. In addition to this, the statement that Elizabeth I had humble maternal relatives in Norfolk also appears to have been a misreading of the sources, with a nineteenth-century commentator on Strickland's claims pointing out that these humble maternal relatives were actually members of the Boleyn family in Norfolk rather than kin to any unidentified stepmother. There is really no evidence to support a claim that Elizabeth Howard died in 1512 and, instead, a great deal of evidence to suggest that she was the Countess of Wiltshire who died in April 1538 and was buried at Lambeth, which was, of course, the burial ground of the Howards, with Howard mourners in attendance. Elizabeth appears in sources with reasonable regularity after 1512 although, as set out above, she spent a considerable portion of her time in the country, attending to the education of her children.

The first of Elizabeth's three children to leave home was her younger daughter, Anne. Anne Boleyn's childhood came to an end abruptly in the summer of 1513 when she was sent to Brussels to take up a position as one of the maids in the household of Margaret of Austria. This was a very prestigious post and can only have come about through the friendship that had developed between Margaret and Thomas during his embassy the previous year. Soon after Anne's arrival, Margaret wrote personally to Thomas Boleyn to confirm that his daughter had arrived safely and to state that Anne 'was very welcome to me, and I hope to treat her in such a fashion that you will have reason to be content with it; at least be sure that until your return there need be no other intermediary between you and me than she; and I find her of such good address and so pleasing in her youthful age that I am more beholden to you for having sent her to me than you are to me'.[42]

Anne quickly learned French, as her father, who was himself fluent in the language, had hoped, writing to him proudly in French from Margaret's court. Elizabeth must also have been with pleased with reports of Anne's progress. It is not impossible that Anne met Henry VIII for the first time in August 1513 when Margaret moved her court to Lille to meet with the English king and his retinue, which included Thomas Boleyn. Her time in Brussels was brief and in late 1514 she left Margaret to serve the new Queen of France.

While Thomas was responsible for launching the career of the couple's younger daughter, Elizabeth was the driving force behind the debut of her eldest child. In 1514, when Henry VIII's sister, Mary Tudor, was sent to France to marry the aged King Louis XII, she was attended by Mary Boleyn who obtained a permanent position in her household.[43] Elizabeth's half-brother, Lord Berners, was appointed as chamberlain to Mary Tudor, while her brother, the Earl of Surrey, also attended the wedding in France, making it highly likely that it was Elizabeth who was able to use her family connections to ensure that her eldest daughter did not miss out on such a sought-after and highly prestigious position. Mary Boleyn was soon joined by her sister, Anne, in France, apparently against the wishes of her father, who had hoped that she could remain in the Netherlands. By 1514 both of her daughters had left home, which may account for the fact that references to Lady Boleyn at court increase after this period. For Elizabeth's two daughters, it was to be their time in France that defined their characters and their futures in the years to come as they developed their careers as courtiers.

6

MARY BOLEYN, ROYAL MISTRESS

While Elizabeth Howard Boleyn was rumoured to have been a mistress of Henry VIII, it is certain that her eldest daughter, Mary Boleyn, shared the king's bed. Mary has been subject to an upsurge in interest in recent years, with two biographies recently released.

Mary Boleyn began her career in France. Henry VIII's sister, Mary Tudor, was betrothed in childhood to Charles of Castile, the future Holy Roman Emperor and Catherine of Aragon's nephew. Although the groom's aunt and guardian, Margaret of Austria, Regent of the Netherlands, was enthusiastic about the match, Charles's two grandfathers, the Emperor Maximilian and Ferdinand of Aragon, were less enthusiastic, employing delaying tactics when Henry pressed for the marriage. In 1514 the English king finally lost patience, breaking the betrothal and, instead, engaging his beautiful young sister to the 'feeble old and pocky' Louis XII of France.[1] The bride was, unsurprisingly, unenthusiastic, but she gave her consent. She travelled to France in October 1514 with a large train of attendants, including Mary Boleyn.[2] She would have attended the royal marriage in the cathedral at Abbeville on 9 October and also the new queen's Coronation later in the month. For Mary, this was a prestigious appointment, and she was soon joined by her sister, who journeyed to France direct from Brussels.

Soon after the wedding, Louis caused consternation in his wife's household by sending most of her English attendants home, including the new queen's governess, Lady Guildford. Both Boleyn sisters found favour with the French king, perhaps due to Anne's language skills, and they were allowed to stay. Louis was besotted with his beautiful young bride and, apart from the disagreement over her attendants, the marriage was harmonious. It was also particularly short, with Louis, exhausted by his efforts to keep up with his wife, dying on 1 January 1515, leaving his son-in-law and kinsman, Francis of Angoulême, as King of France.

As the king's widow, Mary Tudor was expected to spend time in seclusion, moving with her household to the palace of Cluny. Both Boleyn sisters were with her and were witnesses to the dramatic events that unfolded during the French queen's period of mourning. France had the Salic law, which barred the inheritance of women or of men descended from the royal line through women, something which meant that Louis's two daughters were unable to succeed to the crown, with Louis's heir male, Francis, marrying Louis's eldest daughter as a courtesy. It was therefore of paramount importance to Francis that Mary did not bear a son and he took an active interest in the widowed queen's establishment at Cluny. Francis had some romantic interest in Mary himself, with rumours of an attraction between the two before Louis's death. Francis was warned not to take any action for fear that he should father a child with her which would be attributed to Louis, leading to him remaining 'plain Comte d'Angoulême, and never King of France'.[3] Once it was clear that Mary was not pregnant, the licentious new king did indeed make advances towards his wife's stepmother, something which must have increased the attitude of unease that pervaded at Cluny. Francis was also anxious that Henry would bestow Mary in marriage with Charles of Castile, something that would be dangerous to France, and he therefore encouraged her in her affection for Charles Brandon, Duke of Suffolk, who had come to bring her home to England. With Francis's encouragement and her own fears that her brother would arrange a second match for her, Mary did the unthinkable and secretly married Suffolk. When Henry found out, he was furious, but he soon accepted the *fait accompli*, with the couple returning to England in May 1515. Her two Boleyn attendants, Mary and Anne, had been witnesses to all that had happened at Cluny. Anne definitely did not return home to England with Mary Tudor, instead transferring to the household of the new French queen, Claude. Mary's whereabouts are less certain. She may have also moved to Claude's household, although there is no record of her there. Alternatively she may have returned to England with Mary Tudor or soon afterwards.[4] In any event, Mary Boleyn's relations with King Francis must have been of only a brief duration, occurring during the early months of 1515.

The new Queen of France was fifteen and a rather unprepossessing figure. During her marriage she suffered near-annual pregnancies which ruined her health and also ensured that she was unable to have any real presence at court, instead being overshadowed by her husband's more dynamic mother, Louise of Savoy, and his sister, Marguerite of Angoulême. Claude was pious to the point of saintliness. Francis always showed his wife respect in public, but he was notoriously licentious. Chasing women was one of his chief pastimes and, according to a near contemporary, Seigneur de Brantôme, the best way to please him was

> by offering to his view on his first arrival a beautiful woman, a fine horse and a handsome hound. For by casting his gaze now on the one, now on the other and presently to the third, he would never be a-weary in that house, having there the three things most pleasant to look upon and admire, and so exercising his eyes right agreeably.[5]

Following Francis's accession, there were reports of the ladies of his court that 'both maids and wives, do oft-times trip, indeed do so customarily'. This was an exaggeration, but there is no doubt that Francis I's court was an easy place for a woman to lose her virtue if she so chose.

The hostile Elizabethan writer, Nicholas Sander, claimed that, at the French court, Anne Boleyn became known as 'the English mare, because of her shameless behaviour; and then the royal mule, when she became acquainted with the King of France'. Sander believed that Anne had disgraced herself in France by indulging first in sexual relations with members of Francis's court and later with Francis himself. It must however be remembered that it was also Sander who claimed that Anne had first been sent to the Continent after disgracing herself in a relationship with her father's butler and Sander's tales can certainly be dismissed as fanciful.

While there is no evidence that any hint of scandal ever attached itself to Anne Boleyn, who appears to have acquitted herself well and honourably during her years in France, becoming French in all but birth, there is some evidence that Mary Boleyn's reputation was not entirely spotless. It is not at all impossible that Sander confused the two sisters in his account and that there was therefore a grain of truth in his claims of an 'English mare' and a 'royal mule'. Francis I, in spite of his love of women, was not known for his gallantry, later describing Mary Tudor as 'more dirty than queenly'. Some years after both Boleyn sisters had left his court, he recalled Mary Boleyn 'as a very great whore and infamous above all'.[6] It is possible that Francis referred to Mary's later affair with Henry VIII in this remark, although, given that he himself had a number of mistresses, it is unlikely that an affair with one monarch would be enough for Francis to brand Mary quite so viciously. It therefore does seem more likely that he was aware of Mary being considerably more promiscuous than her two marriages and affair with Henry VIII would suggest. When Anne Boleyn visited the French court in late 1532 she and Francis sat together and spoke privately for some time, indicating that they were indeed acquainted and that the French king remembered his first wife's former maid. Given his comments on Mary Boleyn, he is also likely to have recalled her. Although the evidence is highly limited, it does seem likely that she had something of a reputation for promiscuity while in France and that the king himself was aware of this, suggesting an affair with him or, at least, members of his court close to him. If Sander's comments are considered to have any basis in fact then it is possible that Mary slept with Francis himself, although she cannot have been more than a casual lover for the King of France. The evidence, such as it is, suggests that Mary embarked on her career as a royal mistress while in France and that she did not keep herself chaste.

Whispers of misconduct may account for the fact that she does not appear again in the sources until 1520. Her sister, Anne Boleyn, would later be rusticated from court for carrying out an illicit relationship with Henry Percy, spending some years at home at Hever. This would have allowed any rumours to die down. Alternatively, since there is no evidence of her actually returning to England in 1515 Mary may have remained in France as her recent biographer has suggested, staying at Brie-sous-Forges with an acquaintance of her father's, well away from the court.[7] That Mary's conduct was not widely known is clear from her appointment in the household of Catherine of Aragon by 1520. However, her sexual experience may have served to pique Henry's interest in his wife's new attendant when whispers of Mary's reputation did begin to reach England. The sixteenth-century Nicholas Sander believed that Henry had seen Mary on visits to her mother and ordered her to be brought to court so that he could ruin her.[8] More likely, however, Elizabeth Howard Boleyn was able to use her own court connections to secure a place for her eldest daughter. It was at court that Henry VIII first became interested in Mary Boleyn.

Unlike her sister, Anne Boleyn remained in the household of Queen Claude, flourishing in the cultured atmosphere of the French court. There is very little record for her time with Claude. She probably took part in the queen's Coronation in May 1516 at St Denis, as well as her state entry to Paris. She also became acquainted with Francis's sister, the accomplished Marguerite of Angoulême, who was later known for her support for the religious reform movement. Anne may, perhaps, have first become exposed to these ideas with Marguerite. One critical writer claimed that it was while she was in France that she first 'embraced the heresy of Luther'. Given that Anne's own father and brother also supported reform, however, this must be questionable: religious reform was highly fashionable in the early sixteenth century and Anne could very easily have come upon the ideas in her own home before she embarked on her court career.

Anne had a number of opportunities to meet with her father during her time in France. In early 1519, for example, Thomas was part of a mission to France headed by the Bishop of Ely and the Earl of Worcester which coincided with the birth of Claude's son, Henry, Duke of Orleans. Thomas Boleyn attended the christening, an event that Anne is also likely to have attended. Both of Anne's parents, her sister and many other family members attended the grand meeting between Henry and Francis in June 1520, known as the Field of the Cloth of Gold.[9] Once again, Anne's own attendance is not recorded, but, given her language skills, she is very likely to have attended Claude, who played a prominent role in the celebrations. Over 6,000 people attended Francis and his queen at their base at Ardes, while a similar number attended Henry at the English camp at Guisnes. For Anne and the other Boleyn women present, the Field of the Cloth of Gold must have been a grand spectacle, with the two kings seeking to outdo each other in magnificence and display.

If Anne had not previously seen Henry VIII while in the household of Margaret of Austria, this would have been the first time that she laid eyes on her future husband who, while still in his late twenties, remained a glittering and splendid figure, acquitting himself well in dancing and sporting prowess at the meeting. On more than one occasion Henry dined with Claude while his French counterpart visited the English queen. Anne Boleyn would have been one of the French ladies who danced before the English gentlemen, while Mary Boleyn would have done the same to entertain Francis and his men. It may have been an uncomfortable meeting for Mary and the French king. John Fisher, Bishop of Rochester, later praised the queens for being 'accompanied with so many of other fair ladies in sumptuous and gorgeous apparel' at the meeting: Anne and Mary Boleyn, their mother, Elizabeth, and aunt, Anne Tempest Boleyn, took their places among these women to take part in the dancing and feasting which accompanied one of the most costly, and grandest, events of Henry VIII's reign, which Bishop Fisher declared to be 'wonderful sights as for this world'.

Mary Boleyn was already married when she attended the English queen in France, taking William Carey as her husband on 4 February 1520. Carey, who was a similar age to his bride, was a younger son of Thomas Carey of Chilton Foliat in Wiltshire. The family were prominent in the local gentry, with Thomas Carey sitting as a Member of Parliament in Henry VII's reign. Through his mother, William Carey was related to the Earl of Northumberland. By 1519 he had joined the court, serving in the king's household. With his association with the king, Carey represented a solid, but not brilliant, match for the daughter of the ambitious Thomas Boleyn. It may be that Carey was the best match that Mary could obtain following her behaviour in France. Alternatively, the couple, who were both resident at court, may have made a love match, although Carey's later acquiescence with regard to her affair with Henry VIII does not suggest a man deeply in love with his wife. More likely Carey's court connections and kinship with the Earl of Northumberland were sufficient for her family. Mary's father had, after all, risen through his court service and he may have hoped that his son-in-law would do the same. Neither Mary nor Anne Boleyn were heiresses, and, as Anne's later relationship with Henry Percy showed, neither was of great worth on the aristocratic marriage market. There is no evidence that Mary's marriage was arranged to cover a relationship with the king. In February 1520 Henry's mistress, Bessie Blount, who had borne his son, Henry Fitzroy, in June 1519, was in Essex, awaiting the birth of a second child who can probably be attributed to the king.[10] As with all his affairs, Henry was discreet when he began his relationship with Mary, something which makes the dating of his affair very difficult. William Carey began to receive significant royal grants early in 1522, suggesting that the affair may have begun around that time.[11] Given that Henry VIII's mistress, Bessie Blount, was married off at around the same time, it would seem plausible to date his interest in Mary to the waning of his interest in the mother of his only acknowledged illegitimate son.

Henry VIII later admitted that he had enjoyed a love affair with Mary Boleyn and there is no reason to doubt that the pair were lovers. It seems unlikely, as recently asserted, that Henry raped Mary, forcing her to begin an affair with him.[12] This was a very serious charge, even for a king: Henry's grandfather, Edward IV, allegedly held a dagger to the throat of a young widow, Elizabeth Woodville, intending to force himself upon her. When she resisted, he stopped short of the act, instead marrying his intended victim. Henry VIII did not force himself upon Anne Boleyn when she resisted him, something that suggests that he was no rapist. His ancestor, King John, earned notoriety in the early thirteenth century, partly for allegedly forcing himself upon noblewomen, something which helped to earn the enmity of his barons. Although a king, Henry

VIII was not free to act outside the constraints of society and the rape of a gentlewoman who was closely related to a number of prominent figures is simply implausible. Mary Boleyn would have been a willing occupant of the king's bed, particularly as, in 1522, the king was still a very handsome specimen, renowned as one of the most handsome princes in Europe.

Details of the pair's relationship are scant, although Mary featured prominently in a court masque in March 1522. Her husband's acceptance of the relationship was bought with a number of royal grants, including the keepership of New Hall in Essex, a fine palace that Henry had used as his base when visiting Bessie Blount at her residence at Blackmoor Priory: the significance of the palace's connection with a former mistress was probably not lost on Mary or her husband.[13] In July 1522, Carey and another courtier were jointly granted the valuable wardship of one Thomas Sharpe of Canterbury, allowing them to make use of his lands and income.[14] This was followed by other grants, including a pension of 50 marks per year. It may have been due to Mary that her father was made treasurer of the household in April 1522 and a Knight of the Garter in April 1523. This honour was followed in June 1525 when Thomas Boleyn was created Viscount Rochford on the same day that Henry created his illegitimate son, Henry Fitzroy, Duke of Richmond. Thomas's promotion, although it could be seen as the reward for his years of royal service, is more likely linked to the king's relationship with Mary, particularly since he would later acquire two earldoms due to Henry's love for his younger daughter.

When discussing Mary Boleyn and her relationship with Henry VIII, the question must of course be asked as to whether either of her two children, Catherine and Henry Carey, can be considered to have been fathered by the king. Henry VIII acknowledged only one illegitimate child during his lifetime, his son, Henry Fitzroy, by Elizabeth Blount. However, there is good reason for believing that Fitzroy's sister, Elizabeth Tailboys, may also have been born to the king and other children have also been attributed to him.[15]

Henry Carey's birth date of 4 March 1526 is known due to the evidence of William Carey's inquisition post mortem.[16] Catherine's birth date is less clear although she was appointed as a maid of honour to Anne of Cleves at the end of 1539, an appointment for which she must have been at least twelve years old. Catherine married in 1540 and her first child was born in 1541, something that would suggest a birth date of around 1524.[17] This is supported by the portrait of a heavily pregnant woman which is usually identified as Catherine and is inscribed with the date 1562, as well as recording that the sitter was thirty-eight.[18] The lady strongly resembles an effigy known to be Catherine and there is no reason to doubt the identification, indicating that 1524 is likely to be correct.

It has recently been pointed out in one academic study that the paternity of Mary Boleyn's children remains ambiguous.[19] Henry VIII did not have problems in impregnating his sexual partners, simply that the pregnancies rarely produced healthy male offspring, and it is therefore not impossible that he produced more surviving children than previously acknowledged. There were certainly contemporary rumours as to their paternity, with the Vicar of Isleworth stating during his examination by the royal council on 20 April 1535 that 'Mr Skidmore did show to me young Master Carey, saying that he was our sovereign lord the king's son by our sovereign lady the queen's sister, whom the queen's grace might not suffer to be in the court'. A sexual relationship with Mary Boleyn potentially invalidated Henry's marriage to her sister, something that would make both Henry and Anne reluctant for Mary's children to be seen as of royal blood.

There is some evidence of royal favour shown to the Carey children which has been pointed out by historians. Following their marriage, Catherine Carey and her husband, Francis Knollys, were the beneficiaries of an Act of Parliament which gave them joint ownership of the Knollys manor of Rotherfield Greys; this was a method of providing for a favoured female courtier without actually incurring any expense himself that Henry had earlier utilised in relation to Elizabeth Blount following her marriage. It has also been suggested that Henry Carey may have been raised with his cousin (or half-sister) Princess Elizabeth, given their later closeness and the fact that he was later created Baron Hunsdon by Elizabeth, a reference to one of her known childhood residences.

Another suggestion that the Carey children might have been commonly believed to have been fathered by Henry VIII is found in Sir Robert Naunton's *Fragmenta Regalia*. Naunton was born in 1563 and had connections to the court of Elizabeth I, eventually serving as secretary of state to James I. In an anecdote concerning Elizabeth's favourite, Robert Dudley, Naunton recorded that:

And for my Lord Hunsdon [Carey], and Sir Thomas Sackville, after Lord Treasurer, who were all contemporaries, he was wont to say of them that they were of the tribe of Dan, and were *noli me tangere*, implying that they were not to be contested with, for they were indeed of the queen's nigh kindred.[20]

On the face of it, this remark refers only to the fact that both Hunsdon and Sackville, who was related to the Boleyns but not descended from Mary Boleyn, were considered to have a special position at court due to their relationship to the queen's maternal family. However, the reference to the tribe of Dan is an interesting one. In the Book of Deuteronomy, Moses called Dan a 'lion's whelp' and this has been taken to mean that a reference to the Careys as the tribe of Dan might also suggest their descent from a lion – the king himself.[21] Another point that should be raised in relation to this is the line *noli me tangere*, or 'touch me not'. While again, this can be given its literal meaning to demonstrate the special status of the queen's maternal kin, it is also potentially another covert reference to the Careys' paternity. In a well-known poem by Sir Thomas Wyatt, which clearly refers to Henry VIII's pursuit of Anne Boleyn, the poet included the line '*Noli me tangere*, for Caesar's I am' in reference to the king's possession of Anne Boleyn. Given the continuing popularity of Wyatt's poems in the later sixteenth century, this reference would have been widely known: it is just possible that the words '*Noli me tangere*', as uttered by Dudley, were also meant to imply that the Careys belonged to 'Caesar' or Henry VIII.

There is a difficulty in interpreting the tribe of Dan remark to refer to the paternity of the Carey children. In the Book of Genesis, Jacob referred to Dan as a serpent that bites a horse's heels to make the rider fall backwards, while he instead calls his fourth son, Judah, a 'lion's whelp'.[22] It is therefore clear that Dan was not the only lion's whelp among the sons of Jacob and a reference to the tribe of Dan in order to infer royal paternity in the sixteenth century need not have been immediately apparent. In addition to this, Dudley, who was politically opposed to the Careys, might have meant to refer to their treachery in his remark, referring to them as biting a horse's heels to make a rider fall backwards.

Another counter-argument to the tribe of Dan remark is that it may have been meant to have another connotation. The tribe is listed in the Book of Numbers as the largest of the twelve tribes of Israel, and it has been estimated that there were approximately 103 members of the Carey family alive during the reign of Elizabeth I due to the great fertility of Henry and Catherine Carey.[23] Given that Elizabeth always showed these cousins great favour, it is likely that their high numbers were resented at court and this could certainly have been the rationale behind Dudley's remark. Also, of course, Dudley was not born when Henry VIII and Mary Boleyn were conducting their affair and, while he might have heard rumours and even had some more specific knowledge from the queen herself, he was hardly in a position to know for certain whether the Carey children were the king's. Henry VIII, after all, never acknowledged them. It is therefore possible that, even if he did indeed mean to imply their potential royal paternity in his remarks, he may only have been repeating rumour and not speaking from actual fact. That said, however, Elizabeth I would presumably have been aware if the Careys were her half-siblings and it is not at all impossible that she could have imparted this information to her favourite.

William Carey received a royal grant on 20 February 1526, twelve days before Henry Carey's birth.[24] One historian who considered that both Carey children were the king's considered that 'significantly, this royal grant included the borough of Buckingham which was granted to William Carey "in tail male". It is impossible not to be struck by the coincidence of this entailment to a male "heir", just twelve days before the date of record on which William Carey's wife gave birth to a male child said to be the king's son.'[25] However, it would seem implausible that this grant was intended to provide for the king's own son, given that this 'son' had not yet been born, with Mary's second pregnancy as likely to result in a daughter as her first. It would seem more arguable that the child that Mary was carrying was her husband's, unlike her earlier daughter who can be attributed to the king. William Carey's quiet acceptance of his wife's relationship with the king had to be bought, as can be seen by the royal grants to him. It seems likely that it was also agreed that the king would make some provision for Carey's own heir, perhaps as a reward for Carey raising the king's daughter as his own. The entail on male heirs for this grant was in order to ensure that Catherine Carey, whom the king knew to be his daughter and intended to provide for in due course, would not inherit. Instead, the property would pass to the sons that Mary Boleyn would bear her husband.

A similar pattern occurred with Bessie Blount. While the king acknowledged her first child, Henry Fitzroy. Her second child, a daughter born nearly two years before her marriage, was raised as a child of her husband, Gilbert Tailboys, something which caused considerable family friction when that daughter unexpectedly inherited the Tailboys' patrimony.[26] Where a husband acquiesced to his wife's relationship with the king in return for offices and lands, there was little reason for him to not also raise an illegitimate daughter of the king's as his own, particularly if the king agreed to provide for this daughter at her marriage as he appears to have done for Catherine Carey. Such a husband is, however, highly unlikely to have agreed to raise a son in a similar manner, since that son would inherit his property at his death. This must be the strongest evidence that Henry Carey was not the king's son, although his sister may well have been a royal daughter. It has been suggested that Mary and Carey had a non-sexual marriage, with their relationship merely being a sham to cover her love affair with Henry VIII.[27] There is no evidence to support this. Mary may have abandoned sleeping with her husband during her relationship with the king but, equally, she may not, something which would further throw the paternity of at least her eldest child, Catherine Carey, into doubt.

Anne Boleyn left Claude's household early in 1522, returning to England as negotiations were opened for her marriage with James Butler in order to settle the Ormond inheritance. Like her sister, she found a place at the English court, something that was not surprising given her importance to the king's administration of Ireland. Her sister may also have helped secure her position. Mary is highly likely to have been instrumental in arranging for Anne to take a prominent role in a court masque held at Greenwich within weeks of her arrival in March 1522. The masque was to be one of the most spectacular of Henry's reign, with a large mock castle built within the palace for the occasion. Once the guests were seated, eight ladies wearing gowns of white satin and caps of gold and jewels appeared at the top of the castle, representing the virtues of beauty, honour, perseverance, kindness, constancy, bounty, mercy and pity. Henry's sister, Mary, the former Queen of France, played Beauty. Mary Boleyn played Kindness, a virtue that aptly reflects her character. Even more appropriately, as it turned out, Anne took the role of Perseverance. Jane Parker, who may already have been betrothed to the sisters' brother, George, also took part, although her virtue is not recorded. The eight ladies defended their castle with rosewater and comfits as it was stormed by eight lords dressed in cloth of gold and blue satin. Eventually, the lords drove away a further eight women dressed to represent vices, with the virtues then coming down joyously from their tower to dance with the gallants. Anne's partner is nowhere recorded. Henry, who was one of the participants, probably danced with his sister or, perhaps, Mary Boleyn. This was Anne Boleyn's court debut but she and her future sister-in-law, Jane Parker, must have been overshadowed by the radiant Mary Boleyn.

As well as ensuring the appointment of her sister as one of the dancers in the masque, Mary may also have used her influence on behalf of Jane Parker. Surprisingly, there are few sources relating to the life of Jane Parker, who would later become the notorious Lady Rochford. Jane was the daughter of Henry Parker, who as the son of Alice Lovel, the heiress to the Morley family, was created Lord Morley by the king in 1520.[28] The Parker family, like the Howards, had been conspicuous in their support for Richard III at Bosworth Field, with Jane's grandfather, Sir William Parker, serving as the last Yorkist king's standard bearer in the battle. Given this association William's son, Henry, was lucky to gain a patron in Henry VII's mother, Lady Margaret Beaufort, who took him into her household as a carver or cupbearer.[29] Margaret, who was a noted supporter of scholars and the universities, may have recognised Henry's intelligence as he became one of the most noted scholars of his day. He remained devoted to the memory of his patron, years later writing a highly flattering memoir of her for her great-granddaughter, Mary I. Margaret was fond of the young Henry, arranging for him to marry Alice St John of Bletsoe, who was the daughter of her half-brother. The couple had three surviving children, Henry, Margaret and Jane, with the earliest mention of Jane in surviving sources being her participation in the Greenwich masque in 1522. This suggests that she had already obtained a court position, something that was not too surprising given the fact that her mother was a first cousin of the king's father. William Cavendish, who had been resident at court during the 1520s, later put words into Jane's mouth, claiming:

Brought up in court all my young age,
Withouten bridle of honest measure,
Following my lust and filthy pleasure.[30]

While this account was written with the hindsight of Jane's scandalous fall, Cavendish is likely to have known her and it may be accurate. The account suggests that she spent much of her youth at court and, perhaps, enjoyed a less than spotless reputation. No scandal has been linked to Jane before the last year of her life, but it should be noted that the court was a place where flirtations were rife and conduct could be somewhat free. The Imperial ambassador, Eustace Chapuys, for example, famously noted that he doubted that Henry VIII's third wife, Jane Seymour, could have been a virgin at the time of her wedding given that she had spent some years at court.

Very little evidence survives relating to Jane's childhood. Her father was a noted scholar who made translations of a number of important works. As such, it can be assumed that Jane received some sort of education, particularly as her signature on a surviving letter indicates that she was literate.[31] A list of some of Jane's possessions compiled in 1536 contained references to three books:

a primer bound with silver and gilt, a book covered in black velvet and with a clasp of silver and a book covered in crimson velvet.[32] Jane was interested in education, with a letter from a William Foster surviving from 1536 in which he called Jane the 'most special patroness of my study'.[33] She remained close to her father after her marriage, with him continuing to guide her religious education. In a dedication written to the Princess Mary, for example, Lord Morley noted that the princess had translated a prayer of St Thomas Aquinas when she was aged eleven in 1527 or 1528. Morley commented that the prayer 'is so well done, so near to the Latin' that he marvelled at it that he had caused it to be copied into the books of his wife and his children 'to give them occasion to remember to pray for your grace'.[34] Jane's loyalty to her father, who was a friend to Princess Mary, caused her problems with her husband's family in the years following her marriage.

The Morleys enjoyed close connections with the Boleyns, which probably explains how the match came to be arranged. Jane's grandmother, Alice Lovel, had taken Elizabeth Howard Boleyn's brother, Sir Edward Howard, as her second husband, while Jane's sister married Thomas Boleyn's nephew, John Shelton. Jane and George's marriage agreement was signed on 4 October 1524, with the couple known to have been married by the autumn of 1525 at the latest.[35] At the end of 1526 Thomas Boleyn received £33 6s 8d from a servant of Jane's father: a reasonably substantial sum which suggests that it was connected to the agreement made at the time of the marriage.[36] Jane also later claimed that 'the King's Highness and my Lord my father paid great sums of money for my jointure to the Earl of Wiltshire [Thomas Boleyn] to the sum of 2,000 marks'.[37] From this, Jane was assured an annual income of 100 marks in the event that she was widowed during her father-in-law's lifetime, to increase to 300 marks per annum on his death.[38] The king's involvement in her jointure suggests that he may have been involved in the negotiations for the match, perhaps to please his mistress, Mary Boleyn. Certainly, in the early 1520s Jane was socially superior to her husband, who was still a teenager. George had served as a royal page as a child and, in 1522, received the grant offices in Tunbridge jointly with his father, later also receiving the grant of a manor in Norfolk.[39] This may, perhaps, have been to make him a more attractive proposition to the Morley family, although within a few years of the marriage the fortunes of the Boleyn family dramatically increased.

At the time of Jane Parker's marriage to George Boleyn, his sister, Mary, was the pre-eminent member of the family at court. The end of her relationship with the king is nowhere recorded, but it was probably midway through 1525, perhaps shortly before the ennoblement of Thomas Boleyn, but before Mary conceived Henry Carey, who should be considered her husband's child. This coincides with the return of her sister, Anne, to court, who was the woman that supplanted Mary in the king's affections. Nicholas Sander claimed that Mary saw the king's waning affection for her and his interest in her sister and, becoming jealous, went to the queen

and bade her be of good cheer; for though the king, she said, was in love with her sister, he could never marry her, for the relations of the king with the family were of such a nature as to make a marriage impossible by the laws of the Church. 'The king himself,' she said, 'will not deny it, and I will assert it publicly while I live; now, as he may not marry my sister, so neither will he put your majesty away.'[40]

Sander is a highly prejudicial source but, on occasion, his work contains elements of the truth. It is certainly not impossible that there was some jealousy between the two sisters as Mary watched herself be supplanted in favour of her younger sister, Anne Boleyn.

Part 3
Queen Anne Boleyn: 1526–1536

7

THE KING'S NEW LOVE

Mary Boleyn was not the only Boleyn woman to attract amorous attention at court in the 1520s, with her sister, Anne, arriving home from France in 1522 after she was recalled to England to marry James Butler and settle the Ormond inheritance. Anne, like her father, had no enthusiasm for this solution and she soon set about arranging her own higher-status marriage.

Anne Boleyn had been absent from England for nearly a decade by 1522. With her French grace and manners she immediately caused a stir at court, with one favourable sixteenth-century biographer, George Wyatt, commenting:

> In this noble imp, the graces of nature graced by gracious education, seemed even at the first to have promised bliss unto her aftertimes. She was taken at that time to have a beauty not so whitely as clear and fresh above all we may esteem, which appeared much more excellent by her favour passing sweet and cheerful, and these, both also increased by her noble presence of shape and fashion, representing both mildness and majesty more than can be expressed.[1]

Unlike her sister, Anne did not conform to contemporary ideals of beauty, with dark hair and skin and dark eyes. Even those commentators hostile to her agree that there was something unusual and compelling about her which made up for any defects in her appearance. The later sixteenth-century writer, Nicholas Sander, after slandering Anne with claims of a number of monstrous deformities, admitted that 'she was handsome to look at, with a pretty mouth, amusing in her ways, playing well on the lute, and was a good dancer. She was the model and mirror of those who were at court. For she was always well dressed, and every day made some change in the fashion of her garments.'[2] Anne seemed more French than English in her homeland and became one of the leaders of fashion at court, with George Wyatt commenting that she artfully hid a minor defect on the tip of one of her fingers with stylish, long hanging sleeves which were soon copied by the women of the court.[3]

Although Anne was nominally promised to James Butler, no steps were taken to bring matters to a conclusion, and within a few months of her arrival she had acquired a considerably more prominent suitor in the shape of Henry Percy, heir to the Earl of Northumberland.[4] Percy, a young man of a similar age to Anne, was a member of Cardinal Wolsey's household. It was soon noted that, whenever Wolsey came to court, his young attendant would visit the queen's chamber to 'fall in dalliance among the queen's maidens'. He soon turned his attention solely to Anne herself and, according to William Cavendish, who was a contemporary of Percy's in Wolsey's household, 'there grew such a secret love between them that at length they were engaged together, intending to marry'.

There is some doubt as to the extent that matters reached between Anne and Percy as they conversed privately in the queen's apartments. Wolsey, although a regular visitor to the court, was not usually resident there and so meetings between the couple must have been fairly snatched in nature, particularly as Percy or Anne would have been called away by their respective employers when service was required. In 1532 Percy's wife, Mary Talbot, claimed that her marriage was invalid due to her husband's earlier binding betrothal to Anne, something which would have made her own marriage invalid. This corroborates Cavendish's account and, while a somewhat desperate attempt to end her own unhappy marriage, is likely to have some truth to it, particularly as by 1532 Anne was the king's own fiancée and, as such, any claim that she was effectively already married would have been a very dangerous one to make. A letter survives from Percy, written at the time of Anne's fall to the king's then chief minister, Thomas Cromwell, which refutes any betrothal, with Percy claiming that

> this shall be to signify unto you that I perceive by Sir Raynold Carnaby, that there is supposed a precontract between the queen and me; whereupon I was not only heretofore examined upon my oath before the Archbishops of Canterbury and York, but also received the blessed sacrament upon the same before the Duke of Norfolk, and other the king's highness' council learned in the spiritual law; assuring you Mr Secretary by the said oath, and blessed body which afore I received, and hereafter intend to receive that the same may be to my damnation, if ever there were any contract or promise of marriage between her and me.[5]

This letter, which was written the day before Anne's death when five men had already been executed for their perceived romantic associations with her, must be taken with some caution. Even Percy's oath on the sacrament is not conclusive, in spite of the highly religious time he lived in. He was in fear of his life at the time: if he admitted to a betrothal with Anne then he was confessing to failing to inform the king that the woman he had married was actually unavailable, something that jeopardised the succession and was treason under the first Act of Succession passed in 1533. Another of Anne's early suitors, Thomas Wyatt, was arrested at the time of her fall and, although not charged, Percy probably watched his fate with alarm. Henry VIII annulled his marriage to Anne in the days before her execution, although the pretext for this annulment is not certain, with sources variously claiming that it was due to Anne's earlier betrothal to Percy or, alternatively, due to the king's own relationship with Mary Boleyn.[6] The relationship between Anne and Percy probably did extend to a formal promise to marry, something which, when made by two adults, was as binding as marriage itself.

Percy's love for Anne is clear, particularly as, socially, she was far beneath him. Anne's feelings are less certain. She had a high view of her own worth and the idea of becoming Countess of Northumberland must have appealed to her. Percy was of a similar age to Anne and there is evidence that she did indeed have feelings for him. The roots of her enmity towards Cardinal Wolsey lie in the Cardinal's role in breaking the relationship and, while this could have been due more to Anne's disappointment at the loss of Percy's status rather than his person, the evidence suggests that there was more to it than this. Anne was deeply involved in the fall from power of Cardinal Wolsey in 1529 and when Henry finally gave the order for him to be arrested in 1530, it was Percy who was sent to take him into custody, with Cavendish commenting significantly that Anne sent 'her ancient suitor' to do the deed. This vindictiveness suggests that she was still angry over the loss of Percy, in spite of the fact that, by 1530, she knew that she was to become queen. It therefore seems highly likely that the couple were indeed in love. Percy was one of the peers who sat in judgement on Anne at her trial in 1536, but it proved too much for him. He was taken ill before the trial of Anne's brother which followed.

Anne and Percy were unable to keep their relationship secret, with news of it soon reaching the king. Although Henry, at that stage, had no interest in Anne, he was angered by the proposed match, perhaps due to the disparity in their status or the fact that it jeopardised the Ormond settlement. Henry instructed Wolsey to break the engagement, with the cardinal immediately sending for Percy and rebuking him for his presumption. The young man, who burst into tears, gallantly attempted to defend his fiancée, declaring that

> I considered that I was of good years, and thought myself
> sufficient to provide myself with a convenient wife whereas
> my fancy served me best, not doubting but that my lord my
> father would have been right well persuaded. And, though
> she be a simple maid, and has but a knight to her father, yet
> she is descended of right noble parentage. For by her mother
> she is near to the Norfolk blood: and on her father's side
> lineally descended from the Earl of Ormond, he being one of
> the earl's heirs general.

Although the Boleyns had come far since their humble origins at Salle, by the early sixteenth century they had not come far enough to please Percy's father, the sixth Earl of Northumberland. On receiving a message from Wolsey, Northumberland hurried south, whisking his son away to marry Mary Talbot, the daughter of the Earl of Shrewsbury. Anne was sent home to Hever in disgrace, vowing that 'if it lay ever in her power she would work the Cardinal as much displeasure as he had done her'.

Anne Boleyn was finally able to return to court in 1525 when she resumed her position in the queen's household. She soon found another admirer. The courtier and poet Sir Thomas Wyatt came from an old Kentish family. His father, Sir Henry Wyatt, was associated with Sir Thomas Boleyn, with them both being created knights of the Bath at Henry VIII's Coronation in 1509 and receiving the joint appointment of constable of Norwich castle in 1511. Given the similarity of Christian names, it is not impossible that Boleyn was Thomas Wyatt's godfather: the honour could have been returned with Boleyn's second son, Henry, who did not survive infancy, who shared a Christian name with Sir Henry Wyatt.

By 1525, Thomas Wyatt was a prominent figure at court, with a firm friendship with the king.[7] Although he had, by then, been unhappily married for some years, he and Anne engaged in a flirtation, with Wyatt finding himself attracted to her appearance and intrigued by her 'witty and graceful speech, his ear also had him chained unto her, so as finally his heart seemed to say, I would gladly yield to be tied for ever with the knot of love'. Anne was well aware that there was no future in her relationship with Wyatt but she may well have been attracted to him and saw little harm in engaging in a little courtly love with him.

The evidence for Wyatt's interest in Anne survives both in a biography of Anne written by his grandson, George Wyatt, as well as in Thomas Wyatt's own poems. To Wyatt, Anne was the exotic 'Brunet' who featured in some of his surviving poems. In one poem, written some time after the end of their relationship, Wyatt declared that

Be sign of love. Then do I love again,
If thou ask whom, sure since I did refrain
Brunet that set my wealth in such a roar
The unfeigned cheer of Phyllis hath the place
That Brunet had: she hath and ever shall[8]

That this poem refers to Anne is evident from the fact that the third line quoted above originally read 'Her that did set our country in a roar'. Given that she later refused absolutely to become the king's mistress, it seems highly unlikely that she would have consented to become the mistress of Sir Thomas Wyatt, regardless of how attractive he was.

According to George Wyatt, it was Anne's relationship with Wyatt which first led to her coming to the attention of the king, with the two men competing for her affections.[9] While the couple were conversing one day, Wyatt playfully stole a small jewel from Anne, which she kept hanging on a lace from her pocket. Aware that the jewel would be recognised and that it would be presumed that she had given it to him, she immediately requested that it be returned, but Wyatt refused. Shortly afterwards, Henry VIII, who, after the end of his affair with Mary Boleyn, was looking for a new mistress, was flirting with Anne when he took a ring from her to wear on his little finger. He was still wearing it a few days later when he became engaged in a game of bowls with Wyatt. Henry, who had by then determined to make Anne his mistress, declared that he had won a game when it was clear to all present that he had not. Pointing with the finger on which he wore the ring, he declared, 'Wyatt, I tell thee it is mine,' a reference that his opponent knew full well was to Anne Boleyn rather than the game of bowls. Wyatt, determined not to be beaten, replied, 'If it may like your majesty to give me leave to measure it, I hope it will be mine.' He then took Anne's jewel from around his neck, making a great show of using it to measure the distance between the balls. Henry recognised the jewel at once and declared, 'It may be so, but then am I deceived,' before stalking away in anger.

Anne must have had a job excusing herself to the king following this incident and it marks the end of her flirtation with Wyatt. The poet was well aware that he could not compete with the king, with one of his most famous poems, in which he referred to the pursuit of Anne as that of a deer in the chase, making his decision to abandon her clear:

Whoso list to hunt: I know where is an hind
But as for me, alas I may no more;
The vain trevail hath wearied me so sore,
I am of them that farthest cometh behind.
Yet may I by no means my wearied mind
Draw from the deer, but as she fleeth afore
Fainting I follow, I leave off therefore,
Sithens in a net I seek to hold the wind.
Who list to hunt, I put him out of doubt,
As well as I may spend his time in vain,
And graven with diamonds in letters plain
There is written her fair neck round about:
'*Noli me tangere* [i.e. touch me not], for Caesar's I am,
And wild for to hold, though I seem tame.'[10]

While Wyatt and other nameless suitors quickly abandoned their pursuit when the king made his own interest plain, Anne was far from willing to abandon herself to the king's love.

By 1526, Henry VIII was still only in his mid-thirties and in his prime. The evidence of Anne's relationship with Thomas Wyatt indicates that she had an eye for a handsome man and she must have been flattered by the king's interest in her, as well as likely being attracted to him herself. In spite of this, Anne had seen how the king had treated her sister, abandoning her when he had tired of her with very little reward for the loss of her reputation and honour. Anne valued herself too highly to consent to become any man's mistress, even the king's. While Henry VIII made a public show of his affection for her in February 1526 by arriving at a joust wearing the motto 'Declare I dare not', she rebuffed his attempts to persuade her to consummate their relationship, eventually retreating home to Hever when the pressure became too great. If Anne hoped that this would lead to Henry forgetting her, she was mistaken, with the king's ardour only increased by her aloofness. Once at Hever, she found herself pursued by letters from the king, which she cannot but have found flattering with their declarations of his ardent love for her.

Seventeen of Henry's letters to Anne survive and, while her replies do not, it is clear that she was not uninterested in his suit although she always refused to become his mistress. In one early letter, Henry wrote,

My Mistress and friend, my heart and I surrender ourselves into your hands, beseeching you to hold us commended to your favour, and that by absence your affection to us may not be lessened: for it would be a great pity to increase our pain, of which absence produces enough and more than I could ever have thought could be felt, reminding us of a point in astronomy which is this: the longer the days are, the more distant is the sun, and nevertheless the hotter; so is it with our love, for by absence we are kept a distance from one another, and yet it retains its fervour, at least on my side.[11]

At the same time, he sent Anne his portrait set into a bracelet so that he would remain constantly in her thoughts.

Henry was desperate for Anne to return to him, remonstrating with her in one letter for the fact that he had been told 'that you would not come to court either with your mother, if you could, or in any other manner'. He found her aloofness, which contrasted with the other women he had desired, baffling, declaring hurt that

which report, if true, I cannot sufficiently marvel at, because I am sure that I have since never done anything to offend you, and it seems a very poor return for the great love which I bear you to keep me at a distance both from speech and the person of the woman that I esteem most in the world; and if you love me with as much affection as I hope you do, I am sure that the distance of our two persons would be a little irksome to you.

Henry, aware that Anne was determined to safeguard her honour, was looking for ways to persuade her back into his presence. His suggestion that she come to court chaperoned by her mother demonstrates that claims that Elizabeth Boleyn had a poor reputation are misguided. Elizabeth was not always present at Hever, as her visit in 1526 to her friend, Lady Lestrange, at Hunstanton in Norfolk shows. Kent was certainly her base, however, as a letter from the French ambassador from October 1528 shows. The ambassador commented that he did not think that Anne, who was then acknowledged as the king's fiancée, would 'yet leave her mother in Kent'.[12] Thomas Boleyn's accounts for the last two months of 1526 record that he purchased three hogsheads of wine for the house at Hever, as well as paying for carriage to the castle, demonstrating the presence of the family there.[13]

Anne also had other potential chaperones at court since, in January 1526, 'Mr Boleyn' and his wife, along with Mr Carey and his wife, Mary Boleyn, were listed as being entitled to lodgings at court when they were present, due to the men's attendance on the king.[14] 'Mr Boleyn' is probably Anne's brother, George, since the same document also refers to 'young Boleyn'. Henry would later rely on Jane Seymour's brother and sister-in-law to chaperone her during their courtship and it is therefore clear that there were suitable members of her family present at court to protect her honour if Anne so wished.

For Anne, Henry's suggestion of a chaperone was not enough to ensure that she retained her good reputation, particularly since his letters are full of frustrated sexual desire. In one, he wrote that 'I wish you between my arms'. In another, it appears that it was only after Henry finally offered Anne marriage that she consented to some kind of physical relationship, with the king writing in a later letter, after he had begun his attempts to divorce his wife, that 'I would you were in mine arms, or I in yours, for I think it long since I kissed you'. In another letter after the divorce had begun, Henry declared that he was 'wishing myself (especially of an evening) in my sweetheart's arms, whose pretty dukkys [breasts] I trust shortly to kiss'. There is no evidence that the pair actually consummated their relationship until late in 1532, when it was finally clear that their wedding was imminent.

With Anne's refusal to yield to him, Henry continued to cast around for a proposal that she would accept, finally writing with the unprecedented offer that

> if it pleases you to give yourself body and heart to me, who have been, and will be, your very loyal servant (if your rigour does not forbid me), I promise you that not only the name will be done to you, but also to take you as my sole mistress, casting off all others than yourself out of mind and affection, and to serve you only.

This was highly significant. In effect, the king was offering to make her his official mistress, in the same model as often employed by the French kings. If Anne had accepted, she would have had some status at court, with Henry's assurances that he would remain faithful to her. For Anne, however, this could not be enough and, with the example of her sister, she was well aware of how quickly the king's interest could wane when he had achieved what he wanted, regardless of any promises made. She indignantly refused, leaving Henry with only one other option if he wanted to consummate his relationship with Anne: marriage.

Henry's letters to Anne make it clear that he was deeply in love with her and he could not bear to live without her. At some point early in 1527 he finally capitulated, offering her marriage. Henry did not put this offer in writing, instead waiting until he was able to speak to her in person. According to George Wyatt, Anne insisted on time to consider her answer – a prudent decision given the fact that the offer was almost unprecedented, with only Henry's grandfather, Edward IV, alone among the Kings of England marrying a woman who had refused to become his mistress. George Wyatt claims that

Anne was reluctant to marry Henry as she loved Queen Catherine.[15] It is more likely that she wanted time to discuss the matter with her parents and to consider the seriousness of the king's offer, which was fraught with difficulties. For Sir Thomas Boleyn and his wife, news of the proposal must have filled them both with surprise, although Thomas was apparently 'not a little joyful' at the news, something which may have helped Anne in her decision.[16] Anne was probably attracted to Henry as a man, as well as enticed by the possibility of becoming a queen and, eventually, and apprehensively, she sent him her assent, along with the present of a jewel shaped like a maiden in a storm-tossed ship to signify her turmoil. For Henry, this was the answer to his prayers and he replied happily, saying,

> I thank you very cordially, not only for the handsome diamond and the ship in which the lonely damsel is tossed about, but chiefly for the fine interpretation and the humble submission which your kindness has made of it; thinking well that it could be very difficult for me to find occasion to merit it if I were not aided by your great indulgency and favour, for which I have sought, seek, and will ever seek, by everything in my power.

Henry then continued, declaring that

> the demonstrations of your affections are such, the beautiful words of the letter so cordially couched, as to oblige me ever truly to love, honour and serve you, begging you to continue in the same firm and constant purpose, assuring you that so far from merely returning your devotion I will out-do you in loyalty of heart were that possible, and you, with no bitterness in yours, can further that end; praying also that if at any time I have offended you, you will give me the same absolution as you yourself demand; again assuring you that henceforward my heart shall be dedicated to you alone, with

a strong desire that my body could also be thus dedicated, which God can do if he pleases.

Henry signed his letter 'H seeks AB no other', with Anne's initial enclosed in the drawing of a heart. For the first time in his life, he was deeply in love and it is difficult to see how Anne could not have returned at least some of this fervour.

With the exception of one doubtful letter written at the time of her fall, there is only one surviving letter which purports to have been from Anne to Henry VIII. This letter, which exists as an Italian translation of a supposedly lost original, is highly doubtful but, if genuine, does indeed suggest that Anne returned the king's love and was as eager to marry Henry the man as Henry the king:

It belongs only to the august mind of a great king, to whom Nature has given a heart full of generosity towards the sex, to repay by favours so extraordinary an artless and short conversation with a girl. Inexhaustible as is the treasury of your majesty's bounties, I pray you to consider that it cannot be sufficient to your generosity; for if you recompense so slight a conversation by gifts so great, what will you be able to do for those who are ready to consecrate their entire obedience to your desires? How great soever may be the bounties I have received, the joy that I feel in being loved by a king who I adore, and to whom I would with pleasure make a sacrifice of my heart, if fortune had rendered it worthy of being offered to him, will ever be infinitely greater.

The warrant of maid of honour to the queen induces me to think that your majesty has some regard for me, since it gives me the means of seeing you oftener, and of assuring you by your own lips (which I shall do at the first opportunity) that I am, Your majesty's most obliged and very obedient servant, without any reserve, Anne Boleyn.[17]

This letter should be treated with caution but may, perhaps, be accurate, albeit with its tone altered by translation into Italian and then back into English.

It is clear that Anne fully committed herself and her future to the king from the early months of 1527. Both she and Henry hoped that they would be able to quickly marry and consummate their relationship and, on 5 May 1527, Henry gave a banquet at court in honour of the French ambassadors and publicly led Anne out as his dancing partner for the first time. Twelve days later a secret ecclesiastical court opened in London to try the validity of the king's marriage, based on the fact that Catherine of Aragon had been the widow of Henry's elder brother.

8

ANNE BOLEYN & THE KING'S GREAT MATTER

Anne and Henry could never have envisaged in May 1527 that it would be nearly six long years before they were able to marry. Henry always argued that his conscience was troubled by his marriage to his sister-in-law and that he believed that his lack of surviving sons was due to the fact that the Bible, in the Book of Leviticus, stated that a man who married his dead brother's wife would be childless. While the couple had a surviving daughter, the eleven-year-old Princess Mary, in Henry's eyes, the lack of a son was effective childlessness. The fact that, through his sexual relationship with Mary Boleyn, he had placed himself within the same degree of relatedness (the first degree of affinity) with Anne as he was with Catherine, was immaterial to Henry, although it did not escape the eyes of some of his contemporaries. To be on the safe side, Henry did, in fact, ask the pope for a dispensation to marry a woman within the first degree of affinity, while at the same time disputing the validity of the earlier dispensation obtained for his first marriage.

In spite of the absurdity of his position, Henry knew that he had a good chance of succeeding if his church council of May 1527, which was convened by Cardinal Wolsey, could give sentence quickly. Unfortunately for Henry and Anne, news of the court quickly leaked out, with Catherine and the ambassadors of her powerful nephew, the Holy Roman Emperor Charles V, learning of the proceedings within hours. Catherine, not surprisingly, immediately asked her nephew to alert the pope, forcing Wolsey to adjourn the court on 31 May. With the adjournment, it became clear to Anne and Henry that they would have to seek the divorce directly from the pope. Unfortunately for them, news arrived that, on 16 June 1527, the Emperor had sacked Rome and was holding the pope as a virtual prisoner. With family honour at stake, Charles, who hardly knew his aunt, had no intention of allowing her to be discarded, ensuring that, while Henry had the upper hand in England, it was Catherine who held sway in Rome. Henry did not fully appreciate this at first, apparently hoping that the Emperor's support could be bought. In this he was to be disappointed, with Charles unequivocally informing Henry's ambassadors that

> he was sorry to understand of the intended divorce, adjuring the king (for the rest) by the Sacrament of Marriage, not to dissolve it or, if he would needs proceed therein, that the hearing and determining of the business, yet, might be referred to Rome, or a General Council, and not be decided in England. Adding further, that he would defend the Queen's just cause.[1]

Charles's own wife was the daughter of a man who had married two sisters and then their niece in turn (who were in fact Charles's two aunts and his sister respectively) and it was certainly not in his interests to allow his aunt to be discarded as Henry wished.

Anne, who was resident at court during the summer of 1527, must have found herself in a very difficult position as news of the king's desires began to leak out. As a member of Catherine's household, she was constantly in her mistress's presence, something which must have been uncomfortable for both women. According to George Wyatt, Catherine was able to find ways to subtly attack her opponent, for example often insisting that her rival join her as she played cards with the king so that Anne would be forced to display her deformed fingertip to Henry as she held her cards. During one game Catherine finally confirmed that she knew full well what Anne's ambitions were, with Wyatt recording:

> And in this entertainment of time they had a certain game that I cannot name then frequented, wherein dealing, the king and queen meeting they stopped, and the young lady's hap was much to stop at a king; which the queen noting, said to her playfellow, My lady Anne, you have good hap to stop at a king, but you are not like the others, you will have all or none.[2]

By 1527, Catherine had been married to Henry for nearly twenty years, devoting her life to him. She had tended to ignore Henry's affairs in the past, but she recognised Anne as a dangerous rival from the beginning. For her part, Anne was hostile towards Catherine and her daughter, with the records of her conduct not showing her in a very good light. According to the Imperial ambassador, Eustace Chapuys, for example, Anne supposedly declared at Christmas 1530 to one of Catherine's ladies that 'she wished all the Spaniards in the world were in the sea'.[3] When her companion upbraided her, Anne continued, saying that 'she did not care anything for the queen, and would rather see her hanged than acknowledge her as her mistress'. In her defence, Anne was sorely tried by Catherine's supporters at court, with Chapuys for one always referring to her in his despatches as 'the Lady' or 'the Concubine', even after she had become queen. Anne was also furious to find that, some years into her relationship with the king, Catherine still performed the traditional wifely duty of making his shirts.[4] The three were forced to live in close proximity to each other until 11 July 1531, when Anne and Henry secretly left Windsor with a small retinue, leaving Catherine behind. In spite of the queen's protestations, the separation proved permanent and she and Henry never met again. Anne continued in her antagonistic relationship with her predecessor, at one stage requesting that Catherine's jewels be sent to her for her own use.[5] To this, Catherine gave the cutting response that 'it was against her conscience to give her jewels to adorn a person who is the scandal of Christendom'. On being expressly asked by the king, she was forced to relinquish them.

At the same time that he dispatched his ambassadors to the Emperor, Henry also sent agents to speak to the pope himself. While the pope met with Henry's ambassadors, there was little he was actually prepared to do and, after the first embassy failed, Henry sent Edward Foxe and Stephen Gardiner to the pope at Orvieto to further press his claims. Anne followed Foxe and Gardiner's progress with interest, expecting them to keep her in touch with events directly. In a letter written by Anne to Gardiner on one of his journeys to Italy in April 1529, for example, she expressed the hope that this mission would be more pleasant to her than his first which had come to nothing and which 'for that was but a rejoicing hope, which causing the lie of it does put me to the more pain, and they that are partakers with me, as you do know, and therefore I do trust that this hard beginning shall make a better ending'.[6]

On their first visit to Italy, Foxe and Gardiner found the pope in a pitiful state, protesting his loyalty to Henry but begging for more time. Foxe returned to England in April 1528 and rushed straight to Greenwich, arriving on the evening of 28 April. On his arrival, Henry commanded him to go straight to Anne's chamber where Anne, eager to hear his news, made 'promises of large recompense' to the diplomat.[7] While they were talking, Henry entered the chamber and Anne left the room, allowing them to speak privately for a few minutes in which Foxe informed the king that the pope had privately told him that he might be prepared to confirm a sentence of divorce given in England. This was excellent news for the couple and Henry called his fiancée in to tell her himself. Overjoyed, the couple kept Foxe with them for most of the evening. Even better news followed a few weeks later when the pope, after considerable pressure from Gardiner, finally agreed to send a papal legate, Cardinal Campeggio, who was Bishop of Salisbury and known in England, to hear the case in Henry's own kingdom.

Both Anne and her mother kept abreast of news of the divorce. Elizabeth was resident with her daughter at court in March 1528 while the king was engaged in daily hunting expeditions. On 3 March Thomas Heneage, a former servant of Wolsey's who had recently joined the king's household, was intercepted by Anne and her mother at dinner time.[8] Anne immediately complained to Heneage that she felt that the cardinal had forgotten her since he had failed to send her a token with his most recent messenger, a man named Forest. Heneage sought to reassure her that the cardinal had had his mind on other matters and had simply forgotten, something which is unlikely to have pleased Anne. Elizabeth, who was listening to the conversation and had evidently been in a position to speak personally to Forest, then stepped in, complaining that she had asked Forest to request a 'morsel' of tuna from the cardinal and that she had not yet received it, therefore requesting it again through Heneage. Although couched in civil language, it is clear that both women considered themselves to have been slighted by the cardinal and it is not at all impossible that Elizabeth was also opposed to the cardinal's dominant position in England. The pair appeared together again in the depositions of Elizabeth Barton, the nun of Kent, following her arrest. She claimed that Anne had desired that she remain at court and that Elizabeth had sent to her personally to ask her to attend Anne herself.[9]

Whether this means that Elizabeth actually gave credence to the nun's claims is debatable and it appears more likely that she, like Anne and Henry, was trying to ascertain whether the nun could be persuaded to slip quietly back out of public notice. There can be no doubt that Anne and her mother were emotionally very close. We have Anne's own testimony for her affection for her mother, with a letter from Anne to her friend, Lady Wingfield, written at some point between 1529 and 1533, stating, 'Assuredly, next mine own mother, I know no woman alive that I love better.'[10]

Throughout the years of the divorce, Anne largely appears to have remained on good terms with her parents, with her father's accounts from the last months of 1526 recording that he had paid over £3 to settle a bill she owed.[11] By this time Thomas lived in some style at court, with his accounts showing a payment of £4 to the king's goldsmith. He purchased black satin for a doublet for himself, as well as making payments to his sister, Lady Shelton, brother, William, and his wife. That the couple remained close to Elizabeth's family is clear from the gift of a hogshead of Gascon wine to her stepmother, the Dowager Duchess of Norfolk. As the years dragged by Anne's mood became more tense, leading to quarrels with both Henry and members of her own family. She fell out with her uncle, the Duke of Norfolk, in early 1530 and also made an enemy of her aunt, Norfolk's estranged wife, who was a staunch supporter of Catherine of Aragon, requesting that the duchess be sent home 'because she spoke too freely, and declared herself more than they liked for the queen'.[12]

Anne also quarrelled with her father in the summer of 1532 when she refused to intercede for the life of a young priest who had been condemned for clipping coins.[13] Anne, in typically outspoken manner, 'told her father that he did wrong to speak for a priest as there were too many of them already'. The disagreement was not lasting, although there is evidence of some continuing bitterness in comments made by Thomas during Anne's first pregnancy in

1533. Anne had a particularly fiery character, at one point publicly quarrelling with Henry over Cardinal Wolsey and threatening to leave him, something that caused the king to burst into tears.[14] Henry did sometimes become frustrated with Anne, complaining privately to Norfolk that Anne was 'not like the queen, who had never in her life used ill words to him'. Norfolk certainly agreed with this, having already privately commented that Anne would be the ruin of all her family. Henry was always the one to make amends, with a report reaching Rome early in 1531 that the king had desperately summoned some of Anne's relatives to court to beg them in tears to help him make his peace with her after one quarrel. It would seem likely that these unspecified relatives included Elizabeth. Both Thomas and Elizabeth benefited from their daughter's position: in 1529 Thomas was finally created Earl of Ormond, as well as receiving the English title of Earl of Wiltshire, which had once belonged to his great uncle. It is telling that, at the banquet to celebrate the ennoblement, Anne took the place of the queen. At the same time, Anne's brother took the courtesy title of Viscount Rochford, while Anne began to style herself as 'Lady Anne Rochford'.[15]

Anne's brother, George, and his wife Jane Parker Boleyn benefited from her relationship with the king. As the king's prospective brother-in-law, George naturally acquired a certain status at court. He was in receipt of royal favour, receiving an annuity in 1528, as well as being appointed as keeper of the palace of Beaulieu in Essex. Jane gave the king a New Year's gift in 1532 when she made him the present of four caps.[16] Henry reciprocated with gold plate. While lists of the king's New Year's gifts are fragmentary, Jane is known to have given Henry a shirt with an embroidered silver collar in 1534, suggesting that she was enough in the king's thoughts to be regularly included in his New Year's gift lists. Jane and George lived in some style. A short list of some of Jane's possessions compiled in 1536 records that she possessed a rich wardrobe, including a pair of sleeves of crimson velvet decorated with goldsmith's work and another of yellow satin.[17] She owned a pair of knitted stockings of white silk, decorated with gold, kept specifically for masques. At the time of her death Jane had some fine plate, such as a pair of silver flagons and a ewer of silver parcel gilt.[18] Her jewels included a black enamelled brooch with six small diamonds and a gold brooch decorated with a cameo. At some point during their marriage George and Jane also acquired a rich bed of painted wood, which was decorated with burnished gold gilt and furnished with hangings of white satin, decorated with tawny cloth of gold and George's devices as Viscount Rochford.[19]

Although the pope bowed to Henry's demands to some extent in the summer of 1528, he was still in the Emperor's power and had no intention of offending Catherine of Aragon's nephew. Unbeknown to Henry and Anne, Campeggio was under strict instructions to delay matters as much as possible and his progress towards England was painfully slow. He had still not set out by the end of June, some weeks after it was first agreed that he would be sent, when Henry and Anne suddenly found that they had greater problems to contend with. Throughout the Tudor period, there were a number of sudden outbreaks of sweating sickness, which was a highly contagious disease that struck down people suddenly, particularly attacking the young and healthy. In June 1528 there was an outbreak in London, which quickly infected much of the city. The sweating sickness was a terrifying disease, with the French ambassador commenting that 'one has a little pain in the head and heart; suddenly a sweat begins; and a physician is useless, for whether you wrap yourself up much or little, in four hours, sometimes in two or three, you are dispatched without languishing'.[20] Henry, who was always terrified of disease and conscious of his lack of a male heir, was in a state of high anxiety as the sweat began to ravage the city. Even his love for Anne was not enough for him to brave infection and practically, although hardly romantically, he sent her away when she was exposed to the disease, while he fled to safety.[21]

Although Henry was not prepared to risk infection for Anne, he quickly wrote to her to reassure her of his continuing love for her and his concern for her health:

> The uneasiness my doubts about your health gave me, disturbed and alarmed me exceedingly, and I should not have had any quiet without hearing certain tidings. But now, since you have as yet felt nothing, I hope, and am assured that it will spare you, as I hope it is doing with us. For when we were at Walton, two ushers, two valets de chamber, and your brother, fell ill, but are now quite well; and since we have returned to our house at Hunsdon, we have been perfectly well, and have not, at present, one sick person, God be praised; and I think, if you would retire from Surrey, as we did, you would escape all danger. There is another thing that may comfort you, which is, that, in truth, in this distemper few or no women have been taken ill, and, what is more, no person of our court, and few elsewhere, have died of it.[22]

Anne heeded Henry's advice and returned home to Hever. However, reports that she had escaped the fever were premature and, soon after, Henry wrote anxiously that

> there came to me suddenly in the night the most grievous news that could arrive, and I must need lament it for three reasons: the first being to hear of the sickness of my mistress, whom I esteem more than all the world, and whose health I desire as my own, and would willingly bear the half of your illness to have you cured; the second, for fear of being yet again constrained by my enemy absence, who until now has given me every possible annoyance, and so far as I can judge

is likely to do worse, though I pray God rid me of a rebel so importunate, the third, because the physician in who I most trust is absent at a time when he could do me most pleasure; for I hoped through him, and his methods, to obtain one of my chief joys in this world, that is to say, that my mistress should be cured.

Henry sent his second-best doctor to Hever, something which, given that he was concerned about infection himself, is testament to his deep love for Anne: he desperately wanted her to recover. Thomas Boleyn also contracted the sweating sickness that summer at Hever and it must have been a relief for his wife, who was almost certainly present, when they both recovered. The family did not escape unscathed, with Mary Boleyn's husband, William Carey, succumbing to the sweat that summer.

The death of her young husband was a shock to Mary Boleyn and left her financially exposed. Anne promised her sister that she would do something for the family following Carey's death, approaching the king about her 'sister's matter', which the king faithfully promised in one of his letters 'to write to my lord my mind thereon, whereby I trust that Eve shall not have power to deceive Adam; for surely, whatsoever is said, it cannot so stand with his honour but that he must needs take her, his natural daughter, now in her extreme necessity'.[23] It appears from this that Anne had sought Henry's assistance in ensuring that Thomas Boleyn would take on financial responsibility for his eldest daughter in her time of necessity.

William Carey's sister, Eleanor, was a nun at the aristocratic convent at Wilton which, in the summer of 1528, was without an abbess due to the death of its previous head. Anne approached Henry to request that he appoint Eleanor Carey as abbess. Anne's promotion of Eleanor placed her in direct and open conflict with Cardinal Wolsey for the first time, as he instead supported the candidacy of the prioress, Isabel Jordan. Nonplussed at the king's support of Eleanor, Wolsey carried out an investigation into her conduct, evidently aware that there was a scandal to be found. He then reported his findings to a shocked Henry who, in spite of his six wives and break with Rome, was a deeply pious man, and who wrote immediately to Anne to inform her that he could no longer support her sister's kinswoman:

As touching the matter of Wilton my lord Cardinal hath had the nuns before him and examined them, Master Bell being present, which hath certified me that for a truth she [Eleanor Carey] hath confessed herself (which we would have had abbess) to have had two children by two sundry priests and further since hath been kept by a servant of the Lord Brook that was. And that not long ago; wherefore I would not for all the gold in the world cloak your conscience nor mine to make her ruler of a house which is of so ungodly demeanour, nor I trust you would not that neither for brother nor sister I should so destain mine honour or conscience; and as touching the prioress or dame Eleanor's eldest sister though there is not any evident case proved against them, and that the prioress is so old that of many years she could not be as she was named, yet notwithstanding, to do you pleasure I have done that neither of them shall have it; but that some good and well disposed woman shall have it.

Whether the revelations about Eleanor Carey were a surprise to Anne or not is unclear: Wilton had long been used by noble families as a convenient place to house daughters who, for some reason or another, had proved unmarriageable, something that meant that many of the nuns had little or no vocation for the religious life. Anne was further infuriated when Wolsey ignored the king's commands regarding Wilton, appointing Isabel Jordan to the position in spite of Henry's prohibition. This was a dangerous game for the cardinal to play and Henry immediately wrote to admonish him, declaring his fury at Wolsey ignoring his express commands and then trying 'to cloak your offence made by ignorance of my pleasure' when, as Henry pointed out, he had told the cardinal himself that 'his pleasure is that in no wise the Prioress have it, nor yet Dame Eleanor's eldest sister for many considerations'.²⁴ Although matters were soon smoothed over with an apology from Wolsey, the damage had been done in spite of Henry writing to assure his minister that 'seeing the humbleness of your submission, and though the case were much more heinous, I can be content for to remit it, being right glad, that, according to mine intent, my monitions and warning have been benignly and lovingly accepted on your behalf'.

During the early years of the divorce, Wolsey and Anne had always taken great pains to appear friendly towards each other due to the fact that both were aware of the great influence the other had over the king. A number of Anne's letters to Wolsey survive, demonstrating that she was prepared to flatter and work with him if necessary, for example in one letter writing, 'After my most humble recommendation, this shall be to give unto your Grace, as I am most bound, my humble thanks for the great pain and travail that your Grace doth take in studying by your wisdom and great diligence how to bring to pass honourably the greatest wealth that is possible to come to any creature living.'²⁵ In spite of the pair's politeness towards each other, there was significant underlying hostility. Wolsey's servant, Cavendish, claimed that the cardinal referred to Anne as 'the Night Crow' and as a 'continual serpentine enemy about the king', complaining of her influence over Henry and her ability to limit his access to the king. For example, on one occasion Anne arranged a hunting trip and picnic for the king to ensure that he would not be available to see the cardinal on a day that he came up to court. For his part, Wolsey was also looking for ways to bring Anne down, at one stage reporting her to the king for her possession of William Tyndale's *Obedience of a Christian Man*, which was banned in England as heretical.[26] On hearing that Wolsey intended to denounce her for this, Anne rushed to the king to inform him that she had marked out points that she thought would interest him, heading off the cardinal's complaints that the work should not have been in her possession in the first place. Due to her regular presence beside the king at court, to which Wolsey was only a visitor, it is no surprise that Anne soon gained the upper hand. It was the failure of the Blackfriars trial of his marriage that truly brought about the cardinal's ruin.

Anne remained at Hever throughout the summer of 1528, evidently recuperating from her illness, with Henry writing unhappily that 'as touching your abode at Hever, do therein as best shall like you, for you know best what air doth best with you; but I would it were come thereto (if it pleased God), that neither of us need care for that, for I ensure you I think it long'.[27] While away from court she continued to keep abreast of news, particularly seeking details of the progress of Cardinal Campeggio's journey towards England.

Campeggio finally arrived in London in October 1528 and immediately retired to his bed with gout. This was a major disappointment to the couple and Anne, who had been intending to remain in the background during the legate's visit, returned to London for Christmas. This time she had her own apartments at court as she did 'not like to meet with the queen', an arrangement which must have been something of a relief for all three parties involved in the divorce.[28] Campeggio finally rose from his sickbed in early 1529 and set about trying to fulfil his secret orders from the pope to 'persuade the Queen to a Divorce; and dissuade the King from it, as having either way the end he proposed: yet he failed in both'.[29] Campeggio then tried to persuade Catherine to become a nun, a solution that actually had a good deal of merit as it would both have allowed Henry to remarry and ensured that Catherine retired with her honour and the legitimacy of her former marriage to the king and her daughter unchallenged. However, Catherine was a pious woman and could not bring herself to feign a vocation that she did not have. She was also in love with her husband and desperately hoped that he would return to her, something which could never permit her to retire and to allow her position to be taken by Anne Boleyn. Campeggio found both husband and wife unshakeable in their respective beliefs, commenting of Henry that he was so convinced that his marriage was void that 'if an angel was to descend from heaven he would not be able to persuade him to the contrary'.[30] It quickly became apparent to Campeggio that the matter would need to be tried.

Both Catherine and Henry were busy in their preparations for the trial of their marriage. Through his examination of the original papal bull of dispensation, Wolsey thought that he had found a flaw in that the wording said that Catherine's first marriage had been 'perhaps' consummated. Henry pounced on this, with his lawyers arguing that if Arthur and Catherine had indeed consummated their marriage then her second marriage to her brother-in-law could never have been valid. Catherine always claimed that she had been a virgin at the time of her marriage to Henry, but the king was able to find a number of witnesses to testify against her. George, Earl of Shrewsbury, for example, was happy to testify that he had been present when Arthur had been conducted to Catherine's bedchamber on their wedding night and that he had always supposed that the marriage had been consummated.[31] A further testimony by Sir Anthony Willoughby was more damaging, with Willoughby claiming that Arthur had spoken to him the morning after the wedding, saying, 'Willoughby, bring me a cup of ale, for I have been this night in the midst of Spain.' The teenager had also later boasted that 'it is good pastime to have a wife'. Given Catherine's deep religious faith, it seems unlikely that she was lying. Certainly, Henry had originally believed that he had found her a virgin on their wedding night. In any event, Catherine was able to surprise everyone by producing a copy of a papal brief which was held in Spain and which overcame all the difficulties that Wolsey had identified in the papal bull. While Henry made strenuous efforts to obtain the original from Spain, declaring it to be a forgery, Catherine sensibly refused to request it from her nephew. At stalemate, Anne retired from court in the early summer of 1529 with a trial of the marriage finally convening at Blackfriars in June 1529.

Both Henry and Catherine were cited to appear before Campeggio and Wolsey on the first day of the trial on 18 June 1529. To everyone's surprise, Catherine heeded the summons and sat in her chair on the opposite side of the hall to Henry. As the court was opened, Catherine stood up and walked over to the king, kneeling at his feet. The queen was well aware that the court was not impartial and she immediately appealed to Rome for the case to be heard there, making a long and emotional speech to her husband:

> I beseech you for all the love that hath been between us, and for the love of God, let me have justice and right, take of me some pity and compassion, for I am a poor woman and a stranger born out of your dominion. I have here no assured friends, and much less impartial counsel, I flee to you as to the head of justice within this realm. Alas! Sir, wherein have I offended you, or what occasion of displeasure have I deserved against your will and pleasure - now that you intend (as I perceive) to put me from you? I take God and all the world to witness that I have been to you a true, humble and obedient wife, ever comfortable to your will and pleasure, and never said or did anything to the contrary thereof, being always well pleased and contended with all things wherein you had any delight or dalliance, whether it were in little or

much. I never grudged in word or countenance, or showed a visage or spark of discontent. I loved all those whom ye loved only for your sake whether I had cause or no, and whether they were my friends or my enemies. This twenty years or more I have been your true wife and by me ye have had divers children, although it hath pleased God to call them out of this world, which hath been no default of me.[32]

Catherine continued, insisting that Henry had found her a virgin at their marriage. She begged him to let her remain as his wife. Finally, as a mortified Henry sat watching, she stood and left the hall, refusing all commands that she return with the words that 'it makes no matter, for it is no impartial court for me, therefore I will not tarry'.

The trial continued without Catherine and Henry was soon pushing Campeggio to give judgement. Finally, aware that he could delay no longer, Campeggio stood and said that he would give no judgement, instead revoking the case to Rome.[33] This announcement infuriated Anne and Henry and caused uproar at court, with the king's brother-in-law, the Duke of Suffolk, declaring that 'cardinals never did good in England'. Anne was as furious as the king and, at dinner one day, spoke openly against Wolsey, turning towards Henry and declaring, 'Is it not a marvellous thing to consider what debt and danger the cardinal hath brought you in with all your subjects?' Anne claimed that Wolsey had done enough to warrant execution and, while Henry tried weakly to defend him and declared that he perceived that Anne was 'not the cardinal's friend', she countered that 'I have no cause to be. Nor hath any other man that loves your Grace. No more has your Grace, if ye consider well his doings.'

Henry had relied on Wolsey for many years by 1529, but he was furious with the cardinal's failure to secure for him his greatest desire. Following Cardinal Campeggio's departure from England, he was surprised to find that his bags were searched at Calais on the suspicion that he was carrying money to facilitate Wolsey's flight to Rome. On 9 October 1529, Wolsey was charged with taking orders from a foreign power (i.e. the pope) and forced to surrender the great seal and his position as chancellor of England. He was also ordered to retire to his house at Esher, although was not arrested, spending the next few months attempting to engineer a return to court. Wolsey knew that the best way to assuage Henry's anger was by appealing to the king's greed and he ordered that accounts should be prepared of all his possessions so that they could be surrendered to the king. Anne and Henry travelled secretly to York Place to view their new possession and Anne must have felt triumphant to see that all the cardinal had once owned now belonged to her and the king. Wolsey on the other hand was forced to make use of borrowed dishes, plate and cloth at Esher. Henry remained unsure about Wolsey and, at Christmas 1529, sent his own physician to attend the cardinal, who had fallen ill. At the same time, he insisted that Anne sent the fallen minister a token of comfort which she complied with, sending a golden tablet. Henry also sent Wolsey four cartloads of gifts at Candlemas.

Anne and her uncle, the Duke of Norfolk, continued to press Henry to abandon the cardinal and, finally, at Easter 1530 Wolsey was ordered to travel to his diocese of York. Wolsey was staying at Cawood in November 1530 when Henry Percy, who had by then become Earl of Northumberland, arrived to arrest him for treason. This was Anne's final revenge and, following his arrest, the cardinal was taken towards London with his legs tied to his horse. He was a broken man, stating that 'had I served God as diligently as I had done the king, he would not have given me over, in my grey hairs'. On 29 November 1530 Wolsey died at Leicester. It was suggested that he took poison to avoid a more shameful death, although he may also simply have died an old and broken man, aware that his fall from grace was to be made permanent. Anne and her family rejoiced in the minister's fall, and by the end of 1530 it was clear to everyone that she was queen in all but name.

As early as December 1528 the French ambassador had commented of Anne that 'greater court is now paid to her every day than has been to the queen for a long time. I see they mean to accustom the people by degrees to endure her, so that when the great blow comes it may not be thought strange.'[34] As the years wore on, Henry increasingly began to despair of receiving an annulment from the pope and he and Anne instead began to look around for other solutions. In September 1532 Henry felt secure enough to create Anne Lady Marquis of Pembroke with land grants worth 1,000 pounds a year. It is of particular note that in the patent conferring the title on Anne, the title and lands were stated to descend to her male heirs, rather than the more usual specification that it must be legitimate male heirs. This is a clear indication of a change in the nature of Anne and Henry's relationship and suggests that they had already begun to, or were close to, finally consummating their relationship. In October 1532 the pair visited Calais on a visit to Anne's old acquaintance, Francis I of France. Although no suitable French lady had been found to greet her (and suggestions that she be met by Francis's mistress were treated with short shrift by the English) Anne acquitted herself well, dancing before Francis in a masquing costume of cloth of gold and crimson tinsel satin.[35] She was accompanied in the visit by both her sister, Mary, and her sister-in-law, Lady Rochford, with the two women dancing alongside the future queen.

By mid-January 1533 Anne would have begun to suspect that she was pregnant and, in spite of rumours of an earlier marriage ceremony, it appears that the couple finally wed in considerable secrecy on 25 January 1533 at Whitehall Palace. Word of the marriage soon began to leak out and, on 23 February 1533, Chapuys wrote to the Emperor to inform him that he had heard that the couple had married privately with only Anne's parents, brother, two friends and one of the king's priests in attendance. Chapuys's sources were not entirely accurate since he asserted that it was Cranmer himself who had performed the ceremony, something which the archbishop himself denied in a private letter to a friend.[36] It is not impossible that the Boleyns might have been able to attend the wedding. An alternative account, however, considers that the ceremony was attended by only two members of the king's Privy Chamber and Anne's friend, Lady Berkeley, while it was officiated over by Henry's chaplain, Rowland Lee, who received the office of Bishop of Lichfield for his pains.[37] Whoever attended the marriage, it is certain that, by the end of January, Anne was indeed married to the king, with only weeks to wait until she was finally acknowledged as Queen of England.

9

ANNE THE QUEEN

Although Anne and Henry finally felt secure enough to marry in January 1533, they were both aware that, in the eyes of the world, Henry was still married to Catherine of Aragon. While Henry preferred to secure his divorce through a sentence given by the pope, at Anne's urging he was prepared to look at other solutions.

Although Chapuys referred to Anne and her father as 'more Lutheran than Luther himself', it is more correct to say that both shared the humanist ideals of promotion of the scriptures in the vernacular.[1] While both were interested in religious reform, this does not necessarily equate them with Protestantism, which, in any event, was still in its infancy during Anne's lifetime. Anne owned a French Bible and, as queen, kept an English version on display for her household to read.[2] She was also, not surprisingly, anti-papal. As well as owning a copy of Tyndale's *Obedience of a Christian Man*, which she had shown Henry, Anne possessed Simon Fish's anti-clerical work, *The Supplication of Beggars*, which criticised the cult of purgatory and the payment of ecclesiastical fees.[3] More pertinently for Anne, Fish argued that the king's laws could not be enforced against the pope's as the chancellor was generally a priest. Few others would have dared to show Henry such 'heretical' works and he began to take an interest.

In 1531 the king made his first move against the pope, insisting that the English clergy, in order to avoid a charge of praemunire (i.e. prioritising papal law above the king's) recognise him as sole protector and supreme head of the Church of England.[4] The value of this title was limited by the qualification that Henry was only supreme head 'as far as the law of Christ allows', but it was the first step towards the break with Rome. Henry also instigated an attack on church revenues levied in England and was presented, in August 1532, on the death of the conservative Archbishop of Canterbury, William Warham, with the perfect opportunity to secure his annulment.

Warham's death cleared the way for a more reform-minded successor, with Henry's choice falling on the unknown Thomas Cranmer. Cranmer had been appointed as one of the king's chaplains in January 1532, almost certainly on Anne's recommendation. He had previously been a member of Thomas Boleyn's household. He held strong reformist views and was already secretly married when he accepted the post of Archbishop of Canterbury early in 1533. As soon as he was appointed, a request was made to the pope for the bulls confirming Cranmer's appointment and the pontiff, anxious to do anything to appease Henry, unsuspectingly dispatched them in March 1533.[5] Soon after they arrived, Cranmer repudiated his oath of loyalty to the pope. Already, the groundwork had been laid for the divorce with the Act in Restraint of Appeals, which was passed by Parliament in February 1533 and stated that matrimonial cases should not be tried by appeal to Rome, instead remaining within the jurisdiction of the Church of England.[6]

As a result of this, in early May 1533, Cranmer travelled to Dunstable, close to Catherine's residence at Ampthill. Not surprisingly, the queen refused to attend a Church court to try the validity of her marriage. Cranmer pressed on regardless, giving sentence on 8 May 1533 that Henry's first marriage had been invalid from the start.[7] Cranmer informed Henry and Anne personally of the sentence, hurrying back to London in order to prepare for the new queen's Coronation.

Anne had found it impossible not to drop hints of her marriage even before it was officially recognised, for example informing stunned observers that she had a craving for apples which the king had assured her meant that she must be pregnant. The official announcement was finally made on Easter Saturday 1533, by which time Anne must have been visibly pregnant. According to Chapuys, she made a grand statement of her new status:

On Saturday, Easter Eve, dame Anne went to mass in Royal state, loaded with jewels, clothed in a robe of cloth of gold friese. The daughter of the Duke of Norfolk, who is affianced to the duke of Richmond, carried her train, and she had in her suite 60 young ladies, and was brought to church, and brought back again with the solemnities, or even more, which were used to the queen. She has changed her name from marchioness to Queen, and the preachers offered prayers for her by name.[8]

For Anne, it was the culmination of all her hopes and she adopted the motto 'the Most Happy'. Although she was secure in the king's love, Anne's queenship was not accepted by everyone in England and there was a good deal of muttering among the people. It was perhaps in retaliation to this that Anne could not resist a further attack on her predecessor, ordering her chamberlain, Lord Burgh, to seize Catherine's barge and remove and mutilate her arms and badges.[9] It was this barge that Anne used to make her ceremonial procession to the Tower of London on the first day of her Coronation festivities.

On 29 May the Mayor of London and representatives of all the crafts arrived by water at Greenwich, travelling in barges decked with colourful banners. Anne may have reflected on just how far the Boleyns had risen since her great-grandfather had fulfilled the office of mayor himself less than a century before as she watched the company assemble. At 3 p.m. she walked out to her own barge, sailing down the river in procession to be met, at Tower wharf, by a great gun salute, louder than anyone could remember. Henry also came out of the Tower to greet his wife 'with a noble loving countenance' and the couple retired inside to the royal apartments.[10] An enormous crowd had come out to watch Anne's procession and, while Chapuys claimed that the crowd 'showed themselves as sorry as though it had been a funeral', this was not the majority verdict.[11] In general the mood was one of celebration. The couple spent the next day quietly at the Tower.

The ceremonies recommenced on 31 May when Anne set out for Westminster in a grand procession. She sat in a litter of white satin with a canopy of cloth of gold carried above her head.[12] Immediately after her rode twelve ladies on horseback dressed in cloth of gold. Anne's mother, Elizabeth, followed with her stepmother, the Dowager Duchess of Norfolk, in a chariot covered in cloth of gold before a further twelve mounted ladies followed dressed in crimson velvet, with the remaining ladies riding in three golden coaches. Anne wanted her family around her, and both her sister and sister-in-law are likely to have been among the ladies in the procession. Jane, Lady Rochford, was certainly present in London, with one member of the court writing to George Boleyn, who was then in France, to inform him that Anne's Coronation had honourably passed and that he could shortly expect a letter from Jane containing news from the court.[13]

Anne's route through London on 31 May took her past a number of pageants designed to demonstrate the glory of Anne and the Tudor dynasty.[14] One displayed a castle. As Anne watched, a white falcon, representing her own falcon emblem, descended from the sky. As the bird landed, a child stepped forward to recite a poem on the glory of the falcon and, by analogy, Anne. An angel then descended to crown the falcon, before another child praised the queen, declaring, 'Honour and grace be to our Queen Anne!' The crowd was not entirely positive, with Anne apparently complaining to the mayor that few members of the crowd uncovered their heads or cried God save the Queen.[15] However, in the main, the ceremonies went well. The following day Anne was crowned in Westminster Abbey by Archbishop Cranmer.

Once the ceremony was over Anne and Henry began to prepare for the birth of their child. That summer, the annual progress was curtailed due to Anne's advancing pregnancy and, instead, she and her ladies spent much time enjoying entertainments in her chambers.[16] Anne's rivalry with Catherine of Aragon had not ceased with her predecessor's banishment and she asked Henry to send to his former wife to demand a rich triumphal cloth which she had brought from Spain to be used as a christening robe.[17] Not surprisingly, Catherine refused to hand over her personal property, declaring that she would not grant such a favour 'in a case so horrible and abominable'. Anne must have been angered by her predecessor's refusal, but she can hardly have been surprised. She soon had other things to worry about when it emerged that Henry had taken advantage of her pregnancy to take a mistress, as he had so often done before during his first wife's pregnancies. Unlike Catherine, Anne was not prepared to ignore Henry's indiscretion and 'she used some words to the king at which he was displeased', to which he responded that 'she must shut her eyes, and endure as well as more worthy persons, and that she ought to know that it was in his power to humble her again in a moment more than he had exalted her'.[18] Anne had held Henry enthralled for six years and must have been shocked at his anger towards her. The couple were quickly reconciled and it was with great ceremony that Anne took to her chamber at Greenwich on 26 August 1533 to await the birth of the expected prince.

Henry's grandmother, Lady Margaret Beaufort, had created a set of ordinances for a royal birth, which Anne would have been at pains to follow. Margaret decreed that, a month before the birth the queen should retire to a female world. Anne relied on her sister to attend her after the premature end of her final pregnancy in January 1536 and it therefore seems likely that her mother, sister and sister-in-law would have been present with her in 1533. If so, they would have attended Anne when she went into labour, giving birth to a daughter at 3 p.m. on 7 September 1533. The sex of the child was a blow for both her parents and was greeted by them with 'great regret'.[19] Henry's initial reaction was to cancel the grand tournament that he had planned to celebrate the birth of his son, although after a few days the couple accepted their daughter more happily. The baby was healthy and was proof of Anne's fertility. In spite of rumours that the child was to be named Mary in order to fully usurp the place of her elder half-sister, she was instead christened Elizabeth, probably primarily after Henry's mother, Elizabeth of York, although by happy coincidence also the name of her maternal grandmother.[20] In the few brief years that she had with her, Anne proved to be a fond mother, regularly visiting the child in her own household and taking decisions in relation to her education.[21] In spite of her fondness for the child, however, Anne knew that she would quickly be expected to conceive again and bear the king a son.

Anne used her position as queen to further the religious reform movement in England. According to her chaplain, William Latymer, as soon as she became queen, she called her chaplains to her, telling them that she had 'carefully chosen you to be the lanterns and light of my court'. She continued,

I require you, as you shall at any time hereafter perceive me to decline from the right path of sound and pure doctrine, and yield to any manner of sensuality, to await some convenient time wherein you may advertise me thereof: the which I promise you to accept in very thankful part, addressing my self wholly to reformation and yielding good example to others, for the discharge of my own conscience. And as to the rest of my court, I straightly charge you vigilantly to watch their doing, curiously to mark their proceedings, lives and conversations, diligently to advertise them of their duties, especially towards almighty God, to instruct them the way of virtue and grace, to charge them to abandon and eschew all manner of vice; and above all things to embrace the wholesome doctrine and infallible knowledge of Christ's gospel, aswell in virtuous and undefiled conversation as also in pure and sincere understanding thereof.

Given Anne's notoriously fiery temper, it seems unlikely that any of her chaplains would have dared admonish her for any perceived sin. However, there is no doubt that Anne wanted to preside over a household at the forefront of religious reform and that she wanted her chaplains to ensure that everyone within her household followed her lead.

As well as promoting the reading of the scriptures in the vernacular, she also sought to dispel religious superstitions. For example, sending commissioners to Hailes Abbey to investigate the relic of the blood of Christ held there. On it being discovered to be either red wax or duck's blood, she had it removed. Anne was charitable, distributing alms to the poor people of towns that she visited. Both she and her brother paid to maintain scholars at Cambridge. Anne's patronage was not always welcomed, with a letter from the queen to a Dr Crome complaining that she was 'marvelling not a little that, albeit heretofore we have signified unto you at sundry times our pleasure concerning your promotion unto the parsonage of Aldermany, within the city of London, which we have obtained for you, yet you hitherto have deferred the taking on you of the same'.

Dr Crome was a little less eager than Anne that he should take the post, but the queen was prepared to accept no protests. She wanted him there and there he must go, ending her letter by stating that 'our express mind and pleasure is that you shall use no farther delays in this matter'.

Anne conceived a second child early in 1534 and, by April, she was visibly pregnant.[22] The birth was expected at some point in the summer with Anne sending her brother to France in July to request that a proposed meeting between Henry and Francis could be delayed until after she had delivered her child so that she could also attend.[23]

While Anne was awaiting the birth of her second child at court, a family drama was taking place in the countryside involving her sister, Mary. By 1534, Mary had been a widow for nearly six years. She had spent much of the intervening years in the company of her sister, although it is clear that she had not entirely abandoned her own interests as, in the spring of 1534, she secretly married a servant, William Stafford, who, while a gentleman, was far beneath her socially. Mary herself provided an account of her reasoning for the match, declaring in a letter to the king's chief minister, Thomas Cromwell,

> Consider, that he was young, and love overcame reason; and for my part I saw so much honesty in him, that I loved him as well as he did me, and was in bondage and glad I was to be at liberty: so that, for my part, I saw that all the world did set so little by me, and he so much, that I thought I could take no better way but to take him and to forsake all other ways, and live a poor, honest life with him.[24]

Mary knew that Stafford was no match for the queen's sister and that he was poor, with little income of his own, but she touchingly believed that, with only the opportunity to prove himself, he could indeed become a success:

For well I might have had a greater man of birth and higher, but I assure you I could never have had one that should have loved me so well, nor a more honest man; and besides that, he is both come of an ancient stock, and again as meet (if it was his grace's pleasure) to do the king a service, as any young gentleman in his court.

Unfortunately for Mary, her family were not inclined to see William Stafford's virtues, focussing only on the disparity of rank. There is some suggestion that Mary came to regret her hasty match to some extent, in spite of the fact that she later protested that 'and seeing there is no remedy, for God's sake help us; for we have been now a quarter of a year married, I thank God, and too late now to call that again'. Although Mary stated that she would not change her conduct, it is perhaps telling that she was unable to find a way to tell her family of what she had done, instead letting them find out in the worst possible way.

Anne relied on her sister to attend her during childbirth and she recalled Mary to court to attend her in the summer of 1534 with her approaching confinement. Mary received this summons with a heavy heart, travelling up to court with her new husband. Given that she later indicated that she had been married only for three months, it seems likely that they had been forced by circumstances to marry so hastily, with Mary already visibly pregnant when she arrived at court, something which suggests a pregnancy considerably more advanced than three months. Mary perhaps hoped that the publicity of the court would deflect the worst of her family's anger. If this was the case, she was mistaken. Her parents, brother and uncle, the Duke of Norfolk, were horrified, with Mary later lamenting to Cromwell,

And I beseech you, good master secretary, pray my lord my father and my lady be so good to us, and to let me have their blessings and my husband their good will; and I will never desire more of them. Also, I pray you, desire my lord of Norfolk and my lord my brother to be good to us. I dare not write to them, they are so cruel against us; but if, with any pain that I could take with my life, I might win their food wills, I promise you there is no child living would venture more than I. And so I pray you to report by me, and you shall find my writing true, and in all points which I may please them in I shall be ready to obey them nearest my husband, whom I am most bound to; to whom I most heartily beseech you to be good unto, which, for my sake, is a poor banished man for an honest and a godly cause.

Mary hoped to appease her family by confirming that she wanted nothing more from them than their blessing, suggesting that she hoped that some of their anger was financial.

While Mary was saddened by the response of her parents, brother and uncle to her marriage, she was also deeply worried by the reaction of her sister. For Anne, who was always portrayed as an upstart, the fact of her sister's marriage to a servant was infuriating and the worst of the anger directed at Mary came from the queen. On seeing her sister, Anne ordered that she and Stafford be banished from the court, refusing to give them the opportunity to plead their case. When she wrote to Cromwell, Mary confirmed that

I am sure it is not unknown to you the high displeasure that both he and I have, both of the king's highness and the queen's grace, by reason of our marriage without their knowledge, wherein we both do yield ourselves faulty, and do acknowledge that we did not well to be so hasty nor so bold, without their knowledge.

That it was Anne rather than Henry who was the driving force behind the banishment is clear from Mary's assertion:

> And good master secretary, sue for us to the king's highness, and beseech his highness, which ever was wont to take pity, to have pity on us; and, that it will please his grace of his goodness to speak to the queen's grace for us; for, so far as I can perceive, her grace is so highly displeased with us both that, without the king be so good lord to us as to withdraw his rigour and sue for us, we are never like to recover her grace's favour: which is too heavy to bear.

Henry had, after all, forgiven his own sister her hasty marriage to the Duke of Suffolk and, as a romantic at heart, is unlikely to have been angry for long at his former mistress's love match.

For Mary, the loss of her sister's favour was devastating both on a financial level and also personally. Although there is little evidence for their relationship, Mary often appears to have been at court and the sisters were evidently close. Mary herself claimed that a permanent loss of her sister's love would be 'too heavy to bear', something that suggests that she was saddened at the potential loss of her sister. However, Mary's letter also suggests a tone of defiance and rivalry, which was understandable given the elder sister's former relationship with the king. Mary made a less than subtle criticism of her sister when she informed Cromwell that 'if I were at my liberty and might choose, I ensure you, master secretary, for my little time, I have tried so much honesty to be in him, that I had rather beg my bread with him than be the greatest queen in Christendom. And I believe verily he is in the same case with me; for I believe verily he would not forsake me to be a king.' For Mary, love conquered all other considerations, even if it meant her financial ruin and the loss of her family.

Above: 2. Blickling Hall, Norfolk. Blickling became the seat of the Boleyns in the fifteenth century. A later house now stands on the site of the Boleyn family residence.

Below right: 3. Blickling church. The parish church, sited next to the manor, would have been familiar to the early Boleyn women.

Below left: 4. The Boleyn chantry chapel in Norwich Cathedral. William Boleyn asked to be buried here, close to his mother, Anne Hoo Boleyn.

Above left: 5. Isabel Cheyne Boleyn from her memorial brass at Blickling church. Isabel, who was the daughter of William Boleyn and Anne Hoo, was buried at her family home following her early death.

Above right: 6. Anne Boleyn, eldest daughter of William Boleyn and Margaret Butler, from her memorial brass at Blickling church. Anne died in childhood and a younger sister, Anne Boleyn, Lady Shelton, was later named after her.

Above left: 7. The remains of the funeral monument to Anne Hoo Boleyn in Norwich Cathedral. Sadly, the memorial brass for the first Anne Boleyn has long since disappeared.

Above right: 8. Cecily Boleyn from her memorial brass at Blickling church. The sister of Geoffrey Boleyn, Lord Mayor of London, joined him at Blickling following his purchase of the manor.

9. Hever Castle, Kent. Margaret Butler Boleyn spent her last years at Hever, which was also the family home of her son, Sir Thomas Boleyn.

Below: 10 & 11, *Next page:* 12, 13, 14. Anne Boleyn, Lady Shelton, and her husband, Sir John Shelton, depicted at various stages of their lives in stained glass at Shelton church, Norfolk.

Opposite page, top left: 15.
Thomas Boleyn, Earl of Wiltshire
and Ormond, from his memorial
brass at Hever. Thomas was an
ambitious courtier who promoted
the court careers of his two
daughters, Mary and Anne Boleyn.

Opposite page, top right: 16. A
portrait commonly identified as
Thomas Boleyn. Thomas made a
socially advantageous marriage to
Elizabeth Howard, whose father
later became the 2nd Duke of
Norfolk.

Opposite page, middle: 17. The
tomb of Anne Boleyn, Lady
Shelton, and her husband, Sir John
Shelton, from Shelton church,
Norfolk.

Below left: 18. The Howard family arms displayed over the gates of Framlingham Castle. Elizabeth Howard Boleyn was proud of her Howard lineage.

Below right: 19. Thomas Howard, 3rd Duke of Norfolk, from his tomb at Framlingham. Elizabeth Howard Boleyn's brother sat in judgement on her son and daughter at their trials in May 1536.

Above left: 20. Francis I of France. The French king is reputed to have been Mary Boleyn's lover, referring to her as a great whore and infamous above all others.

Above right: 21. Sir Thomas Wyatt, who wanted to be the lover of both Anne Boleyn and her cousin, Mary Shelton.

Left: 22. Henry VIII in his youth. The king was renowned as the most handsome prince in Europe, although there is no truth in the rumours that Elizabeth Howard Boleyn served as one of his mistresses.

Above: 23. Mary Boleyn was the mistress first of Francis I and then Henry VIII.

Next page: 24. Anne Boleyn's dark eyes captivated the king when he had tired of her sister, Mary.

ANNA BOLLINA · · · VXOR · HEN · VII

Above: 25. *The Clouds that Gather Round the Setting Sun.* Anne Boleyn was instrumental in bringing about the fall of Thomas Wolsey, with the cardinal referring to her as a 'serpentine enemy'.

Below left: 26. Henry VIII gave Anne a fine clock during the years of their courtship.

Below right: 27. Thomas Cranmer, from his memorial in Oxford. The Archbishop of Canterbury annulled the marriage of Henry VIII and Catherine of Aragon and crowned Anne Boleyn.

Above left: 28. Hans Holbein's design for a Coronation pageant for Anne Boleyn, with her falcon badge prominently displayed.

Above right: 29. Anne Boleyn's falcon badge without its crown, carved as graffiti at the Tower of London.

Above left: 30. A rare survival of the entwined initials of Henry VIII and Anne Boleyn from King's College Chapel, Cambridge.

Above right: 31. The entwined initials of Henry VIII and his third wife, Jane Seymour, from Hampton Court. Henry tried to erase all memory of his second wife, Anne Boleyn.

Above: 32. A romantic depiction of the execution of Anne Boleyn. The queen was beheaded with a sword – a kinder death than a clumsy axe.

Below left: 33. Princess Mary. Anne Boleyn, Lady Shelton, found her young charge a troublesome burden when she was appointed as her governess.

Below right: 34. Catherine Howard, the queen whose indiscretions led Jane Boleyn to the block.

35. Traitor's Gate. Anne Boleyn was taken to the Tower of London by water and reputedly passed through this gate.

36. The Tower of London. Anne Boleyn, her sister-in-law, Jane Boleyn, and daughter, Princess Elizabeth, were all imprisoned in the ancient fortress.

37. A memorial marking the supposed site of the scaffold on Tower Green where both Anne and Jane Boleyn died.

Above: 38. The Bishop's Palace at Lincoln, where Jane Boleyn led Thomas Culpepper to a secret nocturnal meeting with the queen.

The Lady Henegham

Right: 39. Mary Shelton. The daughter of Lady Shelton was a poet with remarkably modern views about love, becoming a mistress of Henry VIII in her youth.

40. Henry Howard, Earl of Surrey, who was reputed to have been romantically involved with his friend, Mary Shelton.

41. Catherine Carey and her husband, Sir Francis Knollys, from their memorial at Rotherfield Greys in Oxfordshire.

42. The six daughters of Catherine Carey (and one daughter-in-law). Lettice Knollys, the second daughter, is first in the line depicted at Rotherfield Greys.

43. Robert Dudley, Earl of Leicester, from his tomb in Warwick. Dudley was Elizabeth I's greatest favourite, with speculation that the pair would marry.

44. Lettice Knollys from her tomb in Warwick. Lettice's royal cousin never forgave her for secretly marrying Robert Dudley.

45. Robert Dudley, the only child of Lettice Knollys' second marriage, who died young.

Top: 46. Hatfield House. Elizabeth I was resident at the palace when she discovered that she had become queen.

Above: 47. Princess Elizabeth as a child.

Right: 48. Elizabeth I as queen. Anne Boleyn's daughter was the greatest, and the last, of the Boleyn women.

Mary's disgrace lasted for some time after her banishment from court. The records are unfortunately silent on the fate of Anne's child and it would appear that she suffered a stillbirth that summer. Given that there is no record of Mary's own child, it would appear that she also lost a baby, something that would have allowed relations to thaw to some extent. There is no record of Mary being back at court until early 1536 when she attended her sister during her third and final pregnancy. It appears that the two had mended their relationship, although it took time for the wounds to heal. According to reports, Mary was the only person that Anne would allow to attend her in her grief at the loss of her miscarried son.[25]

Mary was not the only Boleyn to find herself in disgrace in 1534, with Jane Parker Boleyn also suffering banishment from court at the time. Although Anne and Henry were reconciled after he first took a mistress in the summer of 1533, Anne, who had been the sole object of the king's desire for so long, found it impossible to tolerate her husband's infidelity as her predecessor had done. For Henry, part of Anne's attraction had been her refusal to yield to him and, therefore, with the consummation of their relationship, an element of her fascination for him ended. Instead, he reverted to his familiar pattern of taking a mistress during his wife's pregnancies. In September 1534, Chapuys reported that

ever since the king began to entertain doubts as to his mistress's [Anne's] reported pregnancy, he has renewed and increased the love which he formerly bore to another very handsome young lady of this court; and whereas the royal mistress, hearing of it, attempted to dismiss the damsel from her service, the king has been very sad, and has sent her a message to this effect: that she ought to be satisfied with what he had done for her; for, were he to commence again, he would certainly not do as much; she ought to consider where she came from, and many other things of the same kind.

The king's reaction to Anne's anger in 1534 was worse than that in 1533 and may have been the first indication that Anne no longer fully occupied the king's heart. She was certainly alarmed enough about the new mistress to attempt to take action against her, enlisting the help of her sister-in-law, Jane Rochford, to help her. Jane was regularly resident at court during the first year of her sister-in-law's queenship and, with the banishment of Mary Boleyn, may well have found her royal kinswoman coming to rely on her more than usual. Anne and Jane certainly appear to have felt that they had common enough interests to conspire together for Henry's mistress to be exiled from court. The details of the plot do not survive, with Chapuys speculating that it was to have the rival sent away 'through quarrelling or otherwise'. Unfortunately, for the two women, the plot was unsuccessful, with Jane bearing the brunt of the king's anger and being sent home from court in disgrace early in October 1534. The length of Jane's exile is nowhere recorded, although Chapuys referred to her dismissal on 19 December 1534, implying that she was still kept away from court. This is the last time that the records show Jane acting with her sister-in-law, and Anne's failure to protect her from banishment may have caused Jane an estrangement, particularly as Anne escaped all censure. Chapuys certainly implied that it was Jane who suffered for Anne's complaints against the mistress, recording that 'neither is there any further sign of the king's ill-humour towards the Lady's relatives, except that which is naturally connected with their occasional quarrels; though it must be said, Rochford's wife was dismissed from Court owing to the above mentioned cause'.

Jane Rochford remains a shadowy figure in the sources. However, there is a hint that she may have become publicly opposed to her sister-in-law's interests by the last months of 1535.

Henry's eldest daughter, Mary, had been denied her title of princess and declared to be illegitimate on the annulment of her parents' marriage, something which was not widely supported in England. In October 1535, while the court was absent from London, a number of women went to watch Mary as she was moved from her lodgings at Greenwich and, weeping, declared her to be 'princess' (and thus, impliedly, heiress to the crown in spite of the Act of Succession which named Princess Elizabeth as heir). This protest, although hopeless, attracted attention, with the ringleaders being imprisoned in the Tower. Not surprisingly, given the fact that Henry did not want to draw attention to support for his eldest daughter over his younger, the incident receives very little attention in the sources. However, the Bishop of Tarbes did briefly record its details in a despatch. Interestingly, a marginal note which relates to the information on the ringleaders states 'Millor de Rochesfort et millord de Guillame', something which has been interpreted to suggest that Jane and her kinswoman, Lady William Howard, were the two women imprisoned.[26] This evidence has been described as 'not convincing', although it is generally assumed that Jane and her husband were estranged by the end of 1535.[27] Other evidence also supports the fact that Jane, in spite of her position in the Boleyn family, was friendly towards Princess Mary.

Jane's father, Lord Morley, remained devoted to the interests of Henry VIII's eldest daughter throughout his lifetime, dedicating a number of his works and translation projects to her. Mary's fragmentary privy purse expenses from the late 1530s and 1540s also indicate an association. Lord Morley presented the princess with a New Year's gift in 1537, 1538, 1540 and 1543 (a year in which a book was presented).[28] The princess reciprocated with the gift of a book in January 1544.[29] In December 1537 she also made a payment to one of Lord Morley's servants, suggesting that they had delivered a message or a gift from their master.[30] The princess held the family in high enough esteem to stand as godmother to a child born to Jane's brother Henry and his wife in January 1537, making a payment to Mistress Parker's nurse and midwife in gratitude for her safe delivery.[31] Following the fall of Anne Boleyn there is also considerable evidence that Jane herself was in favour with the princess. Like her father, Jane gave Mary New Year's gifts in 1537, 1538 and 1540. That she had earlier been in the habit of giving the princess gifts is clear from the sum of 5 shillings paid by Mary in January 1537 for 'mending of the clock which my lady's grace had of my Lady Rochford'.[32] In February of that year Mary gave Jane 12 yards of expensive black satin for a gown, while that April she rewarded a servant of Jane's, suggesting that the pair communicated when not together.[33] Similar payments to Jane's servants were made in April 1538 on two separate occasions.

The evidence suggests that Jane sympathised with the king's eldest daughter, making a public show of support for her while she was still exiled from court and probably still angry with the queen. Although the evidence is tenuous it is generally considered that Jane was estranged from her husband's family by the end of 1535. Certainly, any show of sympathy for Mary from Jane would not have endeared her to Anne Boleyn.

10

PRINCESS MARY & THE QUEEN'S AUNTS

As the queen, Anne was placed in charge of arranging the household of her daughter, Princess Elizabeth, as well as the arrangements made for the care of her teenage stepdaughter, Princess Mary. Understandably, when it was decided that the two girls were to share the same household, Anne was determined that it should be headed by those loyal to her, appointing her mother's half-sister, Margaret, Lady Bryan, as Elizabeth's lady mistress and her father's two sisters, Anne Boleyn, Lady Shelton, and Alice Boleyn, Lady Clere, as its chief female officers. Her uncle, Sir John Shelton, was appointed as steward of the household, something that meant he was in charge of their domestic guard.[1]

The elder Anne Boleyn was the sister of Sir Thomas Boleyn. She married a Norfolk neighbour, Sir John Shelton, whose family was closely connected with her own. The family was a prosperous and well-respected one, with at least one member of every generation knighted since a Ralph de Shelton fought for Edward III at the Battle of Crecy.[2] They had lived at Shelton in Norfolk, which is now a small village, since at least the early thirteenth century, taking their surname from the manor.[3] As prominent Norfolk families, the Boleyns, Sheltons and Cleres were highly interconnected and the marriage was arranged to complement that of her sister, Alice, to Sir Robert Clere. Sir John Shelton was prominent in the county, serving as sheriff before their marriage, which took place in 1512 when John was in his mid-thirties and Anne some years younger.[4] The couple settled at Shelton Hall, which survives today as a ruin.[5] In Lady Shelton's time it was a grand building surrounded by a high, towered wall and a moat.

Towards the end of his life Sir John Shelton commissioned fine stained-glass windows for the chancel at Shelton Church. The windows survive today and depict John's parents, as well as John and Anne at three stages in their lives. The earliest chronologically shows the couple kneeling in church facing each other on separate panes of glass. John is depicted as a long haired, heavy-featured and well-built young man, dressed in a fine robe of red, a long furred collar and hanging sleeves. Anne is dressed stylishly for the end of the fifteenth century, wearing a tight-fitting red dress with hanging sleeves and a black hood with a veil. Her dress is low-cut and her features youthful and more delicate than her husband's.

In the second depiction chronologically, the couple again face towards each other but on separate panes. Both kneel in church with open prayer books before them. Sir John looks older in this image, with long fair hair and a heavy beard. Beneath his heraldic mantle he wears armour, suggesting that he was depicted at around the time of his marriage in 1512, when England was at war with France. Anne also looks more mature, with a serene expression. Beneath a long heraldic mantle displaying the Boleyn family arms and bull motif, she wears a fine green dress, decorated with gold. She also wears a long gold gable hood, which was highly fashionable early in Henry VIII's reign.

The final depiction shows the couple as they would have appeared towards the time of John's death in 1539 when he was sixty-two.[6] Unlike the other depictions, the couple are portrayed close together on the same pane of glass. Touchingly, as John kneels with clasped hands, he gazes at his wife while Anne solicitously reaches out to his shoulder with her hand. John looks considerably older in this depiction, with shoulder-length grey hair surrounding an entirely bald crown of the head. By this time he had shaved off his beard, although he retained a moustache. Once again John wears a rich red gown decorated with fur, while Anne wears a tight red dress decorated with gold. Anne's face, which appears beneath a long black cap, is older, with a loving expression as she gazes at her husband. Clearly the couple were fond of each other, something that is also demonstrated by the high number of children born during their marriage. As well as their heir, John, the couple produced sons Thomas, who served as a groom porter of the Tower, and Ralph.[7] There were a number of daughters, with both the eldest, Amy (or Emma), and the second, Elizabeth, remaining unmarried. Margaret married a Thomas Wodehouse, while Gabrielle became a nun. The youngest was Mary Shelton.

Alice Boleyn married as his second wife Sir Robert Clere of Ormesby, who was some years older than her and had already served as Sheriff of Norfolk in 1501.[8] He was wealthy and had been knighted by the future Henry VIII in 1494, when the prince was still an infant.[9] The couple were married at some point before 1506, with Margaret Butler Boleyn paying a dowry of 500 marks in exchange for Sir Robert's promise of a substantial dower for his wife in the event that she was widowed.[10] Sir Robert, who had continued to be prominent into the reign of Henry VIII and attended the great meeting between the English and French kings known as the Field of the Cloth of Gold in 1520, lived to a venerable age, dying in 1529. He was pious and asked in his will that his executors should arrange 100 Masses for his soul. He also requested that if anyone had proved that he had wronged them then his executors should compensate them.

Alice bore three sons, with the eldest, John, later having the good fortune to inherit Blickling through his mother when the direct line of the Boleyn family died out. Alice Boleyn Clere survived her husband by some years, dying in 1539. It is a testament to

the fact that she took pride in her Boleyn lineage that the arms of
the City of London were proudly displayed among other heraldry
on the Clere brass at Ormesby.[11] Evidently Alice and her family
saw no stigma in the fact that the family fortune was founded on
trade and the endeavours of her grandfather, Sir Geoffrey Boleyn,
who, as a former Lord Mayor of London, was able to make use
of the arms of the city. Alice found favour under her niece, Queen
Anne Boleyn, who appointed her to assist her elder sister, Anne
Boleyn, Lady Shelton, in the management of the household of
Princess Mary in 1533. In her will, which was dated to October
1539, Alice made a bequest of a gold rosary to her youngest son,
Thomas, 'which Queen Anne gave me', something which suggests
that she, for one, did not consider her niece's marriage to have
been invalid.[12] She was also close to her siblings and their children.
Without any daughters of her own, she made bequests to a number
of her nieces, such as her emerald ring, which was passed to her
eldest surviving sister's daughter, Elizabeth Shelton. To her grief,
Alice's second son, Richard, died young. She therefore divided the
bulk of her estate between her surviving sons, John and Thomas,
making particularly careful provision for Thomas, the youngest of
the three brothers.

Alice's motivation for taking a post in Princess Elizabeth's
household is not easy to understand, given that, following the
death of her husband she had been left a very wealthy woman. On
Sir Robert's death, Alice received twenty manors as her jointure,
including her marital home of Ormesby, which her husband
instructed should be fully equipped for her use.[13] She also received
a house at Norwich together with plate and household stuff to
allow her to live comfortably in her widowhood. Alice certainly
had no financial need of the appointment. Additionally, she must
have been aware that any position with the king's bastardised
daughter, Mary, was likely to be troublesome and even potentially
politically dangerous. It may simply be that she was fond of her

niece, who is known to have made her personal presents, and agreed to the appointment as a favour to her. She may also have been pressured by her sister, Anne Boleyn Shelton, to assist her in the governance of the ex-princess.

Queen Anne Boleyn was a devoted mother to her daughter, reputedly refusing to let her out of her sight and having a special cushion produced for the infant to lie upon when she sat in state as queen.[14] It must therefore have been a wrench for her when, in December 1533, Elizabeth was given her own household and sent in great state to live at a variety of smaller palaces outside of London. Both Anne and Henry remained in regular contact with their daughter, visiting her often and delighting in showing her off to the world. A visit to Elizabeth in April 1534 was typical, with Sir William Kingston, one of the gentlemen present, declaring that the baby was 'a goodly child as hath been seen, and her Grace is much in the king's favour as a goodly child should be'.[15] In March 1534 Elizabeth was officially declared heiress to the crown by Parliament, with the same enactment ruling that her elder half-sister was illegitimate and unfit to inherit the crown.

Mary had not been permitted to see her mother since 1531, although the pair continued to correspond secretly, with Catherine writing in September 1533 to warn her daughter that she had heard that 'the time is come that Almighty God will prove you'.[16] Catherine's information was sound and that same month the princess's household servants were ordered to remove their livery and replace it with that of the king: a public announcement of her illegitimacy.[17] Henry also sent a deputation to Mary to order her to relinquish her claim to be Princess of England, something that she absolutely refused to do.[18] Mary's refusal infuriated Anne and Henry, with the king ordering that his eldest daughter's household be broken up in November 1533, and that she move to join Elizabeth as a maid of honour, something that was deeply humiliating for Mary.[19] Mary was allowed to take only a few attendants when she set out to join Elizabeth in December, with her governess, the Countess of Salisbury, being refused permission to remain with her.[20] Instead Anne appointed her aunts, Lady Shelton and Lady Clere, to have governance over the former princess, something that demonstrates that she was closer to them than another aunt, the Duchess of Norfolk, whom she had had banished from court for sending secret messages of support to Catherine of Aragon.

Mary was taken to join Elizabeth with only two maids: something that must have been humiliating for a girl who had once been heiress to the crown. Upon her arrival, her defiance continued, declaring when asked if she would like to pay court to the princess that 'she knew of no other princess in England but herself; that the daughter of Madame de Pembroke was no princess at all'.[21] When the Duke of Suffolk refused to carry a message to the king in which she referred to herself as Princess of Wales, she simply told him, 'Then go away, and leave me alone.' Lady Shelton and Lady Clere must have realised that they would have their work cut out with Henry's eldest daughter. As a punishment for her disobedience, Mary's two maids were discharged, leaving her with only one serving maid to attend her.[22] The maid was also forbidden to taste the princess's food as a safety precaution, something that would later cause Lady Shelton great anxiety.

It is not always possible to determine which of the two sisters was responsible for actions reported in Elizabeth and Mary's household, with Chapuys, for example, referring to Lady Shelton and Lady Clere simply as Anne's aunt or the princess's governess, rather than by name. It appears more likely that his references to Mary's governess are to Lady Shelton, since he would later refer to a letter received by the governess from the queen which is known to have been addressed to Lady Shelton. Regardless of some uncertainty, it is clear that both were considered loyal by their niece, who sent them direct instructions as to how she wished her stepdaughter to be treated. In one despatch, for example, written in February 1534, Chapuys recorded that

> a worthy gentleman of this place has told me that Anne has sent a message to her father's sister, in whose keeping the Princess now is, that she ought not to tolerate her using her title; should she continue to do so she was to slap her face as the cursed bastard that she was. And because the Princess has hitherto been in the habit of breakfasting in her own room, and, when obliged to go down into the hall, has refused to eat and drink anything, the said Anne is in despair, and has for this reason given orders that no food or drink should be served to her in her chamber.[23]

In September 1534 Mary became unwell and Lady Shelton sent for an apothecary whose medicines only made the king's daughter sicker. To Lady Shelton's horror, there were immediately rumours that Mary had been poisoned, particularly since, in accordance with her orders, she refused Chapuys's servant permission to see her when he arrived to enquire about Mary's health. The rumours were treated with such seriousness that the king sent both his own doctor and Catherine's to attend her, as a mark of his good faith towards his daughter.[24] Lady Shelton enjoyed the king's trust, who would later inform Chapuys that she was an expert in 'such female complaints' as Mary was suffering from.[25] By February 1535, when Mary was ill again, Lady Shelton was terrified, weeping at the thought that if anything happened to her charge she would be condemned as her murderer. She was particularly unpopular in London where rumours circulated that she was attempting to poison Mary.

If Queen Anne Boleyn hoped that her aunts would enforce a strict regime with her stepdaughter, she soon found herself both disappointed and frustrated. Lady Shelton, in particular, gradually began to befriend her charge, with both she and her daughters featuring regularly in Mary's accounts when she was back in favour after Anne's fall, something which must indicate that there was no lingering resentment. For example, in January 1544 Mary gave her former governess two cushion covers worth over 7 shillings.[26] Lady Shelton and her daughter-in-law, Margaret, sister of Jane, Lady Rochford, presented New Year's gifts to Mary in 1528 and 1537, while Mary in her turn made presents of cash in 1537 to Elizabeth and Mary Shelton, two of Lady Shelton's unmarried daughters.[27] The princess may well have first come across Lady Shelton's daughters during her time under their mother's charge and she does genuinely seem to have been fond of them. There were further cash gifts to Elizabeth and Mary Shelton in January 1540, while the eldest sister, Amy, received cash in July 1538.[28] Amy also received the valuable gift of an antique brooch from the princess on another occasion.[29]

Not surprisingly, given her links to Lord Morley, Mary was closest to Lady Shelton's daughter-in-law, Margaret Parker, for example standing as godmother for her child in October 1537 and making her a gift of clothing in January of the following year.[30] The gift of a bottle of wine delivered to the princess in June 1543 by 'Mr Shelton's servant' is also likely to have come from his wife.[31] There is clear affection for Lady Shelton, however, who gave the princess the rich gift of two cushion covers garnished with gold and silk at New Year 1543.[32] Clearly, Princess Mary did not bear a grudge against the Shelton family, suggesting that they at least always treated her fairly during Anne Boleyn's time as queen, something that seems to have infuriated Lady Shelton's niece.

There is contemporary evidence that Lady Shelton, while prepared to enforce her niece's orders, was not prepared to enforce them with malice. In February 1534 Chapuys recorded that Mary was being kept with very little to wear, forcing her to send to her father to request funds. At the same time she requested permission to hear mass in the local church, something which was refused her due to the cheers that she received whenever she was seen by the local population.[33] While Lady Shelton was in charge of day-to-day decisions in relation to Mary, she was kept under close scrutiny by other members of the family, with the Duke of Norfolk and her nephew, George Boleyn, summoning her to them to berate her for treating Mary 'with too great kindness and regard, when she ought to deal with her as a regular bastard that she was'. To this Lady Shelton replied that 'even if it were so, and that she was the bastard daughter of a poor gentleman, her kindness, her modesty, and her virtues called forth all respect and honour'.

Lady Shelton was forced to spend a great deal of time with her young charge: in March 1534, when Mary refused to travel with the household to a new residence she was forcibly placed in a carriage with Lady Shelton for what must have been a very uncomfortable journey for them both.[34] Matters were certainly tense. When, in April 1534, Anne and Henry came to visit Elizabeth, they ordered that Mary be kept in her room with an armed guard at the door.[35] The royal couple doubtless had some strong words for Lady Shelton about how they expected her to make Mary behave since she appears to have taken this out on the girl, informing her that 'the king, her father no longer cared whether she renounced her title willingly or not, since by the last statute she had been declared illegitimate and incapable of inheriting, and that if she were in his (the king's) place she would kick her (the Princess) out of the king's house for her disobedience'. Lady Shelton took this harsh line in an attempt to make Mary comply, something that would both make her life easier as governess and protect Mary, given that the king had reportedly threatened her with execution if she would not obey.

As a first cousin of the Holy Roman Emperor Mary was probably safe, although Henry, as her father, was recognised by convention to have absolute control over the disposal of her person. Lady Shelton came under direct pressure from the king to enforce

Mary's conduct. The following month, Henry asked her of Mary 'whether there were signs of her rebellious spirit and stubborn obstinacy being in any way subdued', to which the queen's aunt was forced to reply that 'she continued the same'.[36] Henry then declared, 'Then there must be someone near her who maintains her in her fanciful ideas by conveying news of her mother to her.' Lady Shelton, no doubt anxious to avoid any blame herself, named a maid of the princess who was promptly dismissed: for Lady Shelton, governing Mary was a thankless task and one which she does not seem to have relished.

There was another reason for the strained relationship that developed between Queen Anne Boleyn and her aunt. On 25 February 1535 Chapuys recorded that 'the young lady who was lately in the king's favour is so no longer. There has succeeded to her place a cousin german of the Concubine, daughter of the present governess of the Princess.' Chapuys later made it clear that this lady was 'Madge' Shelton and that while few other details of the affair are known, this Mistress Shelton remained in the king's favour, and presumably as his mistress, for six months.

There is a great deal of debate over who this 'Madge' Shelton was, with two of Lady Shelton's daughters, Margaret and Mary, being possible due to the similarity of their names.[37] The fact that Margaret Shelton is nowhere mentioned in Princess Mary's accounts while her sisters, Amy, Elizabeth and Mary are, probably indicates that Margaret was not known to the princess and is therefore unlikely to have stayed with her parents during their time in the princess's household. This does suggest that it was Mary, rather than Margaret, who was present at court in the household of Anne Boleyn. It is also known for certain that Mary was a member of Anne Boleyn's household, serving as one of her maids.[38] Margaret, on the other hand, is only potentially named by Chapuys as the disputed 'Madge'. Otherwise, her presence at court can only survive in references to a 'Mistress Shelton' who, of course, could just as easily have been Mary.

One thing that might point against the identification of Mary Shelton as Henry VIII's mistress is contained in a letter written by John Husee, the London agent of Lady Lisle on 3 January 1538:

> The election lieth betwixt Mrs Mary Shelton and Mrs Mary Skipwith. I pray Jesu send such one as may be for his Highness' comfort and the wealth of the realm. Herein I doubt not but your lordship will keep silence till the matter be surely known.[39]

Given the reference to the 'wealth of the realm' and the fact that the letter was written a few months after the death of Jane Seymour and before Henry had decided upon a fourth bride, it is possible to interpret Husee's comments as suggesting one of the two women was being considered as a bride for the king. When Henry had first raised the possibility of divorcing Catherine of Aragon there had been rumours that he would marry Bessie Blount and legitimise their son, something that Henry himself never countenanced.[40] His thoughts had only turned to marriage in relation to Anne Boleyn when she had refused to become his mistress, while the Catherine Howard debacle and Henry's doubts as to Anne of Cleves' virginity would later show that he wanted his bride to be chaste. It is therefore improbable that he would consider marrying a woman who had already been his mistress, suggesting that the Mistress Shelton of 1535 was a different sister to the Mistress Shelton of 1538. The lady in 1538 may in fact have been Margaret rather than Mary, as it has now been convincingly argued that 'Mary Skipwith' was actually Margaret Skipwith of Ormesby who, confusingly, also had a sister called Mary.[41] The evidence suggests that Margaret Skipwith, who was married to Bessie Blount's second son in April 1539 and effectively pensioned off by the king, became his mistress in preference to Mistress Shelton. It may therefore be that Henry was seeking a mistress rather than a bride all along, particularly as, by January 1539, negotiations had opened for a foreign marriage. Henry, who appears to have resumed his affairs with both Bessie Blount and Mary Boleyn after their pregnancies might well have been prepared to resume an affair with an earlier mistress in 1538, suggesting that both Mistress Sheltons were the same lady. That Mary Shelton, along with Margaret Skipwith (who was by then Lady Tailbois), were part of a group of ladies invited by the king in August 1539 to view his fleet at Portsmouth, strongly suggests that it was Mary Shelton in January 1539. This and the absence of records for Margaret Shelton, alongside the numerous references to Mary at court, implies that, in both cases, the lady who caught Henry's attention was Mary Shelton.

Margaret may never have been resident at court. Little is known about her life. She married Thomas Wodehouse, Esquire, of Kimberley in Norfolk.[42] Wodehouse was from an old Norfolk family which could be traced back to the reign of Henry I. Margaret's brother, Ralph Shelton, married her husband's sister, Amy, at the same time as her marriage, creating a double alliance. Margaret lived a comfortable but undistinguished life, bearing four sons and four daughters and surviving her husband.[43] The Heraldic Visitations for Norfolk suggest an all too common tragedy for the family, with Margaret's second daughter, Elizabeth, dying young to be replaced by another child named in memory of her. Margaret herself had died before December 1555, as no mention is made of her in the otherwise full list of her siblings contained in their mother's will.[44] Her husband was still living in 1553 when he served as Sheriff of Norfolk, an indication of his prominence in the county.[45] He sat as a Member of Parliament for Great Yarmouth in 1557 and 1558.[46] Margaret's third son, John, was evidently a favourite of his great-uncle, Sir James Boleyn, who left a substantial bequest to him at his death in 1561, on the condition that John married a woman to whom he was already 'handfasted'.[47]

Mary Shelton was beautiful, with Henry's ambassador to the Netherlands later commenting of Christina of Denmark, whom Henry hoped to marry, that 'she resembles one Mistress Shelton that used to wait on Queen Anne' – something that was obviously considered desirable.[48] A surviving drawing by Hans Holbein, depicting Mary, supports this, showing a thin young woman with a distinguished nose, pointed chin and gable hood – something which may suggest that it was produced following Anne Boleyn's death at a time when Queen Jane Seymour was insisting that they were worn at court. Mary resembles her cousin, Queen Anne, in the drawing, something which is likely to have drawn the king towards her. She was well educated and intelligent, with her literary endeavours hinting at a spirit as independent and strong-willed as her cousin the queen. She was also at least eleven years younger than Anne and possibly as much as nineteen years younger.[49] It is therefore easy to see why the king was interested in her. It has been suggested on a number of occasions that Anne herself supplied Mary to the king, reasoning that, if he was going to take a mistress regardless, he might as well take one favourable to her.[50] There is merit in this argument as Henry's mistress in the summer of 1534, who supported Catherine and Mary, undoubtedly caused Anne's position harm, while Jane Seymour, who was equally hostile, actually supplanted her. However, there is in fact strong evidence that Anne was anything but happy with her cousin's relationship with the king.

Anne always reacted angrily to Henry's affairs. Where the lady in question was a member of her household, she had particular power over them, something that the ladies often found to their cost. When Anne found Jane Seymour wearing a locket with a picture of the king round her neck, for example, she snatched it from her forcibly, while on other occasions the two actually came to blows, scratching and fighting. Mary Shelton also felt the force of her cousin's anger. According to Anne's chaplain, William Latymer,

> there was a book of prayers which belonged to one of her maids of honour called Mrs Mary Shelton presented unto her highness wherein were written certain idle posies. She would not be satisfied by any means before she understood certainly to whom the book pertained. The matter was covered a while because of the express threatening of her majesty, but nothing can long escape the piercing eyes of princes, especially in their own palaces, so that at length the pensive gentlewoman (to whom the book appertained) was discovered. Whereupon the queen her majesty, calling her before her presence, wonderful rebuked her that would permit such wanton toys in her book of prayers, which she termed a mirror or glass wherein she might learn to address her wandering thoughts; and upon this occasion commanded the mother of the maidens to have a more vigilant eye to her charge to the end that at all times and in the time of prayers especially they might comely and virtuously behave their selves.[51]

Given that Anne had once exchanged similar verses with Henry in a prayer book of her own, the incident with Mary Shelton's prayer book is highly significant. It is possible that the verses were exchanged with Henry himself. More likely, their discovery was used as a pretext by Anne to allow her to upbraid a cousin who was romantically involved with her husband. The discovery allowed her to attempt to bring the affair to an end by having her cousin more closely watched and, thus, no longer affording her an opportunity to meet with the king. It was a policy that was followed by Anne's later successor as queen, Catherine Parr, in relation to Anne's own daughter. When Catherine realised that her stepdaughter, Princess Elizabeth, was becoming inappropriately involved with her fourth husband, Thomas Seymour, she complained to Elizabeth's governess that the girl had been seen embracing an unidentified man. Elizabeth's governess strongly suspected that this incident had been fabricated by the queen in order to give her a reason for ordering better care to be taken of the princess and it is highly likely that Anne responded in a very similar way in relation to Mary Shelton. Mary's affair with Henry was not long-lasting but the origins of Anne's hostility towards her aunt, Lady Shelton, may lie in her anger over Mary's affair, with Lady Shelton herself angered by the queen's treatment of her daughter. Certainly, by May 1536 Anne was referring to her aunt as someone that she had never loved.

If Anne did not direct Henry's interest towards Mary, it may be that her friend, the poet Sir Thomas Wyatt, unwittingly did. It was Wyatt in his pursuit of Anne that first brought her to the king's attention. By the 1530s he had turned some of his attention towards Mary herself, writing a poem expressing his love for her in which the first letter of each line tellingly spelled out 'Sheltun'. This echoes a similar, earlier poem where the initial letters spelled out 'Anna', which is usually associated with Anne Boleyn. Wyatt met with no greater success in his pursuit of Mary than he had previously done with Anne. In the manuscript in which the poem was written, Mary herself contributed the lines beneath the poem: 'Undesired fancies require no higher Mary Mary Shelton.'[52] That there was some flirtation is clear, with a margin note next to the poem written by Lady Margaret Douglas saying, 'Forget this,' to which Mary replied, 'It is worthy.' As with Anne Boleyn's own relationship with Wyatt, the surviving evidence suggests a playful game of courtly love, particularly as Wyatt was still married and involved in a more lasting affair with another mistress. However, Wyatt had a knack for drawing attention to himself, and those he favoured; perhaps he and Henry had their own game of bowls over Mary Shelton? More likely Wyatt's interest served to bring the teenager into the king's own circle, to the queen's anger and alarm.

Wyatt was not the only suitor interested in Mary. According to a recent work on the mistresses of Henry VIII, she was engaged to Henry Norris, a gentleman in Henry's household to whom he was close.[53] The evidence for this comes from Queen Anne Boleyn herself when, in the Tower following her arrest, she declared that 'Weston told her that Norris came more unto her chamber for her than for Madge'.[54] This 'Madge' may be Mary Shelton if it accepted that she really was known as Madge and that this was not simply a misreading of sixteenth-century handwriting. More certain are Anne's comments regarding Francis Weston 'that she had spoke to him because he did love her kinswoman Mrs Shelton and that she said he loved not his wife; and he made answer to her again that he loved one in her house better than them both; she asked him who is that? To which he answered that it is yourself.' Weston was young and handsome and an affair between him and Mary, in spite of his recent marriage, is not impossible. It cannot have improved her relationship with the queen if Mary considered Anne, albeit unwittingly, to be her rival in love again.

While Anne worried about her troubled marriage, the woman who still believed that she was Henry's true wife was in increasingly bad health in her exile from court. With the annulment of her marriage, Catherine of Aragon had been placed under considerable pressure to use the title of Princess Dowager of Wales. When she had first been officially informed of this in July 1533, she had fully demonstrated to Henry and Anne that she would continue to fight, forcibly scoring through any reference to 'Princess Dowager' in a copy of the orders sent to her and replacing them with 'Queen'. Henry spent the next few years trying to break his ex-wife's will, ordering her removal further and further away from London. This did not always go according to plan, however. One move turned into something of a triumphal progress, with crowds rushing to greet her. In December 1533 when she was ordered to move to Somersham, a house surrounded by marshes which Catherine considered to be 'the most unhealthy house in England', she refused absolutely to go, humbling the Duke of Suffolk who had been sent to enforce the orders in the process.

Catherine could not endure forever, however, and by December 1535 word reached London that she was dying. Her friend, Chapuys, rushed to Kimbolton where she was staying to comfort her, with the former queen piteously declaring her gratitude that 'if it pleased God to take her, it could be a consolation to her to die under my [Chapuys's] guidance and not unprepared, like a beast'.[55] Catherine lingered until 7 January 1536 before slipping peacefully away. Her last actions confirmed her continuing belief in her marriage: she refused to make a will, something that married women were forbidden by law to do, and dictated a letter to Henry, declaring, 'Lastly, I make this vow, that mine eyes desire you above all things'.[56]

Anne and Henry received the news of Catherine's death joyfully, with the king, rightly as it happened, exclaiming, 'God be praised that we are free from all suspicion of war.' The next day he and Anne, along with their daughter, appeared wearing yellow as they were conducted in fine style to Mass before dinner and dancing, with the king behaving like one 'transported with joy'. Anne was as overjoyed as her husband, watching with pride as he carried Elizabeth in his arms, showing her off to the court. Thomas Boleyn, who was present, was equally pleased, declaring that it was a pity that Princess Mary did not keep company with her mother, while Anne exclaimed that she was sorry about Catherine's death 'not indeed because she is dead, but because her death has been so honourable'. It is perhaps not surprising that groundless rumours soon arose that Catherine had been poisoned on Anne's orders. Lady Shelton did not help matters by announcing the death to Mary with no ceremony or preparation, something which must have been devastating to the young woman.[57]

With Catherine dead, Anne decided that she would make one final attempt at befriending her stepdaughter. She had previously made overtures, only to be rebuffed, for example in March 1534 sending her a message as queen, only for Mary to reply that there was no queen in England except her mother, but that she would be grateful if the king's mistress would intercede for her with him. Later, when they were both again in the same house, Anne was thrilled to hear that Mary had curtsied to her, replying that 'if we had seen it, we would have done as much to her'. Unfortunately, Mary's curtsey had been to the altar, something the girl was quick to point out. It is perhaps no surprise that Anne, doing all she could, ranted that she 'intended to bring down the pride of this unbridled Spanish blood'.

Within days of the former queen's death, she had written to Mary saying that 'if she would lay aside her obstinacy and obey her father, she would be the best friend to her in the world and be like another mother, and would obtain for her anything she could ask, and that if she wished to come to court she would be exempted from holding the tail of her gown'.[58] Anne must have felt that this was a very generous offer given the history between the pair, particularly as Mary's loyalties were no longer divided between her parents. Anne was, in January 1536, also pregnant and confidently expecting a son, something which would have rendered Mary almost completely irrelevant. Lady Shelton certainly thought that it would be to both her and Mary's benefit if the princess accepted, 'continually begging and entreating her in the warmest possible terms to reconsider these offers'.[59] It was therefore with fury that Anne received another rebuff from her stepdaughter, firing off a letter to Lady Shelton to complain about her young charge:

Mrs Shelton, my pleasure is that you do not further move the Lady Mary to be towards the King's Grace otherwise than it pleases herself. What I have done has been more for charity than for anything the king or I care what road she takes, or whether she will change her purpose, for if I have a son, as I hope shortly, I know what will happen to her: and therefore, considering the word of God, to do good to one's enemy, I wished to warn her beforehand, because I have daily experience that the king's wisdom is such as not to esteem her repentance of her rudeness and unnatural obstinacy when she has no choice. By the law of God and of the king, she ought clearly to acknowledge her error and evil conscience if her blind affection had not so blinded her eyes that she will see nothing by what pleases herself. Mrs Shelton, I beg you not to think to do me any pleasure by turning her from any of her wilful courses, because she could not do me [good] or evil; and do your duty according to the king's command, as I am assured you do.

While this letter was addressed to Lady Shelton, it was meant for Mary and Anne's aunt showed it to her. Mary was unconcerned, with Chapuys recording that after reading the letter she 'has been laughing ever since', something which was hardly Anne's desired effect.[60] By May 1536 Lady Shelton and her niece had become estranged and this letter does not imply any warmth between the two women. In any event, Anne Boleyn's time as queen was rapidly drawing to a close in January 1536 and Lady Shelton, along with other members of the Boleyn family, took steps to ensure that they were not implicated in the queen's fall.

11

THE FALL OF THE BOLEYNS

When Anne Boleyn had written so harshly about Princess Mary she had been full of hope: her rival, Catherine of Aragon, had died and she confidently expected the birth of a son. In January 1536 she and the other members of her family present at court had no reason to believe that the end of their political dominance was coming, and that it would come with extreme suddenness.

It took Anne over a year to conceive following the end of her second pregnancy, something which must have been deeply worrying for her. Given the claims that emerged at her trial, that Anne had complained that Henry was impotent, it would appear that the difficulty lay with him. However, in the sixteenth century, a failure to produce a child was always the woman's fault and Anne was therefore jubilant when, in the last months of 1535, she realised that she was pregnant once again. Sadly for Anne, this pregnancy proved no more successful than its predecessor and, in January 1536, on the very day of Catherine of Aragon's funeral, she went into premature labour, miscarrying a son at only around three and a half months of pregnancy.[1]

For Anne, the loss of her son was a disaster and she wept bitterly as she lay in her chamber, allowing herself to be attended only by her sister. Henry was also grief-stricken, taking out his anger on

Anne by storming into her chamber to confront her angrily and 'bewailing and complaining unto her the loss of his boy' before saying that he could see that 'he would have no more boys by her' before stalking from the room. Anne had heard these kind of threats before from Henry, such as in their angry confrontations over his infidelity. Soon rumours were flying around court that Henry was claiming that 'he had made this marriage, seduced by witchcraft, and for this reason he considered it null; and that this was evident because God did not permit them to have any male issue and that he believed that he might take another wife, which he gave to understand that he had some wish to do'.[2]

This caused Anne to go on the offensive, trying to shift the blame for the miscarriage to others. On 24 January, Henry had fallen heavily from his horse and had been knocked unconscious. At the time, there was some fear for his life and the Duke of Norfolk was sent to inform Anne of the calamity.[3] Since Henry's death would have resulted in civil war between his two rival daughters, it is easy to see why Anne would have been terrified. According to Chapuys, Anne saw this as one of the principal causes of her miscarriage and 'she wished to lay the blame on the Duke of Norfolk, whom she hates, saying he frightened her by bringing the news of the fall the king had six days before'. However, this argument was largely dismissed as 'it is well known that this is not the cause, for it was told her in a way that she should not be alarmed or attach much importance to it'.

Anne then claimed that her miscarriage had been caused by coming upon Henry sitting with his new mistress upon his knee, with the queen remonstrating with Henry 'that the love she bore him was far greater than that of the late queen, so that her heart broke when she saw he loved others' and she lost her child.[4] For once, Henry was lost for words and, for a few days at least, did feel remorse, leaving his mistress behind at Greenwich when the court moved. Henry's mistress, who was a second cousin of Anne's named Jane Seymour, quickly proved to resemble the queen more closely than anyone would have thought, refusing absolutely to consummate any relationship with the king other than marriage. In the early months of 1536 Anne was still the established queen and she remained in a relatively strong position. Her enemies were, however, beginning to gather around her.

Anne and Henry's relationship continued to be troubled for some time after her miscarriage. According to Chapuys in February 1536 'for more than three months this king has not spoken ten times to the Concubine, and that when she miscarried he scarcely said anything to her'.[5] While this is likely to have been an exaggeration, Henry's relationship with Jane Seymour certainly troubled the queen, with Anne snatching a locket containing Henry's picture from around Jane's neck. Jane Seymour, who was no beauty, captivated Henry with her virtue and the seeming contrast that she presented to Anne. He became devoted to her after sending her a purse full of sovereigns and a letter which she refused to accept, declaring that 'she was a gentlewoman of good and honourable parents, without reproach, and that she had no greater riches in the world than her honour, which she would not injure for a thousand deaths, and that if he wished to make her some present in money she begged it might be when God enabled her to make some honourable marriage'.[6] Jane's message had the desired effect and Henry's 'love and desire towards the said lady was wonderfully increased'.

Jane Seymour was as ambitious as Anne had been and built a strong party around herself, headed by her brother, Edward Seymour, who was made a member of the king's Privy Chamber in March 1536. Anne had made many enemies as queen, with a number of disparate groups falling in together behind her rival. Princess Mary and Chapuys both signalled their support for a new marriage to Jane, with Mary considering that she 'would be very happy, even if she were excluded from her inheritance by male issue'.[7] The addition of Mary's and Imperial support for Jane was dangerous to Anne and worse was to come when Thomas Cromwell also set himself behind Jane.[8] Cromwell had been a member of Wolsey's household and well remembered Anne's animosity towards the cardinal and her role in his downfall: his decision to desert Anne, following a quarrel with her in which she declared that 'she would like to see his head cut off', was therefore unsurprising.

Anne could never have foreseen that such an alliance would ever be possible, with the only common ground of the various parties being their hatred of her. The only main participant in the plot who remained undecided in the early part of 1536 was Henry himself, who had still not entirely decided to abandon his sonless marriage. The death of Catherine of Aragon had allowed both Anne and Henry to hope for a reconciliation with the Emperor and Henry was determined to finally be the victor in their dispute, with Catherine's nephew recognising the legitimacy of his second marriage, regardless of his own bitter feelings towards Anne. In spite of writing to Chapuys that he should not 'treat anything to the prejudice of the late queen's honour, or her [Mary's] legitimacy or right to the succession', Charles had also recognised that Catherine's death largely cleared the obstacles to peace and was prepared to discuss an alliance with Henry.[9] Interestingly, in his instructions to Chapuys Charles also asked his ambassador to find out what Anne herself wanted in order to secure an alliance. Her price was imperial recognition of her marriage and status.

On Easter Sunday 1536, Anne finally received the recognition that she craved from Catherine's own family.[10] Chapuys, who had earlier refused a request from Cromwell to visit her and publicly kiss her, was escorted to Mass by George Boleyn. He must have been aware of what was planned for him since, in his own report, he acknowledged that a great crowd of people were in attendance 'to see how the Concubine and I behaved to each other'. Anne deliberately waited to make her entrance until her brother had manoeuvred the ambassador behind a door, ensuring that Chapuys could not escape until he had done Anne reverence as queen.

This was Anne's moment of triumph and secured for her the final acknowledgement of her royal status. It was also her final triumph. While the Emperor had instructed Chapuys to deal with Anne if necessary, he also asked his ambassador to assure the king of his support if he chose to remarry. Charles, like many in Europe, considered that Catherine's death left Henry a widower.

Catherine's presence had, in fact, protected Anne, in spite of the fact that she, like Henry, wore celebratory yellow at her death. If Henry abandoned Anne during Catherine's lifetime he knew that he would be under pressure to return to his former wife, something that held him to his second bride. On 29 April 1536 Henry finally showed his displeasure in Anne openly by appointing Sir Nicholas Carew, a supporter of Jane Seymour, as a Knight of the Garter, in preference to George Boleyn. Chapuys gleefully reported that 'the Concubine has not had sufficient influence to get it for her brother'. This was probably the moment that Henry decided to commit himself to Jane and abandon Anne; there was no point in going to the expense of commissioning a garter stall for a man he intended to sacrifice.

By 30 April 1536, Cromwell was ready to strike against Anne, inviting Mark Smeaton, a young musician in Anne's household, to dine with him that day.[11] This was a flattering invitation for the low-born Smeaton, and he went gladly, hoping for patronage from the king's minister. He was completely unsuspecting when he arrived at Cromwell's house at Stepney and, rather than being offered a meal, found himself arrested and taken to the Tower for interrogation. Smeaton must have been terrified and there were rumours that he had been racked or subjected to some other torture. In the face of threats, or worse, he admitted to adultery with Anne.

Anne is unlikely to have noticed Smeaton's disappearance and attended the May Day jousts at Greenwich the following day. These were a great affair, attended by the entire court, with Henry sitting close to his queen. Anne may have hoped to speak to her husband and her mood was lighter than it had been for several weeks as she watched her brother and other gentlemen, including Henry Norris, a favourite of the king, and her old favourite, Sir Thomas Wyatt, participate. During the tournament Anne dropped her handkerchief to one of the jousters to allow him to wipe his face, a typical action in the chaste game of courtly love. She noticed nothing amiss and was horrified when, midway through the jousts, Henry suddenly rose to his feet and stalked away without saying a word. This was to be the last time that Anne saw her husband as he swiftly rode away to Westminster Palace, accompanied by only six attendants. On the journey Henry closely questioned Henry Norris, offering him a pardon if he would only confess a crime to the king. Norris was completely taken by surprise and did not give the king the answer that he required; the following morning Norris, like Smeaton before him, was committed to the Tower on a charge of adultery with the queen.

Anne spent an anxious night at Greenwich. The following morning her uncle, the Duke of Norfolk, with several other members of the king's council, came to arrest her. When Anne was told that she was accused of adultery, she immediately exclaimed that she was wronged and begged to see the king, something that was not permitted. She spent much of the day being interrogated, before being taken by water to the Tower of London at 5 p.m. that evening. There is no doubt that Anne was terrified and, on her arrival, she fell to her knees before her interrogators, 'beseeching God to help her as she was not guilty of her accusement, and also desired the said lords to beseech the king's grace to be good unto her'.[12] When Anne asked, 'Shall I go in a dungeon?' she was reassured that she would be staying in the royal apartments which were familiar to her. Nonetheless, she was still very much aware that she was a prisoner and her composure entirely left her for a time.

When Anne arrived at the Tower, she was disconcerted to find that her aunt, 'Lady Boleyn', had been sent to attend her, along with a Mistress Coffin. This Lady Boleyn is usually identified as Anne Tempest Boleyn, the wife of Thomas Boleyn's brother, Edward. As previously discussed, Anne Tempest Boleyn had been a favoured attendant of Catherine of Aragon and she does therefore seem to be a likely candidate for Queen Anne Boleyn's attendant in the Tower, who was far from favourable to her niece.

The alternative candidate would be Elizabeth Wood Boleyn, the wife of Sir James Boleyn. Elizabeth Wood Boleyn had served her niece during her time as queen, something that suggests that the two women enjoyed a friendly relationship.[13] She was reputed to be close enough to her niece for Lady Lisle, the wife of Henry VIII's controller of Calais, to send a token to her in July 1535 in an attempt to obtain a place for her daughter in the queen's household.[14] Elizabeth was evidently not particularly taken with her gift, sending a reciprocal token which Lady Lisle's agent referred to as of little worth. Anne was in the habit of lending sums of money to those with whom she was friendly, such as the Countess of Worcester. At the time of her death, Elizabeth's husband, Sir James Boleyn, owed her £50, a sum that was substantial enough to suggest a friendship: this again does not suggest that his wife can have been the Lady Boleyn at the Tower.[15] Another piece of evidence which counts against her presence in the Tower is that the will of her husband, Sir James Boleyn, which was written in 1561, makes it clear that he died an adherent of the reformed faith, commending his soul to the Holy Trinity, rather than, as had earlier been the custom, to a specific saint or saints.[16] This does not prove that James, or his wife, had earlier been followers of the religious reform which Anne Boleyn certainly adhered to, but it is possible, particularly since James was appointed as his niece's chancellor when she became queen.

The Lady Boleyn who awaited her niece at the Tower was there to spy on the queen and report on her conversation. Queen Anne fully recognised this, complaining to the Lieutenant of the Tower that 'I think much unkindness in the king to put such about me as I never loved'.[17] She was unconvinced by Kingston's answer 'that the king took them to be honest and good women'. Anne replied that 'I would have had of my own Privy Chamber which I favour most', something which again strongly indicates that it was Anne Tempest, who was not one of the queen's attendants, rather than Elizabeth Wood, who was present at the Tower. Lady Boleyn's hostile role was stated by Gilbert Burnet, who wrote in the seventeenth century and appears to have used a lost contemporary account of the fall of Anne Boleyn, written by one Anthony Anthony, who was a Surveyor of the Ordnance at the Tower. He recorded the hostile relationship between the two women, due to the fact that they had long been on 'very ill terms' and that Lady Boleyn went out of her way to obtain evidence against her niece: 'she engaged her into much discourse, and studied to draw confessions from her. Whatsoever she said was presently sent to the court.'[18]

Lady Boleyn and Mistress Coffin were deputed to sleep on a pallet bed in the queen's own chamber: a proximity that cannot have been welcomed by either aunt or niece.[19] To further emphasise the fact that she was under observation, the Lieutenant of the Tower, William Kingston, and his wife slept outside the door. While there was little love lost between the queen and her aunt, it is possible to suggest that Anne Tempest Boleyn had some sympathy for her niece. While Kingston wrote to Thomas Cromwell to inform him that 'I have everything told me by Mistress Coffin that she thinks meet for me to know' he did not record any information actually provided by Lady Boleyn. It was Mrs Coffin who rushed to tell Kingston that Anne had spoken of Henry Norris and his professions of love for her. A few days later Kingston recorded that he had sent specifically for Mistress Coffin and his wife for an update on Anne's conduct, with no mention of Lady Boleyn.[20]

The surviving evidence for Lady Boleyn's conduct in the Tower suggests disapproval of her niece rather than hatred. According to Kingston in one of his reports, Anne complained one evening that 'the king wist what he did when he put such two about her as my Lady Boleyn and Mistress Coffin, for they could tell her nothing of my lord her father nor nothing else, but she defied them all'.[21] In response, Lady Boleyn declared that 'such desire as you have had to such tales has brought you to this'. Clearly Anne could expect little sympathy from an aunt who thought that she had brought her fall upon herself, although Lady Boleyn may not have been quite the enemy the queen believed her to be. Lady Shelton, whom Anne remained estranged from, was also one of the ladies employed as a potential informer on the queen.[22]

Lady Boleyn and Lady Shelton were not the only Boleyn ladies to play a potentially hostile role in the fall of Anne Boleyn. Jane Parker Boleyn, Lady Rochford, is usually assigned a great role in the fall of her husband and his sister. Gilbert Burnet believed that Jane played a major role in providing evidence against her husband and sister-in-law due to the fact that she was jealous of her husband's close relationship with his sister and was 'a woman of no sort of virtue'.[23] Burnet claimed that Jane

carried many stories to the king, or some about him, to persuade, that there was a familiarity between the queen and her brother, beyond what so near a relation could justify. All that could be said for it was only this; that he was once seen leaning upon her bed, which bred great suspicion.[24]

While Jane was indeed involved in a love affair in the last year of her life, her role was that of a procuress rather than a lover. In spite of William Cavendish's claim that Jane had not been a 'chaste wife' and that she was 'in every matter, both early and late, called the woman of vice insatiate' and that she had followed her 'lust and filthy pleasure', there is not actually any evidence that Jane ever took a lover or even contemplated remarrying. If anything, the evidence suggests that she at least outwardly remained loyal to George's memory after his death. Cavendish, who knew her, described her as 'a widow in black'.[25] The evidence of Jane's possessions also suggests that she habitually wore black, something which, given that her widowhood lasted for nearly six years, was far above what was required by convention. In the inventory of some of her goods prepared at the time of George's death, the list of Jane's clothes were colourful and rich, such as sleeves of yellow satin and of cloth of silver.[26] Her clothes listed in inventories carried out at her death were entirely black, such as a kirtle of black velvet and one of black satin. She possessed a gown of black damask and one of black satin and a nightgown of black taffeta.[27] Even the gift of cloth made by Princess Mary in 1537 was black satin. In public, Jane appeared as a grieving widow for the rest of her life. She also appeared publicly as a dutiful wife during George's imprisonment, with the Lieutenant of the Tower recording that Sir Nicholas Carew and Sir Francis Bryan came with a message to George from Jane to 'see how he did' and also to declare that she would 'humbly suit unto the king's highness' on George's behalf.[28] Unfortunately, the letter in which this message was noted was damaged in a fire and the exact nature of Jane's petition is unclear, although it was 'for her husband' and such as that George 'gave her thanks', something which does imply that she offered to speak to the king for his release. This does not suggest hostility between husband and wife.

It is commonly suggested that George and Jane had always had an unhappy marriage. No representation survives of George but he appears to have been a handsome and accomplished man, reputed both as a patron of the religious reform and as a poet, although, unfortunately, no examples of his work survive. There is no surviving record that Jane was ever pregnant or produced any child, something that could suggest that the couple did not commonly live together as man and wife. Equally, one party to the marriage could have been infertile. A George Boleyn, Dean of

Lichfield, who identified himself as a kinswoman of Anne Boleyn's daughter, Elizabeth, was active later in the sixteenth century, suggesting that he could, perhaps, have been an illegitimate son of Lord Rochford's. No other potential illegitimate children have been linked to George, and the Dean of Lichfield could have been a more distant relative. Infertility therefore cannot be ruled out for either party, particularly as it is clear that Jane was well aware of what relations between a husband and wife consisted of, indicating that the marriage would have been consummated. In 1540 Jane, with two other court ladies, gave evidence against the king's fourth wife, Anne of Cleves, to show that Henry's marriage remained unconsummated and to allow him to annul his marriage. According to the ladies, they spoke to the queen, telling her that they wished she was pregnant. A conversation ensued with the ladies declaring 'Madam, I think your Grace is a maid still, indeed'. Anne protested, asking, 'How can I be a maid and sleep every night with the king?', to which Jane replied knowingly, 'There must be more than that,' before agreeing with her companions that if all the king did was kiss his wife goodnight it would be a long time before the queen bore a son.[29]

While the couple's marriage was likely to have been consummated, this is not, in itself, an indication that it was happy. In his *Metrical Visions*, William Cavendish presented a highly unflattering picture of George, putting words into his mouth to declare that:

My life not chaste, my living bestial;
I forced widows, maidens I did deflower.
All was one to me, I spared none at all,
My appetite was all women to devour,
My study was both day and hour,
My unlawful lechery how I might it fulfil.
Sparing no woman to have on her my will.[30]

It was hardly unusual for an aristocratic husband to take mistresses and it was generally considered that a wife should ignore any illicit conduct on her husband's part. However, Cavendish's emphasis on George's licentiousness does suggest that he may have gone further than most, something that would have embarrassed his wife, who, as the daughter of Henry VII's first cousin, probably expected better treatment. Cavendish may, of course, have exaggerated but he does present a reasonably fair picture of Anne Boleyn's brother, stating that George was endowed 'with gifts of natural qualities' among other accomplishments.

The claim, first made by Retha Warnicke in the 1980s, that George was homosexual can probably be discounted.[31] Dr Warnicke based this claim largely on a surviving French manuscript, containing a satirical poem attacking the institution of marriage, which certainly belonged to George and also bears the signature of a 'Marc S'. This Mark was identified as Mark Smeaton, with the argument being that he and George had been involved in a love affair, with Smeaton confessing to adultery with the queen because it was a less shameful death than that which would be inflicted on a homosexual in the period. The identification of 'Marc S' as Smeaton must be fairly contentious as it is highly unlikely that he could have afforded to purchase a work of this quality. However, he did move in the same circles as the Boleyns and so it is possible that he is indeed the Mark in question. It is quite a leap from this to assume that he and the queen's brother were involved in a love affair however, particularly as there is no contemporary evidence to even hint at this. Cavendish also makes it clear that George's licentiousness was directed at women, although he was apparently not particularly discerning as to his sexual partners. It is very possible that George's adultery served to turn his wife away from him, but the evidence does not suggest any noticeable estrangement between the couple; the marriage was consummated, and Jane apparently mourned her husband and tried to intercede with the king on his behalf. None of this suggests any great passion between the couple, but it certainly does not indicate separation or hatred.

As has been pointed out, if Jane was indeed a willing government informer, she was not highly regarded by the king or his council.[32] Following George's conviction for treason, his property was seized, leaving Jane in considerable financial difficulty. The fact that a bed that had belonged to George was in her possession at her death suggests that she did succeed in recovering some of her late husband's property, however the timing and the extent of this recovery is unclear; she may even have purchased the bed for sentimental reasons. Shortly after George's death, Jane wrote to Thomas Cromwell as a 'poor desolate widow without comfort', soliciting his aid in relation to securing a better financial settlement from her father-in-law. Jane wrote,

Praying you, after your accustomed gentle manner to all them that be in such lamentable case as I am in, to be a mean to the king's gracious highness for me for such poor stuff and plate as my husband had, whom God pardon; for that of his gracious and mere liberality I may have it to help me to my poor living, which to his Highness is nothing to be regarded, and to me should be a most high help and succour. And farther more, where that the king's highness and my lord my father paid great sums of money for my jointure to the Earl of Wiltshire to the sum of two thousand marks, and I not assured of no more during the said Earl's natural life than one hundred marks; which is very hard for me to shift the world withal. That you will specially tender me in this behalf as to inform the king's highness of these premises; whereby I may the more tenderly be regarded of his gracious person, your word in this shall be to me a sure help: and God shall be to you therefore a sure reward, which doth promise good to them that doth help poor forsaken widows.[33]

Cromwell did indeed speak of Jane to the king, with both men writing on her behalf to Thomas Boleyn. Royal pressure persuaded Jane's father-in-law to increase her entitlement by a further 50 marks a year, with a reiteration of the promise that she would receive a full 300 marks a year following his death.[34] However, it is highly likely that Thomas's concession was far below what she was hoping for and an indication that she enjoyed no great favour with the king. Shortly after the letter was written she took a post in the household of Queen Jane Seymour, suggesting that she may have been driven to do so due to financial necessity.

There is very little evidence to indicate that Jane and George were estranged at the time of his death, aside from persistent rumours that she had provided information that was used in the case against him and Anne. It may be that the couple's relationship was not happy, particularly if Jane had blamed her banishment from court on George's sister and had then made a public show of support for Princess Mary. The evidence suggests that Jane may have been responsible for some of the accusations levied against Anne and George, but this does not, in itself, suggest that she was vindictive. Such information could have been obtained from the interrogation of a woman who had already spent time in the Tower and was terrified of returning there, particularly if she was already somewhat estranged from her royal sister-in-law. George did not publicly blame his wife for his predicament. Jane is the most likely source of the claims that Anne and George had laughed at the king's clothes and discussed Anne's concerns that he was impotent. She may also have told Cromwell that George had jokingly questioned Elizabeth's legitimacy, something that was treason after the terms of the first Act of Succession.

Jane's role in the fall of Anne Boleyn will always be unclear. Little evidence survives concerning the charges brought against Anne or any of the men with which she was accused. The judge, Sir John Spelman, who sat on the bench during Anne's trial, noted that Anne had originally been accused by Lady Wingfield.[35] Lady Wingfield, who was an old friend of Anne's, had died in either 1533 or 1534, leaving a deathbed statement in which she apparently accused the queen of being morally lax. Although this statement does not survive, it may have related to a premarital affair given the subservient tone which Anne used when she wrote to Lady Wingfield before she became queen. It is not impossible that this related to Anne's relationship with Henry Percy, as suggested by the government's interest in him during Anne's trial. A lack of premarital chastity was a ground for divorce, but it was not treason. Anne was instead the subject of a far more damning allegation by the Countess of Worcester.[36]

According to a letter written by a gentleman present at court during the events of May 1536, 'the first accusers, the Lady Worcester, and Nan Cobham, with one maid more. But Lady Worcester was the first ground.'[37] Nan Cobham has never been identified successfully, but Lady Worcester was a member of the queen's household and noted for her loose conduct. According to a letter written by Lady Worcester to Cromwell in March 1537, Anne had lent her £100, a vast sum, and one in which the countess was 'very loath it should come to my lord my husband's knowledge thereof, I am in doubt how he will take it'. Lady Worcester had a lover and in early 1536, her brother, Sir Anthony Browne, berated her for her immoral conduct. In her anger, the noblewoman blurted out that she was not the worst and that her brother should look to the conduct of the queen herself. This was enough for Cromwell's agents to begin an investigation in Anne's household and, according to Alexander Ales, who was at court during the last weeks of Anne's life, the minister's agents 'tempt her porter and serving men with bribes, there is nothing which they do not promise the ladies of her bedchamber. They affirm that the king hated the queen, because she hath not presented him with an heir to the realm, nor was there any prospect of her doing so.'[38]

Lady Rochford, Lady Wingfield and Lady Worcester were, in fact, not the only women to offer evidence against the queen, with Anne's own terrified words, in which she alternated between weeping and laughing, proving explosive. On her arrival in the Tower, Anne asked Kingston why she was in the Tower and he replied that he did not know. She then asked about her brother, who she had heard had also been arrested, pleading, 'Oh where is my sweet brother?' She then said that she thought that she would be accused with three men, presumably referring to her brother, Norris and Smeaton, who were all prisoners in the ancient fortress. She was still the old Anne, and, while bewailing the thought that Norris and Smeaton had accused her, asked Kingston, 'Shall I die without justice?' When Kingston replied that 'the poorest subject the king hath had justice', Anne burst out laughing.

Anne had always prided herself on her intelligence and self-possession, but in her first few days at the Tower she was a piteous sight, desperately turning over any incident in her mind that could have led suspicion to fall on her. According to Kingston, soon after her arrival,

> the queen spoke of Weston that she had spoken to him because he did love her kinswoman Mrs Shelton and that she said he loves not his wife and he made answer to her again that he loved one in her house better than them both; she asked him who is that? To which he answered that it is your self: and then she defied him.

Francis Weston, who was a popular young man at court, and, like Norris, a member of the king's household, had not previously been the subject of royal enquiry. Anne's words damned him and before nightfall he found himself a prisoner in the Tower. She also discussed her interactions with Smeaton, saying that she had once found him looking sorrowful standing by the window in her chamber. He refused to answer when she asked why he was sad and, annoyed, Anne had declared that 'you may not look to have me speak to you as I should do to a nobleman, because you be an inferior person'. Smeaton then replied, 'No, no, madam, a look sufficed me, and thus fair you well.' While it appears that Smeaton may have had a crush on Anne, this is not evidence of adultery. Anne spoke innocently enough of her brother, saying when it was confirmed that he was also present in the Tower that 'I am glad that we both be so nigh together'. This again could be misconstrued. Anne made no mention of the remaining three men arrested during the investigations: William Brereton, Sir Richard Page and Thomas Wyatt. Page and Wyatt were never brought to trial but Brereton was tried and suffered alongside the rest.

Anne herself was particularly concerned about her mother's reaction to events, lamenting to William Kingston, 'O my mother, thou will die for sorrow.'[39] Given their close relationship, Elizabeth must have been distraught at the arrest of her children although there is no evidence that either she or her husband attempted to intercede on their behalf. It may be that both Elizabeth and Thomas had their own more immediate troubles as, immediately following the arrests, rumours spread throughout Europe that they too had been arrested for a role in Anne's adultery.[40] The couple may well have been fearful of imprisonment, which was a very real threat: five years later Henry would imprison several members of the family of his fifth wife, Catherine Howard, for her lack of chastity at the time of her marriage. It may however have been this threat which caused Thomas to agree to sit in judgement against his children at their trials, a decision which must have been devastating for him.[41]

Many people in England were prepared to believe the worst against Anne, who had never been popular. However, according to Alexander Ales, even Anne's enemies recognised the evidence as circumstantial, admitting that

> it is no new thing, they said, that the King's Chamberlains should dance with the ladies in the bedchamber. Nor can any proof of adultery be collected from the fact that the queen's brother took her by the hand and led her into the dance among the other ladies, or handed her to another, especially if that person was one of the royal chamberlains. For it is a usual custom throughout the whole of Britain that ladies married and unmarried, even the most coy, kiss not only a brother but any honourable person, even in public.

In spite of the flimsy evidence Norris, Weston, Brereton and Smeaton were tried and convicted of adultery with Anne on 12 May. Anne and her brother, due to their status, were tried separately within the Tower itself on 15 May. Lady Boleyn and Lady Kingston accompanied the queen to her trial and sat through proceedings before returning with her to her prison.[42] Anne sat on a special scaffold which had been built for the occasion, facing her peers, who were led by her own uncle, the Duke of Norfolk. Anne's own father and her former love, Henry Percy, sat in judgement on her, something that can have been easy for none of them, even Norfolk, who disliked his niece. Few details survive of Anne's trial although she defended herself vehemently. Sir John Spelman, who was present, claimed that 'all the evidence was of bawdery and lechery, so that there was no such whore in the realm', something which is suggestive of the preconceived view that many present had of her. The list of official charges makes scurrilous reading, with claims that she, 'depising her marriage, entertaining malice against the king, and following daily her frail and carnal lust, did falsely and traitorously procure by base conversation and kisses, touching gifts, and other infamous incitations, divers of the king's daily and familiar servants to be her adulterers and concubines'.[43] She was supposed to have 'allured' her brother 'with her tongue in the said George's mouth', as well as plotting the death of the king so that she would be free to marry a lover. The charges against Anne were outrageous, but the result of the trial was a foregone conclusion. As he pronounced sentence that his sister's daughter should be burned or beheaded 'at the king's pleasure', there were tears in Norfolk's eyes. Henry Percy was suddenly taken ill and unable to participate in George's trial, which followed and in which he was also found guilty.

Anne's five 'lovers' were beheaded together on 17 May. As was customary, the condemned men were permitted to make a speech, with George declaring,

Christian men, I am born under the law, and judged under the law, and die under the law, and the law hath condemned me. Masters all, I am not come hither for to preach, but for to die, for I have deserved to die if I had twenty lives, more shamefully than can be devised for I am a wretched sinner, and I have sinned shamefully, I have known no man so evil, and to rehearse my sins openly it were no pleasure to you to hear them, nor yet for me to rehearse them, for God knoweth all; therefore, masters all, I pray you take heed by me, and especially my lords and gentlemen of the court, the which I have been among, take heed by me, and beware of such a fall, and I pray to God the Father, the Son, and the Holy Ghost, three persons and one God, that my death may be an example unto you all, and beware, trust not in the vanity of the world, and especially in the flattering of the court.[44]

George continued in a similar vein, recognising, as was expected, his worthiness to die, but significantly, not admitting any guilt in the offences for which he died. On the scaffold, none of the men admitted any guilt, with Brereton going so far as to deny any wrongdoing with Anne, declaring, 'I have deserved to die if it were a thousand deaths, but the cause wherefore I die judge not: But if ye judge, judge the best.'[45] The deaths of the five men would have caused Anne to realise that her death was now a certainty. That same day she received word that her marriage had been annulled, either due to her relationship with Henry Percy, or the king's earlier affair with Mary Boleyn. Either way, it cannot have escaped Anne that she was to die for committing adultery when, legally, she had never been married at all.

Such legal niceties were irrelevant for Henry who was already planning his wedding to Jane Seymour. Anne spent the last few days left to her preparing herself for death. She took steps to show the world her innocence of the crimes of which she was convicted, swearing on the sacrament on 18 May before Kingston that she was innocent. After the sentence was passed, Anne was calmer, even making little jokes such as declaring on the evening before her death that she would be known to posterity as 'Queen Anne Lack-Head'. Her execution was slightly delayed by the king making one small concession to the woman that he had previously loved by sending for an expert swordsman from the Continent to carry out her execution. This was a relief to Anne, who declared to Kingston that 'I heard say the executioner is very good, and I have a little neck' before putting her hands around her neck and laughing.

On the morning of 19 May Anne stepped out of her lodgings and made her way to Tower Green, where a crowd of grandees had assembled. Once she was standing on the scaffold, a composed Anne turned to face the crowd, declaring,

Good Christian people, I am come hither to die, for according to the law and by the law I am judged to die, and therefore I will speak nothing against it. I am come hither to accuse no man, nor to speak anything of that whereof I am accused and condemned to die, but I pray God save the king and send him long to reign over you, for a gentler nor more merciful prince was there never: and to me he was ever a good, a gentle, and sovereign lord. And if any person will meddle of my cause, I require them to judge the best. And thus I take my leave of the world and of you all, and I heartily desire you all to pray for me. O lord have mercy on me, to God I commend my soul.[46]

Lady Boleyn was probably one of the four ladies permitted to accompany Anne to the scaffold.[47] One of these ladies, weeping, then stepped forward to cover Anne's eyes with a cloth before the executioner stepped forward.[48] There was no need for a block and, instead, Anne knelt on the straw of the scaffold. While she was praying the headsman stepped up behind her, severing her head with one stroke of the sword.

According to a contemporary account by Lancelot de Carles, following Anne's death her ladies, who were half-dead themselves with grief, but unwilling to let anyone else touch the corpse, wrapped the body in a white covering and carried her to be buried in the nearby chapel within the Tower, laying her next to her brother. If, as seems likely, Anne Tempest Boleyn was indeed one of these ladies, she may have warmed to her niece in the days that they spent in the Tower, at least, as Sir William Kingston did, admiring the queen for the bravery that she showed in the face of her death.

Part 4
The Last Boleyn Women: 1536–1603

12

AFTER ANNE

The fall of Anne Boleyn did not quite bring about the fall of the Boleyn family, although the death of the childless George Boleyn did mean that the direct male line of the family ended with the deaths of Thomas Boleyn and his brothers, none of whom had living sons.

Queen Anne's two aunts by marriage, Anne Tempest Boleyn and Elizabeth Wood Boleyn, both disappeared into obscurity following their niece's death. Since Elizabeth Wood Boleyn was present at court during her niece's time as queen, it is probable that she is the Lady Boleyn who found herself caught up in a scandal concerning the king's niece, Lady Margaret Douglas. Soon after Anne Boleyn's fall it was discovered that Margaret, who was the daughter of Henry's sister, Margaret, Queen of Scots, had secretly married Anne Boleyn's uncle, Lord Thomas Howard. In the examination of one Thomas Smith in relation to this, he declared that Howard would wait until Lady Boleyn was gone from Margaret's chamber, leaving only the Duchess of Richmond to attend the king's niece before he would secretly visit her.[1] Although Elizabeth was quite innocent in the affair, it was dangerous for her name to be mentioned in connection with what the king considered treason.

She was still active in February 1537 when one Richard Southwell wrote to Thomas Cromwell from Yarmouth, concerned that he had heard that Sir James Boleyn, through his wife, was campaigning for one of his offices in the town.[2] This suggests that Elizabeth had remained at court, while her husband was, at that point, in East Anglia. Elizabeth Wood Boleyn was still living in 1553 when her husband arranged a settlement of some of his lands, but she had died by the time of her husband's death in 1561.[3] The couple probably lived comfortably at Blickling, which they acquired following the death of Jane Rochford, who had a life interest.

Sir James Boleyn's will demonstrates that he died wealthy and on close terms with many of his nephews and nieces.[4] He made his will in August 1561, aware that he was 'naturally born to die and pass from this transitory life'. He was concerned that, since he died without children, his bequests would be challenged by his kin. He therefore begged his heirs 'to be content and satisfied with such things as are by me given and bequeathed to them in this my same last will without trouble or vexation of any of them against other for my said goods or lands'. James left personal bequests to his great-niece, Queen Elizabeth I, which strongly suggest that they considered each other to be kin, with James declaring that 'I give and bequeath to my most gracious sovereign lady the Queen's most excellent majesty my basin and ewer all gilt and my written book of the revelations of Saint Bridget. Most humbly beseeching her highness to read and will so ponder the same humbly given.' Rather than being a criticism of the queen for her recent suppression of the Bridgettine House at Syon, it would appear that the gift of the book, and the suggestion that his great-niece read it, was a friendly gesture, particularly since James relied on the queen's support for his favourite niece, Elizabeth Shelton.

Elizabeth Shelton, the daughter of Anne Boleyn Shelton, remained unmarried. By 1561, when she was approaching middle age, she had fallen on hard times. Following his bequest to the queen, James, added, 'Beseeching her said highness to give unto my niece

Elizabeth Shelton having at this day nothing certain wherewith to comfort or relieve herself the four hundred pounds owing to me by her grace.' This £400 was due to James from an annuity that the queen had granted him, to be paid out of the income of a manor in Kent. He then, hopefully, declared, 'Which sums I do for very charity grant and give as before unto my said niece right humbly beseeching her good grace to extend her mercy and goodness unto that poor gentlewoman now utterly destitute and unprovided of friendship or place.' Given that the annuity died with James, only the arrears were actually his to bequeath, not any future income. However, he clearly felt that the queen was likely to benefit a fellow Boleyn daughter, who had fallen on hard times. He also took further steps to ensure that Elizabeth Shelton was no longer quite so destitute or unprovided for, leaving her the sum of 200 marks to be paid in annual instalments of 40 marks. That Elizabeth Shelton was reliant on her uncle and the queen for support suggests that she was, by that time, estranged from the wider Shelton family. Further details on Elizabeth Shelton's life are scant, although she was probably able to live reasonably comfortably on James Boleyn's bequest, particularly since the queen also took pity on her, granting her an annuity of £30 shortly after James's death.[5]

Anne Tempest Boleyn's later life was taken up with arranging the marriages of her four daughters: Mary, Elizabeth, Ursula and Amy. These Boleyn daughters married into the local gentry and lived unremarkable lives, far removed from their famous first cousin. Mary, the eldest, married James, the fifth son of Robert Brampton of Brampton. The second, Elizabeth, married Thomas Payne of Iteringham.[6] The third, Ursula, married a William Pigge of Essex, while the youngest, Amy, married twice, taking first Sir Edward Whinborough and then Nicholas Shadwell of Bromhill as her husbands. By her second marriage Amy is believed to have been an ancestress of the late seventeenth-century poet and playwright, Thomas Shadwell. Anne Tempest Boleyn's date of death is not recorded.

Queen Anne's paternal aunt, Alice Boleyn Clere, was finally able to retire home following her niece's death, leaving her responsibilities with Princess Mary behind. She died in October 1539, probably at her home of Ormesby where she was buried, according to her wishes, with her husband.[7] Alice's eldest son, Sir John Clere, was a soldier, serving first as treasurer of the king's army in 1549 and later serving with the navy.[8] He was on campaign at Orkney in 1557 when he and seventy-nine of his men were drowned in a skirmish. The family remained closely connected to the Boleyns and it was the Cleres who eventually inherited Blickling, with Alice's grandson, Edward, buried in a fine tomb in Blickling church. Alice's sister, Lady Shelton, outlived most of her generation, dying in January 1556. She had been a widow for nearly twenty years and had remained close to her many children. She almost certainly approved when her eldest son, another Sir John Shelton, joined her former charge Princess Mary at Kenninghall in July 1553 when she claimed the throne.[9] Lady Shelton remained close to her own birth family until the end, requesting that her brother, Sir James, should supervise her will.

Contrary to Queen Anne's fears, her mother did not die of sorrow at her fall, although the deaths of two of her three children must have blighted the last years of her life, particularly given her estrangement from her surviving daughter, Mary. There is some evidence that she was reconciled with her daughter, against her husband's wishes, with Thomas refraining from taking any action to Mary's detriment while his wife was still alive. Soon after her death, he abandoned this principle, promising the king that, rather than passing his Ormond inheritance to Mary, he would instead make over his lands to Princess Elizabeth.[10] By waiting until after his wife's death, it is evident that Thomas knew that she would not support this position, even if, as a regular attendant on her daughter, Queen Anne, she had got to know her infant granddaughter.

Thomas Boleyn wrote to Thomas Cromwell from Hever in July 1536 to thank the minister for his 'goodness to me when I am far off, and cannot always be present to answer for myself'.[11] It is clear that, for a time, Anne Boleyn's parents were not welcome at court, although in October 1536 Thomas was commanded by the king to raise troops during the rebellion in Lincolnshire and Yorkshire known as the Pilgrimage of Grace, indicating that he had not been entirely forgotten by his former son-in-law.[12] He was not able to retain his office of Lord Privy Seal, which was passed to Cromwell.[13]

Elizabeth Howard Boleyn did not remain away from court for long, as her presence is recorded in June 1537 when Lady Lisle's agent sought her advice on a question of etiquette.[14] She may already have been in ill health as she was suffering from a severe cough in April 1536 'which grieves her sore'.[15] The couple evidently did not remain at court for long, with Thomas writing letters from Hever in August and September of that year.[16] Thomas Boleyn returned again to court in January 1538 and was 'very well entertained'.[17] Elizabeth accompanied him and was still in London at the time of her death in April 1538, staying in a house near Baynard's Castle.[18] Within a few days of her death, her body was taken from the house in which she died by barge to Lambeth, accompanied by her brother, Lord Edmund Howard, and half-sister, Lady Daubney, as chief mourners.[19] As befitted her rank as a countess and daughter of a duke, Elizabeth's body was conveyed in some state, with torches burning and four banners decorating the black-covered barge. A white cross stood out strikingly against the black.

She was buried at Lambeth, which was close to her brother's London residence and was commonly used as a burial place for members of the Howard family who died in the capital. This burial place shows her continuing pride in her lineage and accounts for the fact that she did not select Hever as her burial place, where her husband later chose to be buried. Thomas Boleyn did not long survive his wife.[20] In spite of rumours that he would marry the king's niece, Lady Margaret Douglas, in July 1538, he did not take a new bride.[21] He died in March 1539 and was buried at Hever with his tomb marked by a fine memorial brass. His funeral was not on the same scale as his wife's, although his fellow Knight of the Garter, Lord Lisle, paid for memorial Masses to be said for his soul.[22]

With the death of his childless only son, Thomas Boleyn's heir male became his brother, Sir James Boleyn. Since he was survived by his daughter, he also had an heir general, who, in theory, inherited all property not entailed on the male line. Since Anne Boleyn died under an attainder and, in any event, her daughter was legally illegitimate, Thomas's only heir general was his eldest daughter, Mary Boleyn, who had survived the fall of her sister and brother. The Crown also had a claim to half of the estates as the beneficiary of Anne's attainder. It has been claimed that Thomas recognised Mary as his heir, allowing her the use of Rochford Hall in Essex, which may have become her main residence.[23] However, there is no real evidence of this and, given Thomas's promise to the king to make Princess Elizabeth his heir, any reconciliation with Mary must be doubtful.

Mary's whereabouts after Anne Boleyn's fall are not known. Her recent biographer suggests that she and Stafford may have spent some years living in Calais, although there is no direct evidence for this; a paucity of references to Mary in the sources can, after all, be explained by her living often away from court, as her equally poorly documented mother had often done.[24] Stafford is recorded as being present in the English-held town in 1539 to welcome Henry VIII's fourth bride, Anne of Cleves, and so, perhaps, Mary joined him. She is not mentioned in any of the substantial surviving correspondence of Lady Lisle, who was the wife of the governor of Calais, friendly with Mary's mother and related to her distantly through marriage, something that does throw a six-year residence in the town into doubt. Mary Boleyn's credit was also low at court in the immediate aftermath of her sister's fall. In a letter written early in 1537, for example, the prior of Tynemouth wrote to Cromwell asking for his house to be released from paying a pension to Mary, who had assisted his predecessor and the priory, stating that she could no longer do any great good to either the prior or the house.[25]

Mary and her husband, William Stafford, were disappointed, for a time, in their hopes of profiting from the Ormond inheritance, of which her venerable grandmother, Margaret Butler Boleyn, remained entitled to an income of 400 marks a year until her death not long after her son's.[26] It took Mary and her husband until April 1540 to finally gain control over her Ormond inheritance, as well as other Boleyn properties such as Hever.[27] Stafford was, by that stage, beginning to rise in royal service, something that may have been due to the king's lingering affection for his former mistress. He rose to the rank of esquire of the body to the king during Mary's lifetime.[28] The couple later sold a substantial portion of their lands to the king, ensuring that they were more financially comfortable than they had hitherto been. There is no evidence that Mary returned to court after her sister's death and she may have lived quietly on her estates. Her wealth increased again in May 1543 when she received the Boleyn family lands previously held by her grandmother, Margaret Butler Boleyn, and sister-in-law, Jane Rochford, as part of their widow's dowers.[29] Mary was still only in her mid-forties but was probably already in ill health, dying on 19 July 1543. She was survived by her second husband and her two children by her first marriage. As a married woman she was unable to make a will, with her property instead divided between her husband and son.[30] William Stafford eventually remarried and continued to have a successful court career, dying as a Protestant exile during the reign of Mary I in 1556.

Although the king perhaps retained the vestiges of affection for Mary Boleyn, it was not her influence that provided for her father's return to court following Queen Anne's fall. Thomas Boleyn's return to royal favour late in 1537 coincided with the king once again taking a romantic interest in Mary Shelton and a desire to please her was probably behind her uncle's rehabilitation. As it happened, the king's interest in Mary proved brief, with him soon moving on to Margaret Skipwith, a contemporary at court. In spite of this, Mary Shelton remained at court, eventually taking a position with Henry's fifth wife, Catherine Howard. With the arrest of her mistress, Queen Catherine Howard, Mary Shelton found herself once again without an appointment at court. Mary was, by 1542, approaching her mid-twenties and, while she was no longer an object of interest to the king, continued to attract suitors. She was a close friend of the king's niece, Lady Margaret Douglas, and his daughter-in-law, Mary Howard, the widowed Duchess of Richmond. The three moved in literary circles, remaining close to the duchess's brother, Henry Howard, Earl of Surrey, and Sir Thomas Wyatt, who died towards the end of 1542.

With Henry Norris's execution with Anne Boleyn in May 1536, Mary Shelton perhaps lost her fiancé. In the 1540s Mary fell in love, with the object of her affections being her first cousin, Thomas Clere, the son of Alice Boleyn Clere. Thomas was the favourite son of his mother and appears to have been well liked by most people that he came across. Mary's love for Clere may actually have caused some conflict with her sister Anne Shelton, who was married to Sir Edmund Knyvet, with the two men coming to blows on one occasion at court. Clere was a close friend and retainer of Henry Howard, Earl of Surrey, the son of the Duke of Norfolk. The pair served together in France, with Surrey later recalling that when he believed himself 'half dead' on the field he handed his friend his will for safe-keeping, something that indicates the level of trust the pair had in each other.[31] Clere was born in around 1518 and was proud both of his Norfolk upbringing and his descent through his Boleyn mother from the earls of Ormond.[32] Few details of his love affair with Mary survive, although it was well known enough for Surrey to include the line 'Shelton for love, Surrey for lord thou chase' in a verse epitaph he composed for his friend. That marriage was not spoken of between the couple was almost certainly due to the fact that they were first cousins: such marriages were highly unusual in early Tudor England, only becoming more common in later centuries. To further complicate matters, Mary Shelton's paternal grandmother had been Margaret Clere, the sister of Thomas's father, so that Thomas was also a first cousin of her father's.[33] This does not mean that the couple did not consummate their relationship, especially since Mary is unlikely to have been a virgin given her affair with the king. She also appears to have had a highly modern view of love, at odds with the conventions of the day.

A remarkable manuscript known as the Devonshire Manuscript survives in the British Library. It contains a large amount of original and transcribed verse, written in at least nineteen different hands. The book is a mixture, with the exchange between Thomas Wyatt and Mary discussed earlier suggestive of courtly love, which was characterised by an exchange of verse.[34] Thomas Clere was one of the contributors, as was Mary's brother-in-law, Sir Edmund Knyvet. Mary, along with her friends, Lady Margaret Douglas and Mary Howard, Duchess of Richmond, were the main contributors. Mary contributed her own compositions to the book, such as one on a woman's failure to cloak her feelings regarding love matters. In the poem, Mary declared that she was unable to 'make a joke of all my woe' and that as she was, so must she appear to the world:

> That though I would it lacked might
> To cloak my grief where it doth grow[35]

Poetry written by women was still a rarity, making Mary something of a trailblazer. There is also evidence that she had radical views about the position of women and the way in which they were portrayed in love matters.

As well as showing remarkably modern views on love, Mary's work in the manuscript has been argued to 'convey her disillusionment with some of the inequalities of her day, particularly in relation between the sexes'.[36] The works that Mary transcribed are particularly illuminating regarding her character. It was Mary who transcribed the series of verses exchanged between the king's niece, Lady Margaret Douglas, and her lover, Thomas Howard, after their secret relationship had been discovered, leading to their imprisonment. Margaret was a close friend of Mary's and she would have had access to the works, possibly even as one commentator has suggested, being in a position to facilitate the correspondence itself, since her brother Thomas was a groom porter of the Tower where Howard was held.[37] The inclusion of the poems, under this analysis, is seen as an act of protest against the Henrician government.

This can be coupled with the medieval verse also transcribed in the manuscript by Mary, much of it written by Chaucer. She did not simply copy the works, instead altering many of them to give them a more feminine slant. For example, in one, Mary altered a line that had originally read 'The cursedness yet and deceit of women' to read 'The faithfulness yet and praise of women'. Other extracts selected (and not amended) also demonstrate the point of view that she was attempting to convey. For example, one passage copied praised the good heart of a woman while condemning a man for speaking openly about their relationship and bringing about the ruin of the woman's reputation. It has been argued that Mary's transcriptions make it clear that she had been part of a scandal and that she had been wronged by one particular man.[38] Given her continuing relationship with Thomas Clere, it was probably not him and it may, perhaps, have been Henry VIII himself given their earlier connection and the evidence of Mary's political opposition to him.

Alternatively it could perhaps be Francis Weston, Henry Norris or even the Earl of Surrey, all of whom have been romantically linked to her. A scandal could account for it taking her so long to find a husband. The transcriptions may also provide evidence for Mary's feelings in relation to her forbidden romance for Clere, making it clear that she believed in the rights of lovers to choose their own partners, regardless of familial or social opposition.

To Mary's grief, Thomas Clere died before his twenty-seventh birthday in April 1545. He was buried at Lambeth, suggesting that he died in London and close to Mary. By 1545, Mary was approaching her late twenties, which was unusual. Her parents already seem to have been at a loss as to what to do with her, with Mary spending time in a convent towards the end of the 1530s.[39] Her sister, Gabrielle, was already a nun at a convent near Norwich, suggesting that the family were pious.

Following Clere's death, Mary may well have begun to be concerned about the future and, in particular, her financial security. She therefore finally decided to marry, taking Sir Anthony Heveningham as her husband. Sir Anthony was in fact a cousin of Mary's, as the son of her aunt, Alice Shelton, although he was not, as Clere had been, also a cousin on the maternal side of her family. Heveningham was an eldest son and the possessor of substantial estates, something which may have assuaged her family's concerns about their close family relationship. In taking a first cousin as her husband, Mary Shelton defied convention to the last, although the need to obtain a papal dispensation for the match had at least been removed following the break with Rome. Heveningham was a widower with two children whose education Mary would have been required to superintend.[40] The couple were married by 1546 when Heveningham settled a number of manors on him and Mary for life, with the remainder to their heirs rather than his elder children, something that provided Mary with financial security but may have been resented by her stepchildren. The couple became close, with Mary bearing several children. Heveningham also asked to be buried with her in the church at Keteringham in Norfolk, the manor on which they settled.

Mary made one further contribution to court life before retiring to Norfolk and obscurity. When her friend, Surrey, was arrested for treason in 1546, it was recommended to the investigators that they 'examine Mrs Heveningham, late Mary Shelton, of the effect of the Earl of Surrey his letter sent unto her, for it is thought that many secrets have passed between them before her marriage and since'. This suggests a continuing close relationship even after her marriage and the possibility must be raised that they were lovers, perhaps coming together in their mutual grief over Thomas Clere. If that is the case, Mary clearly saw Surrey's arrest and execution as the time to settle down into a more conventional life. Her first husband died in 1557 and she quickly took a second husband, a gentleman named Philip Appleyard. She died in 1560, probably aged in her early forties.

Mary Shelton was not, of course, the only Boleyn daughter to remain connected to the court. In late April 1536, as her marriage crumbled around her, Queen Anne Boleyn had taken her little daughter in her arms in the gardens at Greenwich Palace and held her up to Henry as he looked down from an open window.[41] Angry words were spoken between the couple before the queen walked away, defeated, taking Elizabeth with her. This was the last time that mother and daughter saw each other, a separation that had a devastating effect on the young princess. Elizabeth was not yet three at the time of her mother's death and was used to being a cosseted and favoured princess and heiress to the crown. She immediately noticed her demotion in status which came with her mother's death, asking her governess, 'How happs it yesterday Lady Princess and today but Lady Elizabeth?' With her mother's death Henry lost interest in his younger daughter for a time, something that the child keenly felt.[42] Anne's aunt, Lady Bryan, found the change in circumstances so dramatic that she was forced to write to Cromwell begging for clothes for her young charge and stating that 'she hath neither gowns nor kirtle, nor petticoat, nor no manner of linen nor rails [nightdress], nor body stichets [corsets], nor biggens [night caps]'.[43]

Although Elizabeth, like her maternal grandparents, was at court for the celebrations following the birth of Prince Edward in October 1537, it was some years before her father would show any particular interest in her and she was fully welcomed back to court. He never doubted her paternity, however, in spite of Princess Mary's later assertion that she looked like Mark Smeaton, something that is a strong indication of just how little credence the king gave to Anne's 'adultery'. Chapuys had believed at the time of Anne's fall that Elizabeth was to be declared Norris's daughter but this was merely rumour, designed to blacken her mother's name. While he acknowledged her as his child, Henry was not prepared to retain her as his heir and, like her elder half-sister before her, Elizabeth was declared illegitimate in the second Act of Succession, which was passed in the summer of 1536, with her parents' marriage declared to be 'taken reputed and deemed and adjudged to be of no force strength virtue or effect'.[44] Surprisingly, it was left to Princess Mary, who found herself back in favour, but not in the succession, to pay attention to the younger girl, writing to their father that Elizabeth was 'such a child toward, as I doubt not but your Highness shall have cause to rejoice of in time coming'.[45] In the summer of 1536 Elizabeth, along with other members of the Boleyn family, must have seemed of very little consequence.

After the events of May 1536, the Boleyn family was severely depleted, particularly since Sir Thomas Boleyn and his brothers had no surviving male heirs. With the death of Sir James Boleyn in 1561, the male line of the first Geoffrey Boleyn of Salle had entirely died out. In May 1536 there was still one prominent member of the family at court: Jane Parker Boleyn, the notorious Lady Rochford.

13

THE NOTORIOUS LADY ROCHFORD

Jane Parker Boleyn, Lady Rochford, as her surviving letter to Cromwell attests, was left in a perilous financial state after the execution of her husband, George Boleyn, writing to beg assistance as a 'poor forsaken widow'. Although a Boleyn by marriage, her father-in-law had little interest in the childless widow of his only son, no doubt seeing her as a financial burden, It is no surprise, given her long court service and her need for funds, that she quickly took a court post, serving Anne Boleyn's successor as queen, Jane Seymour.

Henry married his third wife, Jane Seymour, within days of Anne's death, immediately ordering that she be given all honours due to her as queen. The facts behind Jane's appointment with the new queen do not survive but, since Jane Seymour herself was a supporter of Princess Mary, it would seem likely that, politically, the two women had interests in common. Jane Rochford's recent biographer has suggested that it was Thomas Cromwell who secured her place, in return for the widow's consent to act as a spy in the queen's household.[1] Although an interesting theory, there is no evidence that Jane was used as a spy, in spite of her promise in her letter that, in the event that Cromwell assisted her, 'God shall be to you therefore a sure reward, which doth promise good to them that doth help poor forsaken widows. And both my prayers and service shall help to this during my natural life, as most bounden so to do.'² In any event, the minister evidently had his own sources close to Queen Jane since his son later married the queen's sister. More likely Jane Rochford, with her long court experience, was a useful attendant for the new queen. Jane Seymour, as the daughter of Margery Wentworth, a first cousin of Elizabeth Howard Boleyn, was also related to Jane Rochford through her marriage to George and may have taken pity on her impecunious kinswoman.

Jane Rochford became friends with the new queen, receiving a gold tablet as a gift from her.³ She would have taken part in most of the ceremonial events of Jane Seymour's brief time as queen, including the ceremonies surrounding her taking to her chamber to await the birth of her child on 16 September 1537. The queen's labour began on 9 October, lasting for two days and three nights until she was finally delivered of a son, to the joy of the king and the country. Jane Seymour was well enough to play a role in the christening on 15 October but she soon sickened. By 24 October the queen's life was despaired of and she died that evening, probably of puerperal fever. Perhaps Jane Rochford was one of the ladies who was blamed by Thomas Cromwell for killing their mistress with kindness by suffering her 'to eat things that her fantasy in sickness called for'.⁴ Jane Rochford was prominent in the funeral procession of the late queen, holding the train of her friend, Princess Mary. With Jane Seymour's death, Jane Rochford's court appointment came to an end. She was glad to secure a new appointment to the household of Henry's fourth wife, Anne of Cleves, who arrived in England in December 1539.

Henry VIII had agreed to marry Anne of Cleves for political reasons, although he had been pleased by a portrait of the German princess prepared by his court painter, Hans Holbein. Unfortunately Henry, who had been used to selecting his bride personally, found himself disappointed in his bride when he met her at Rochester, finding her not as described. Henry only went through with the match for fear of offending Anne's brother, the Duke of Cleves, and efforts to consummate the marriage were unsuccessful. Anne of Cleves, whose heavy German clothes were not to English tastes, tried her best to win her husband's affection, appearing at jousts held to celebrate her marriage 'apparelled after the English fashion, with a French hood, which so set forth her beauty and good visage, that every creature rejoiced to behold her'.[5] Soon after his marriage, Henry began a relationship with Catherine Howard, who was the daughter of Lord Edmund Howard, a brother of Elizabeth Howard Boleyn. Catherine was under twenty when she caught the king's eye and had been raised by her step-grandmother, the Dowager Duchess of Norfolk. As the daughter of a younger son, Catherine, in spite of her grand family name, had few prospects and she was therefore glad to receive an appointment as one of Anne of Cleves's maids. This was probably when she first met Jane, the widow of her first cousin. By July 1540 Henry had taken the decision to end his marriage to Anne of Cleves and marry Catherine Howard, whom he considered to be his pure 'jewel'.

Jane was one of Anne of Cleves's highest-ranking ladies and she, along with ladies Rutland and Edgecomb, had considerable access to the queen in her household. In the summer of 1540, when the king began a trial of his marriage, the three ladies came forward to provide a deposition setting out a conversation that they had allegedly had with Anne on the Wednesday before midsummer at Westminster Palace.[6] The three claimed to have had a long conversation with Anne when they said they wished that she was pregnant. Anne replied that she knew she was not, before revealing an alarming ignorance of sexual matters when she confessed that the king would merely kiss her goodnight before rolling over in bed to sleep when they spent the night together. That this conversation ever took place is highly doubtful. At the time of her divorce Anne's own chamberlain, the Earl of Rutland, required an interpreter to speak with the queen and it is improbable that Anne, who only spoke German, could have understood the ladies and replied in such detail. More likely, given that Henry was seeking an annulment on the grounds of non-consummation, the three ladies perjured themselves on the promise of some benefit. For this testimony to believed, Lady Rochford must have been known to be reasonably close to the queen and respected by her, particularly as the ladies also claimed that on another occasion 'the queen declared to my Lady Rochford, how the king used her the four first nights', demonstrating that on occasion Jane was alone with her mistress and evidently considered a potential confidante. Jane, far from being an infamous and untrustworthy figure as often portrayed, won the affection of both Queen Jane Seymour and Queen Anne of Cleves. With Anne's divorce in July 1540 and Henry's remarriage, she was to quickly win the affection of the final royal mistress that she was to serve.

The summer of 1540 was unusually dry, with cattle dying in great numbers. London suffered as much as anywhere, with the Thames receiving so little rainwater that it was noticeably shallow and saltwater flowed under London Bridge, leading to transport difficulties in the capital.[7] Although his boat trips were curtailed, Henry was enjoying himself, taking Catherine Howard as his bride on 28 July 1540 at Oatlands Palace. Catherine dined that evening under a cloth of estate denoting her new status and, as such, she required a household of ladies to attend her.[8] Jane, as an experienced courtier and Catherine's kinswoman by marriage, was soon appointed to attend Henry VIII's fifth wife, becoming the new queen's closest confidante.

Henry was over thirty years older than Catherine and a poor physical specimen. Although she was in awe of her husband, she was not in love with him and was, in fact, already in love with someone else at the time of her marriage. Catherine met Thomas Culpepper shortly after she arrived at court. He was a member of Henry's Privy Chamber and a man who would have been considered an entirely suitable husband for her. He was young and handsome and the couple may already have been lovers before Catherine became queen. Culpepper does not appear to have been a particularly pleasant character. Shortly before he became involved with the queen he had raped the wife of a park keeper in a thicket of trees while three or four of his men held his victim down.[9] Rape warranted capital punishment in England and Culpepper compounded the crime by killing one of the villagers who apprehended him. In spite of this, the young man was charming and highly personable. The king, who was very fond of him, pardoned him and allowed him to return to court.

Catherine made a present of a chain and rich cap to the man she called her 'little sweet fool'.[10] She was soon also writing him passionate love letters, with her only surviving letter being addressed to her lover. In it, Catherine declared that she was troubled by news of his illness and that 'I never longed so much for [a] thing as I do to see you and to speak with you'.[11] She further added that this thought 'doth comfortly me very much when I think of it, and when I think again that you shall depart from me again it makes my heart to die to think what fortune I have that I cannot be always in your company'. It is clear from Catherine's words that Jane had already become her most trusted confidante and was deeply involved in the affair, writing, 'Praying you that you will come when my Lady Rochford is here for then I shall be best at leisure to be at your commandment.' As a respected and mature widow, Jane's presence allayed suspicion and she was certainly considered an appropriate chaperone for the king's wife. What possessed her to become involved in the affair is unclear as, even without the benefit of hindsight, it must have seemed like madness. Perhaps Jane took pity on the young lovers. Alternatively, she may have looked to gain an advantage over the queen to further her court career. It has been suggested that she acted under direct orders from Catherine.[12] Less likely, Jane's contemporary, Cavendish, putting words into her mouth, believed that,

> And when my beauty began to be shent;
> Not with mine own harm suffced or content,
> Contrary to God, I must needs confess,
> Other I enticed by a sample of my wretchedness.[13]

She may simply have liked her royal kinswoman and was flattered by the confidence that the queen placed in her. It was a highly dangerous game as even Catherine realised. In her letter she begged that Culpepper be good to her male servant who brought the letter as 'I do know no one that I dare trust to send to you'. As queen, Catherine was never alone and always watched, something of which the highly experienced courtier, Jane Rochford, should have been aware. She threw caution to the wind in her behaviour, taking a cramp ring from the queen to send as a token to Culpepper, as well as purchasing a pair of bracelets for the queen to give.[14]

Much of the evidence of Jane's conduct in relation to the queen's love affair survives from Henry VIII's summer progress in 1541 when, for the only time in his reign, he ventured to the north of his kingdom, travelling up into Lincolnshire and Yorkshire with his queen and court. When the details of the affair later began to emerge, Catherine laid the blame squarely at Lady Rochford's door, claiming that she had only embarked on a relationship with Culpepper due to Jane's urgings, with the queen claiming that 'Lady Rochford hath sundry times made instance to her to speak with Culpepper declaring him to bear her good will and favour'.[15] Faced with this nagging and Jane's assurance that Culpepper 'desired nothing else but to speak with her and that she durst swear upon a book he meant nothing but honesty', Catherine claimed that she consented to meet with the young man in a little gallery at the top of the stairs at Lincoln at ten or eleven o'clock at night. There is no doubt that Jane was deeply involved in Catherine and Culpepper's affair, with her contemporary, Edward Hall, recording that it was she who conducted Culpepper to the queen's chamber at Lincoln, where they 'were there together alone, from eleven of the clock at night, till four of the clock in the morning', something which suggests that Jane may have withdrawn to a side room during the meeting. It seems highly improbable that Catherine embarked on her affair only at Jane's urging and, more likely, it was Catherine who urged her kinswoman to secure a meeting.

Once involved, Jane relished her role in assisting the lovers, on one occasion allowing the pair to make use of her own chamber at York.[16] Catherine and Jane were both fully aware of the danger that they were in if they were discovered, with the queen later claiming that she said to Jane, 'Alas madam this will be spied one day and then we be all undone,' to which Jane replied, 'Fear not madam let me alone I warrant you.' Jane was present at most of the couple's meetings, although she would often 'sit somewhat far off or turn her back'.[17] Given the late-night nature of the trysts, she also on occasion fell asleep. She would also sometimes remain in the bedchamber that she shared with the queen while Catherine met with Culpepper in a private place.[18] That Jane was a very active participant in Catherine Howard's treason is clear from the fact that, during the progress, she would take it upon herself to search out the back doors in every house they stayed in, ensuring that Culpepper was able to visit the queen in secret.[19] When they came to Greenwich, she was able to assure her mistress that 'she knew an old kitchen wherein she might well speak with him'.

The end of Catherine's queenship came swiftly and brutally. That autumn, Archbishop Cranmer was approached by a young gentleman named John Lassells who informed him that his sister,

Mary Hall, had been raised with Catherine in the household of the Dowager Duchess of Norfolk and had reported to him that the queen had been 'light of living' and had had sexual relationships with two young men in the household, Henry Manox and Francis Dereham.[20] Cranmer was shocked by what he heard and, on 2 November, handed a letter containing the allegations to the king. Henry was still besotted with his pretty young wife and refused to believe them, instead ordering an investigation in order to clear his bride's name. To his horror, he found that Lassells's claims were true and, devastated, the ageing king burst into tears, demanding a sword to slay his wife himself.

Catherine had been entirely oblivious to all that was happening and she was therefore horrified when, on 4 November, guards burst into her chamber at Hampton Court while she was practising her dance steps. As the musicians fell silent, the stunned queen was told that 'it is no more time to dance'. Both Catherine and Jane must have been terrified, and it was with relief that they greeted the news that only the queen's past life was the subject of the investigations.

Jane is likely to have been aware that Catherine Howard was not the innocent young virgin that Henry VIII had thought he had married, something which became all too evident when the court returned from the northern progress. The Dowager Duchess of Norfolk's household at Horsham had been home to a number of young girls and Catherine mixed with both gentlewomen, such as herself, and servants, sharing a dormitory room with the other unmarried women. Although Catherine received little formal education, her step-grandmother arranged for a neighbour, Henry Manox, to teach her to play the virginals. Manox was far beneath her socially but he seduced the young girl and, according to his later testimony, the couple fell in love with each other. The duchess found them alone together one day and, after beating Catherine, ordered them to separate. The relationship was never consummated but Catherine herself later admitted that 'at the flattering and fair persuasions of Manox being but a young girl suffered him at sundry times to handle and touch the secret parts of my body which neither became me with honesty to permit nor him to require'. Manox was dismissed when the duchess caught him and Catherine alone in her chapel chamber. Probably hoping to marry Catherine, he followed the household when it moved to Lambeth.

Catherine lost interest in Manox at Lambeth when she met a young kinsman of hers, Francis Dereham. Although not of equal status to Catherine, Dereham was higher born than the lowly Manox. He was also young and handsome and a particular favourite of Catherine's step-grandmother. Many of the girls in the duchess's household had lovers and, while the maidens' dormitory was locked at night, the key was easily stolen. The young men of the household were then free to come and go as they entertained their lovers with picnics before sleeping with the girls. Catherine had been very young at the time of her flirtation with Manox, but when she met Dereham she was ready for a full affair. She later admitted that

Francis Dereham by many persuasions procured me to his vicious purpose and obtained first to lie upon my bed with his doublet and hose and after within the bed and finally he lay with me naked and used me in such sort as a man doth his wife many and sundry times but how often I know not and our company ended almost a year before the King's majesty was married to my lady Anne of Cleve and continued not past one quarter of a year or little above.

Catherine and Dereham's relationship was consummated and Dereham later claimed that the pair became engaged, although Catherine, aware of her higher status, denied this. The couple referred to each other as husband and wife and exchanged love tokens, with Dereham lending Catherine the substantial sum of £100.

There was little privacy in the duchess's household and the affair was soon common knowledge. Henry Manox was jealous of the new relationship and wrote to Catherine's step-grandmother setting out the details of the affair. Rather than passing it directly to the duchess, Manox left it on her pew in her chapel where Catherine found it and showed it to Dereham. The precaution of destroying the letter was perhaps not necessary as the duchess already knew of the relationship. According to Katherine Tylney, one of the girls in the household, the duchess once 'found Dereham embracing Mrs Katherine Howard in his arms and kissing her, and thereat was much offended and gave Dereham a blow, and also beat the queen [Catherine] and gave Joan Bowmar a blow because she was present. When Dereham was wanted the duchess would say, "I warrant you if you seek him in Katherine Howard's chamber you shall find him there."' Under interrogation, Catherine signed a confession, admitting to her past and that she had, indeed, had lovers before her marriage to the king.[21]

Catherine's conduct had been immodest, but it was hardly treason since she admitted that her relationship with Dereham had finished nearly a year before the king married Anne of Cleves and had only, in any event, lasted for around three months. She and Jane may therefore have hoped that nothing worse would be discovered. For Jane, the danger that she was in may only have become clear on 13 November 1542 when Sir Thomas Wriothesley, the king's secretary, came to Hampton Court.[22] He immediately set about calling Catherine's ladies, gentlewomen and servants to him in the great chamber. Jane, whose name had not by then been linked to the enquiry, was among the group who met to hear of 'certain offences that she [Catherine] had done in misusing her body afore the king's time'. He then discharged the queen's household and, the next day, Catherine was taken as a prisoner to Syon Abbey while the king decided what to do with her. She was still technically queen, but not accorded the honours associated with the role. Instead, Catherine was permitted only four gentlewomen and two chamberers to attend her, while she was allowed only six French hoods with gold trim but no jewels. Before her name had been mentioned in the enquiry, Jane remained with the queen, with the pair finding time to speak candidly to each other. Jane, terrified, advised Catherine to say nothing of Culpepper, reminding her that her interrogators 'would speak fair to you and use all ways with you but and if you confess you undo both yourself and others'.[23] To hammer home her point, Jane declared that 'I will never confess it to be torn with wild horses'.

Although in her confession Catherine swore that after her marriage she 'intended ever during my life to be faithful and true unto your majesty after', it soon became apparent to those carrying out the investigations that this was not the case, with Culpepper's name soon being mentioned in the enquiry. Catherine always denied that she had actually consummated her relationship with Culpepper, but the evidence certainly suggests that the meetings between the pair were not innocent. Jane herself, in her own deposition, stated that she believed that the couple had sexual relations.[24] The suspicion of adultery was very different to Catherine's pre-marital activity and both Culpepper and Jane were quickly apprehended. Given the fact of Anne and George, Jane can have been in no doubt as to what her likely fate was to be.

Jane already had a certain notoriety as 'the widow of that nobleman who was capitally punished, as you know, for incest with his sister, Queen Anne'.[25] Damned by association, it was easy for her contemporaries to believe in her guilt. When word reached Chapuys, on 19 November, that she had been the 'intermediary agent for such love appointments', he also referred to George's earlier fate in his despatch.[26] It has been suggested that she suffered some kind of nervous breakdown while in prison.[27] According to Chapuys, she lost her reason on the third day of her imprisonment, something that meant that she was not fit to be tried with Culpepper and Dereham early in December as expected.[28] Jane well remembered what had happened to her husband and his sister after they were imprisoned and she must have been terrified. It would have been no consolation to her that the king sent his own doctors to her every day in a bid to ensure that she recovered her reason: this attention was not due to any pity that Henry felt for her. Instead, he wanted to ensure that she had sufficient reason to allow him to try and, in all probability, execute her. Evidently her sanity was still in doubt as, in February, he had Parliament pass an Act that stated that, since it was difficult to tell the difference between real and feigned madness, in cases of treason, the accused could be tried and condemned whether mad or not.[29] There can be no doubt that this was aimed at Jane. It may be that her lack of sanity was rather questionable anyway, particularly as she had lucid intervals.[30] The Act itself noted that madness could be feigned and Chapuys recorded that Jane recovered her reason at 'the very moment' she was told that she was to die.[31] Given that this 'recovery' was made as soon as it became apparent that the king meant to execute her regardless of her state of health, it does seem highly likely that her condition was feigned. She certainly appeared sane enough to bystanders on the scaffold.

At his trial, Culpepper maintained that it was Catherine, through Jane, who had made all the advances and that he had merely bowed to royal pressure to meet with the queen, who had assured him that she 'pined for him, and was actually dying of love for his person'.[32] Trying to shift the blame to Catherine did not save him. Culpepper and Dereham died together at Tyburn on 10 December 1541, for their offences with the queen. Later that month Catherine's uncle, Lord William Howard and his wife, along with Catherine's friend, Katherine Tylney, and others were tried and convicted of assisting her in relation to her affair with Dereham.[33] Catherine's step-grandmother, the aged Dowager Duchess of Norfolk, was sent to the Tower at the same time.[34] Jane and Catherine, in their separate prisons, must have known that it was only a matter of time before their own fates were decided.

Parliament opened on 15 January 1542 to consider the matter of the queen. Although Catherine still had hopes of her life, it was considered ominous that she was still at Syon Abbey, with an increased guard.[35] Unlike her husband and sister-in-law nearly six years before, Jane was not given even the show of a trial, instead being condemned by Parliament in the same Act of Attainder as the queen. It is clear, from its wording, that Henry was as furious with Jane as he was with Catherine, with the Act declaring that

> it may be enacted that the said Queen Katherine and Jane Lady Rochford for their said abominable and detestable treasons by them and every of them most abominably and traitorously committed and done against your majesty and this your realm shall be by the authority of this present parliament convicted and attainted of High Treason; and that ... they ... shall have and suffer pains of death, loss of goods, chattels, debts, farms, and all other things as in cases of high treason by the laws of this your realm hath been accustomed granted and given to the Crown.[36]

Jane was taken to the Tower on 9 February, with the queen following the next day.[37] Catherine, as Anne Boleyn had been before her, was terrified, with it recorded that she 'weeps, cries and torments herself miserably, without ceasing'.[38] There were rumours that this would delay the executions in order 'to give her leisure to recover' as had earlier been afforded to Jane. This speculation was unfounded, and, for both, time had nearly run out. On the evening of 12 February, both women were told that they would die the next day. On hearing that she was soon to die, Catherine composed herself and asked for the block to be brought to her so that she could practice for the morning. Jane's activity is not recorded but her last night alive cannot have been a joyful one.

At around nine o'clock in the morning on 13 February Jane and Catherine stepped out of the Tower together, making a short walk over to Tower Green where a scaffold had been erected. As they walked, they would have been aware that the king's whole council, as well as other invited guests, had assembled to watch them die.[39] As the superior in rank, Catherine was to die first, stepping up onto the scaffold to be beheaded by an axe. Her body was then covered with a black cloth and carried by her ladies to one side, to make space for Jane at the block.[40] It was then Jane's turn and she, like her mistress, was despatched quickly.

There is some dispute over the words spoken by Catherine and Jane on the scaffold. Their contemporary, Edward Hall, merely recorded that they 'confessed their offences, and died repentant'.[41] The French ambassador, on the other hand, recorded that 'the queen was so weak that she could hardly speak, but confessed that she had merited a hundred deaths for so offending the king who had so graciously treated her. The Lady of Rochefort said as much in a long discourse of several faults which she had committed in her life.'[42] Chapuys recorded that 'neither the queen nor Madam de Rochefort spoke much on the scaffold; all they did was to confess their guilt and pray for the king's welfare and prosperity'.[43] Another account, written by Otwell Johnson, a London merchant who witnessed the two women die, claimed that both made Christian ends, and,

uttering their lively faith in the blood of Christ only, with wonderful patience and constancy to the death, & with goodly words and steady countenance they desired all Chritsian people, to take regard unto their worthy and just punishment with death for their offences, against God heinously from their youth upwards, in breaking of his commandment, and also against the king's royal majesty, very dangerously: wherefore they being justly condemned (as they said) by the laws of the realm and parliament, to die, required the people (I say) to take example of them, for amendment of their ungodly lives, and gladly to obey the king in all things, for whose preservation they did heartily pray, and willed all people so to do commending their souls to god, & earnestly calling for mercy upon him.[44]

Given that Catherine was believed to have said little on the scaffold, much of the speech recorded above by Johnson was probably made by Jane. She therefore died a good death by the conventions of the day, appearing remorseful and contrite on the scaffold and admitting that she had sinned.

In death, Jane Parker Boleyn, the last true Boleyn woman to be resident at court, was laid in a humble grave near her husband, George Boleyn, and her sister-in-law, Anne Boleyn, in the chapel in the Tower. Although she was the last notable Boleyn woman, Boleyn daughters continued to be prominent. The most famous of them all, Anne Boleyn's daughter, Princess Elizabeth, was finally welcomed back into the royal family shortly after Jane's death.

14

BOLEYN DAUGHTERS

Following the execution of Lady Rochford, there were no Boleyn women at court. While some of Queen Anne Boleyn's aunts, as well as the daughters of Sir Edward Boleyn, remained living, the Boleyn line that had sprung from Geoffrey Boleyn of Salle at the beginning of the fifteenth century was all but extinct, with the last remaining male-line descendant, Sir James Boleyn, dying in 1561. This was not quite the end of the story and, while not strictly speaking 'Boleyn women' themselves, the daughters of Boleyn women still continued to have a major impact in England for decades after the fall of Queen Anne Boleyn and her family.

Mary Boleyn's daughter, who may have been the child of Henry VIII, reached maturity in the late 1530s. Catherine Carey's whereabouts during her childhood are unknown. Her aunt, Anne Boleyn, took the wardship of her brother, Henry, following their father's death. It has been suggested that Anne placed Henry with her daughter, Princess Elizabeth, after her birth in 1533, something that is indeed possible.[1] Certainly, Elizabeth later created her cousin Baron Hunsdon, the name of one of her childhood residences, and he also married the granddaughter of Lady Herbert of Troy, who was lady mistress of her household between 1537 and 1546. Elizabeth's household accounts survive for the period between

October 1551 and September 1552 and include evidence of her continuing relationship with Henry Carey. In December 1551, for example, she paid 40 shillings 'at the christening of Mr Carey's child', something that suggests that she was godmother.[2] She later paid 20 shillings to Henry himself as a reward for some service.[3] Finally, in April 1552 she received a visit at Hatfield from a Mrs Carey, who can probably be identified as Henry Carey's wife.[4] That this visit was a social call can be seen from the payment made on the same day that Mrs Carey left for some boys who played music to the princess and, presumably, also her guest.

If Henry was indeed placed with Elizabeth then it is possible that Catherine was also raised with her younger cousin. Until her banishment from court in 1534, Mary Boleyn had duties that would have kept her regularly at court. In addition to this, a position with Princess Elizabeth would have been a desirable one for her daughter, something that may well have persuaded Catherine's mother to allow her to live with her niece. Catherine and Elizabeth were very close in later life. For example, a letter from Elizabeth to her cousin survives dating to the 1550s when Catherine was preparing to leave England. The letter is one of the most affectionate that Elizabeth would write, testifying to the close relationship between the pair:

> Relieve your sorrow for your far journey with joy of your short return, and think this pilgrimage rather a proof of your friends, than a leaving of your country. The length of time, and distance of place, separates not the love of friends, nor deprives not the show of good-will. An old saying, when bale is lowest boot is nearest: when your need shall be most you shall find my friendship greatest. Let others promise, and I will do, in words not more, in deeds as much. My power but small, my love as great as them whose gifts may tell their friendship's tale, let will supply all other want, and

oft sending take the lieu of often sights. Your messengers shall not return empty, nor yet your desires unaccomplished. Lethe's flood hath here no course, goof memory hath greatest stream. And to conclude, a word that hardly I can say, I am driven by need to write, farewell, it is which in the sense one way I wish, the other way I grieve.

Your loving cousin and ready friend, Cor Rotto [i.e. Broken Heart][5]

That Elizabeth wrote of her grief and referred to herself as 'Broken Heart' at a parting from Catherine suggests that the two were close and used to spending time together, which testifies to a relationship likely to have developed in childhood and due to their shared Boleyn kinship. There is also very considerable evidence for their close relationship from the facts of their lives. Legend states that Catherine attended her aunt, Queen Anne Boleyn, for some of her time in the Tower, which would have further endeared her to Anne's daughter. Elizabeth was kind to her Boleyn and Howard kin, with her accounts from the early 1550s making it clear that she was in contact with her great-uncle, Edward Boleyn, for example.[6]

A portrait of Catherine depicting her in the later stages of pregnancy and dating to 1562, when she was thirty-eight, shows that, even in maturity, she was a pleasing-looking woman with auburn hair and the pointed features characteristic of many of the Boleyn women. Facially she resembles Elizabeth I, her cousin and, possibly, also her half-sister. Although her gown in the picture is black, something that hints at her staunchly Protestant beliefs, her inner gown is silver, with furs and gold embroidery adorning her clothing. Clearly, like her cousin the queen, she was not so pious that she was prepared to always wear the drab clothes for which Elizabeth had been so praised during her half-brother's reign. A second depiction of Catherine, from a memorial placed in Rotherfield Greys church by her son, shows a woman of very similar appearance although more austerely dressed. Clearly Catherine cared about her appearance and was considered good-looking by her peers. She married young, at the age of only around fifteen or sixteen, a few months after being appointed as a maid of honour in November 1539 in anticipation of the arrival of Anne of Cleves.

Catherine's husband, Francis Knollys, was the heir to an old family who could trace their descent back to Sir Robert Knollys, a soldier during the reign of Edward III.[7] Francis's father, another Sir Robert, was a gentleman of the Privy Chamber to Henry VIII, receiving a lease of the manor of Rotherfield Greys in Oxfordshire from the king, which became the family's principal seat. He had earlier served Prince Arthur.[8] Sir Robert Knollys married Lettice Peniston and Francis was their eldest surviving son, being born in 1514. Francis's first public office was in 1534 when he sat in parliament. He was also one of the gentlemen chosen to welcome Anne of Cleves to England, something which would have facilitated a first meeting with Catherine. Francis proved a reliable royal servant to Henry VIII, for example providing troops for a royal army to be sent to the Netherlands in 1543.[9] He served the king as a gentleman pensioner, as well as holding office under Edward VI. Ideologically, Francis was suited to government under Henry VIII's son, serving as Edward VI's master of horse and taking part in the jousts held to celebrate the young king's Coronation in 1547. He and Catherine resided at Rotherfield Greys after their marriage, which was settled on them jointly by Act of Parliament shortly after their marriage.[10]

It seems likely that Catherine and Francis met at court and, given the very close relationship that they established after their marriage, the suspicion must be that they made a love match. A letter survives from Francis to Catherine, written towards the end of her life, in which he addressed her as 'his loving wife'.[11] Sir

Francis's Latin dictionary also survives, into which were inserted the names and dates of birth of twelve of the couple's children.[12] The births, which ranged from Easter 1541 until May 1562, indicate that the couple must have been frequently together, with only eight years without a recorded birth. It is also possible that two daughters were not recorded in the dictionary, perhaps due to them being stillbirths and not something that their grieving father chose to recall. While the dictionary lists eight sons and six daughters, a memorial plaque in Westminster Abbey which was in place before 1600 states that Catherine bore eight sons and eight daughters, something which is likely to be correct given that Francis died in 1596.[13]

Clearly the marriage was very regularly consummated and most of Catherine's time during her first twenty years of marriage was taken up with childbearing and childrearing, with Catherine paying particular care to the education of her six daughters, Mary, Lettice, Maud, Elizabeth, Anne and Catherine. Catherine probably played a decisive role in naming these daughters. While the second, Lettice, was named for Francis's mother, the first, Mary, was named for Mary Boleyn. Elizabeth may have been chosen for Catherine's royal cousin, with Anne perhaps for her executed aunt. Clearly the Boleyn women were still remembered and of importance to Catherine Carey. The couple were blessed in the health of their children. Only the youngest, Dudley, is known to have died in infancy, surviving only between 9 May and June 1562. Their daughters Mary and Maud are nowhere recorded as adults but, given that they are depicted as adults on the family memorial in Rotherfield Greys church while Dudley is an infant, it would seem likely that they survived to adulthood, albeit remaining unmarried. As set out above, the couple may also have lost two further daughters but, even if this is the case, the loss of only three infants out of sixteen was a remarkable achievement. The love between the couple is also suggested by the fact that, although he outlived her by nearly thirty years, Francis never remarried, remaining a prominent government servant until the end.

While Catherine Carey was first settling down as a wife and mother, her cousin, Princess Elizabeth, also began to take her first steps towards adult life, finally returning to a more acknowledged place within the royal family. On 12 July 1543 the nine-year-old princess was present at the wedding of her father to his sixth bride, Catherine Parr, who was a friend and near contemporary of Princess Mary.[14] Catherine, who had been twice widowed before her marriage to the king, was an experienced stepmother and quickly took the two youngest royal children under her wing, as well as continuing her friendship with her adult stepdaughter. The king and queen kept all three royal children with them in the summer following their wedding, with the Regent of the Netherlands asking in December 1543 whether the five 'continued still in one household'.[15] The answer was unfortunately no, as Elizabeth had displeased her father in some way and been banished from court by the end of the year. That this exile was not permanent was down to the good offices of her stepmother, who continued to speak on her behalf and was able to persuade Henry to allow her to return when he went on campaign in France the following summer.

By the summer of 1544, Elizabeth had grown into a very promising child, as her half-sister, Mary, had predicted. A letter written by the princess to her stepmother survives from that July, demonstrating the girl's erudition and her desire for approval from the woman who was to take the place of her own mother:

Inimical fortune, envious of all good and ever resolving human affairs, has deprived me for a whole year of your most illustrious presence, and not thus content, has yet again robbed me of the same good, which thing would be intolerable to me, did I not hope to enjoy it very soon. And in my exile, I well know that the clemency of your highness has had as much care and solicitude for my health as the king's majesty himself. By which thing I am not only bound to serve you, but also to revere you with filial love, since I understand that your most illustrious highness has not forgotten me every time you have written to the king's majesty, which, indeed, it was my duty to have requested from you. For heretofore I have not dared to write to him. Wherefore I now humbly pray your most excellent highness, that, when you write to is majesty, you will condescend to recommend me to him, praying ever for his sweet benediction, and similarly entreating our Lord God to send him best success, and the obtaining of victory over his enemies, so that your highness and I may, as soon as possible, rejoice together with him on his happy return. No less pray I God, that he would preserve your most illustrious highness, to whose grace, humbly kissing your hands, I offer and recommend myself.[16]

Elizabeth signed her letter 'your most obedient daughter, and most faithful servant, Elizabeth' and it is clear that she already held her stepmother in affection. She spent the summer with Catherine at court. Elizabeth could not, in any event, have been entirely out of favour with her father. In February 1544 Parliament passed the third Act of Succession, on Henry's instructions, which bequeathed the crown first to his son, Prince Edward, and then to any child born to Catherine Parr or a subsequent wife.[17] In default of any such issue, the crown was to pass instead first to Princess Mary and then to Princess Elizabeth, both of whom remained legally illegitimate. Soon afterwards, Henry also commissioned a great painting in which he sat centrally flanked by his third wife, Jane Seymour, and their son, Edward. Standing some distance away but very much included in the picture were the king's two daughters, demonstrating that both Elizabeth and her elder half-sister were once again part of the royal family. The king remained firm to this change of heart for the rest of his life, reiterating the new order of succession in his will, as well as leaving both his daughters wealthy with substantial marriage portions. Elizabeth continued to flourish under the care of her royal stepmother and, with the death of Henry VIII in January 1547, joined the queen's establishment at Chelsea permanently.

The queen dowager had intended to marry Jane Seymour's brother, Thomas Seymour, before the king had first declared an interest in her back in 1543 and, with her husband's death, the two quickly renewed their relationship.[18] Seymour was consumed by a deep hatred for his elder brother, Edward Seymour, who had become Edward VI's protector and had been created Duke of Somerset. He was determined to obtain a royal bride, although it does not appear that his choice first fell on his former love. Within weeks of Henry VIII's death there were rumours that he intended to marry Princess Mary, with the Imperial ambassador going so far as to raise the matter with the princess.[19] Elizabeth's elder half-sister certainly had no intention of marrying an English commoner, laughing when the rumours were mentioned and declaring that 'she had never spoken to him in her life, and had only seen him once'. The king himself wanted his uncle to marry his former stepmother, Anne of Cleves, who was an expensive burden on the government.[20] Thomas Seymour never countenanced marrying Anne of Cleves and there is little evidence that he truly looked upon Princess Mary. There is, however, a suggestion that he was interested in taking Elizabeth as his bride.

Two letters exist which imply that Thomas Seymour showed an interest in marriage to Elizabeth. Both letters are highly debatable as they survive only as Italian copies in a seventeenth-century work. It is indeed possible that they are genuine but, without the originals, they must be treated with caution. According to the first letter, supposedly written by Seymour on 25 February 1547 and addressed to the princess,

I have so much respect for you my Princess, that I dare not tell you of the fire which consumes me, and the impatience with which I yearn to show you my devotion. If it is my good fortune to inspire in you feelings of kindness, and you will consent to a marriage you may assure yourself of having made the happiness of a man who will adore you till death.[21]

Elizabeth's response stated,

The letter you have written to me is the most obliging, and at the same time the most eloquent in the world. And as I do not feel myself competent to reply to so many courteous expressions, I shall content myself with unfolding to you, in few words, my real sentiments. I confess to you that your letter, all elegant as it is has very much surprised me; for, besides that neither my age nor my inclination allows me to think of marriage, I never would have believed that any one would have spoken to me of nuptials, at a time when I ought to think of nothing but sorrow for the death of my father. And to him I owe so much, that I must have two years at least to mourn his loss. And how can I make up my mind to become a wife before I shall have enjoyed some years my virgin state, and arrived at years of discretion?[22]

The letter ends saying that 'though I decline the happiness of becoming your wife, I shall never cease to interest myself in all that can crown your merit with glory, and shall ever feel the greatest pleasure in being your servant, and good friend'.

In spite of the doubts over the letters, there is strong evidence that Seymour did at least make enquiries into the possibility of a marriage with Anne Boleyn's daughter. On 17 January 1549 the Privy Council reported of Seymour that 'notwithstanding the good advice given to the contrary as well by the said lord protector as others his friends of the Council, practised to have in marriage the Lady Elizabeth, one of his Majesty's sisters and the second inheritor after his Majesty to the crown'.[23] One of the charges later laid against Seymour was that in the early months of 1547 he had sought to marry Elizabeth and that he had resurrected these attempts after Catherine Parr's death 'by secret and crafty means'.[24] Elizabeth's governess also later referred to Seymour as her 'old suitor'. Whether the thirteen-year-old princess had any involvement or knowledge in Seymour's machinations is unclear. In any event, when it became evident that the council would never sanction a marriage between Seymour and the princess he turned his attentions back to Catherine, with the pair marrying in secret within a few months of Henry VIII's death.

With Catherine Parr's marriage, Thomas Seymour effectively became Elizabeth's stepfather and joined her stepmother's household. Although he had been frustrated in his attempts to marry her, he was still interested in his young charge, who in the autumn of 1547 reached the age of fourteen, which was generally considered to be the earliest age for a girl to consummate a marriage in the sixteenth century. The first evidence of an attraction between Elizabeth and Seymour appeared innocent enough to the members of Catherine Parr's household.[25]

The queen dowager loved dancing, often employing musicians to entertain her household. According to Elizabeth's governess, Katherine Ashley, the princess would often choose Seymour as her partner and then 'laugh and pale at it' with embarrassment. Alternatively, she would shyly choose her stepfather before she 'chased him away', too embarrassed to actually step out and dance with him. For Seymour, this was probably the first indication that his wife's young charge was attracted to him and he took full advantage of the situation. Shortly after his marriage he began coming into Elizabeth's bedchamber early in the morning, often before she was even out of bed, 'and if she were up, he would bid her good morrow, and ask how she did, and strike her upon the back or on the buttocks familiarly'. Worse was to happen if the princess was still in bed, with Seymour throwing open the curtains and attempting to step into the bed himself, as Elizabeth shrank back under the covers away from him. It was only when he actually attempted to kiss the girl while she lay in her bed that her governess chased him away, leaving the princess, who appears to have had a crush on her dashing guardian, giggling in her bed. Catherine Parr chose to ignore much of what was happening, but she was not ignorant of her husband's actions. It is significant that, when the household moved to Hanworth, Catherine took to joining him on his morning romps, although she took no part in actually curtailing Seymour's behaviour, merely chaperoning him. On two occasions, the queen and her husband tickled Elizabeth as she lay in her bed. On another occasion, in the gardens, Seymour cut Elizabeth's black dress to shreds while the queen held her still, laughing.

The involvement of his wife in the romps seems only to emboldened Seymour. When the household returned to Chelsea, later in 1547, he renewed his morning visits to Elizabeth's bedchamber, with the young girl often jumping out of bed and hiding when she heard the door being unlocked. The fact that Seymour had a key to Elizabeth's bedroom was, in itself, a lapse in propriety on the part of the queen and does suggest that she was completely under the thrall of her husband and unable to see that the slight young girl that she had originally taken under her wing was growing into a woman. When the family moved to Seymour Place in London the visits continued, with Seymour visiting Elizabeth in the morning 'in his night-gown, barelegged in his slippers'. By this time, Elizabeth was anxious about her reputation and would ensure that she was always up and reading, leaving Seymour to go away disappointed.

Elizabeth was right to be concerned about her reputation. From a modern viewpoint, Seymour's conduct with a fourteen-year-old under his care would be considered to be child abuse but this was not how it was viewed by contemporaries, particularly those that remembered Elizabeth's mother and the blackening of her name at her arrest. One contemporary, for example, the hostile Jane Dormer, who was a friend of Princess Mary, recalled to her biographer one of the stories that was current at the time of the Seymour affair. According to Dormer's recollections of Elizabeth,

a great lady, who knew her very well, being a girl of twelve or thirteen, told me that she was proud and disdainful, and related to me some particulars of her scornful behaviour, which much blemished the handsomeness and beauty of her person. In King Edward's time what passed between the Lord Admiral, Sir Thomas Seymour, and her Dr Latimer preached in a sermon, and was a chief cause that the Parliament condemned the Admiral. There was a bruit of a child born and miserably destroyed, but could not be discovered whose it was; only the report of the midwife, who was brought from her house blindfold thither, and so returned, saw nothing in the house while she was there, but candle light; only she said, it was the child of a very fair young lady. There was a muttering of the Admiral and this lady, who was between fifteen and sixteen years of age.[26]

Rumours that Elizabeth bore Seymour a child persisted, and even in the nineteenth century, one writer was able to report with certainty that such a child existed and that Elizabeth was largely to blame for all that happened.[27] It is certain that Elizabeth had feelings for Seymour, but there is no evidence of a sexual relationship. If anything, there was little that Elizabeth could do to avoid her stepmother's husband, with both her governess and the queen encouraging Seymour in his outrageous behaviour. Katherine Ashley later admitted that she had spoken to Seymour in the park at St James's Palace, commenting, 'I have heard ever said that he should have married my lady.' To her credit, Ashley did seek to turn Seymour away from the princess's bedchamber, speaking 'ugly' words to him and eventually complaining to Catherine Parr. The queen again made a 'small matter of it', but even she was growing worried. Finally, early in 1548, Catherine complained to Mistress Ashley that Seymour had informed her that he had 'looked in at the gallery window, and seen my lady Elizabeth cast her arms about a man's neck'. Elizabeth, weeping, denied this charge and Ashley believed her, considering that the accusation had been invented by the jealous queen in order to ensure that the governess would watch her charge more closely. When, in May 1548, Catherine herself caught the pair embracing, Elizabeth was sent away. She never saw the woman who had been a mother to her again, with Catherine dying in childbirth later that year.

For Elizabeth, the loss of her stepmother must have been devastating. In her delirium as she lay dying, Catherine complained that 'I am not well handled, for those that be about me care not for me, but stand laughing at my grief, and the more good I will to them the less good they will to me'. When Seymour attempted to soothe her, she accused him of giving her 'many shrewd taunts'.[28] Elizabeth, who is likely to have heard of Catherine's words from the queen's attendant, Lady Tyrwhit, would have known that they referred to her own relationship with Seymour. Quite apart from her grief at the queen's death, Elizabeth soon learned that it was dangerous to associate with Thomas Seymour. He had continued to plot against his brother following his marriage and, in January 1549 was arrested on suspicion of treason.[29] During the investigations Elizabeth was interrogated, with some of her servants sent to the Tower. She conducted herself well and revealed nothing, but her reputation was damaged. Seymour was executed on 20 March 1549. The incident terrified the princess who, at the age of only fifteen, found herself involved in treason and facing arrest as her mother had done. She spent the rest of her brother's reign conducting herself as a good Protestant maiden and wearing sober black.

Following the death of Edward VI in July 1553, Elizabeth played no role in the attempt to place Lady Jane Grey on the throne, instead riding to congratulate Mary I in London once she had safely attained the throne. Elizabeth had been removed from the succession by her half-brother in favour of Jane and her interests clearly lay with her childless half-sister who was, by then, in her late thirties. She was prominent at the festivities surrounding Mary's Coronation, riding with her former stepmother, Anne of Cleves, in the chariot after the queen's. While, politically, it was prudent for Elizabeth to ally herself with Mary, the relationship between the sisters was often fraught. Mary was determined to see her sister convert to Catholicism and Elizabeth, who favoured Protestantism, finally agreed to attend Mass. She attended Mass for the first time on 8 September 1553 but complained loudly throughout the service that her stomach hurt, disrupting the service and angering the queen. It was a relief to both women when Elizabeth finally left court in December 1553.

Mary I was unmarried when she came to the throne and soon accepted a proposal from her cousin, Philip of Spain. The news of the queen's marriage caused consternation in many parts of England, with a group of gentlemen, led by Sir Thomas Wyatt, who was the son of Anne Boleyn's former suitor, forming a conspiracy to place Elizabeth on the throne. On 25 January 1554, Wyatt rode into the marketplace in Maidstone and issued a proclamation, denouncing the queen's marriage. It was a call to arms that was heeded by many of the men of Kent and Wyatt's force swept towards London. Wyatt refused all of Mary's attempts to negotiate and, by 31 January, the queen had decided to take decisive action herself, going in person to the Guildhall in London to rally the population. Mary, who was so often overshadowed by her younger half-sister, made the speech of her life, declaring that her marriage to Philip was only arranged with the consent and approval of her council, before adding that it would, in any event, only be her second marriage, since

> I am already married to the Common Weal and the faithful members of the same; the spousal ring whereof I have on my finger: which never hitherto was, nor hereafter shall be, left off. Protesting unto you nothing to be more acceptable to my heart, nor more answerable to my will, than your advancement in wealth and welfare, with the furtherance of God's glory.[30]

With Mary's powerful words, spoken with her deep, mannish voice, the Londoners rallied and, when Wyatt reached Southwark on 3 February, he found the bridge defended against him. He spent the next two days trying to cross the Thames before marching his troops to Kingston and making his crossing at the bridge there. When Mary heard of Wyatt's crossing, she panicked and was unable to sleep. By the morning she had composed herself and, when urged to flee, she stood firm, declaring that her army and God would not abandon her.[31] She was right to be confident and Wyatt was quickly captured and his rebellion dispersed. Dangerously for Elizabeth, when Wyatt was tried for treason on 15 March 1554 he implicated her, turning the queen's suspicion firmly towards her half-sister.

The extent of Elizabeth's involvement is not clear but she almost certainly knew of plans for the uprising, perhaps intending to await the outcome of events. On 17 March, Elizabeth was informed that a barge was waiting to take her to the Tower. Terrified, she was determined to delay her departure, begging leave to write to the queen. Elizabeth wrote,

If any ever did try this old saying, that a king's word was more than another man's oath, I beseech your majesty to verify it in me, and to remember your last promise and my last demand that I be not condemned without answer and proof; which it seems now I am, for without cause proved I am by your council from you commanded to go to the Tower. I know I deserve it not, yet it appears proved. I protest before God I never practised, counselled or consented to anything prejudicial to you or dangerous to the state. Let me answer before you, before I go to the Tower (if possible) – if not, before I am further condemned. Pardon my boldness. I have heard of many cast away for want of coming to their prince. I heard Somerset say that if his brother [Thomas Seymour] had been allowed to speak with him, he would never have suffered, but he was persuaded he could not live safely if the admiral lived. I pray evil persuades not one sister against the other. Wyatt might write me a letter, but I never received any from him. As for the copy of my letter to the French king, God confound me if I ever sent him word, token or letter by any means. I crave but one word of answer.[32]

Elizabeth's letter did not change the queen's decision and she was taken by water to the Tower early the next morning. According to the *Chronicle of Queen Jane and Two Years of Queen Mary*, when she entered, Elizabeth declared, 'Oh Lord! I never thought to have come in here as prisoner; and I pray you all good friends and fellows, bear me witness, that I come in no traitor, but as true a woman to the queens majesty as any is now living, and thereon will I take my death.'[33] She went a little further into the Tower and, on seeing the guards, asked the Lord Chamberlain if they were for her. When he denied it, she said, 'I know it is so; it needed not for me, being, alas! but a weak woman.' Even in times of great stress, Elizabeth knew how to win the hearts of those around her. When she had entered the Tower, the Earl of Sussex, who was present, warned the gaolers not to treat her too harshly. For Elizabeth, the terror must have been very real and she cannot have failed to recall the fact that her mother had never left the ancient fortress once taken inside.

Elizabeth was not severely treated in the Tower, although she must have been terrified. She was interrogated, but did not incriminate herself. Wyatt, who was executed on 11 April, denied on the scaffold that Elizabeth was involved in the plot. Eventually, Mary and her council were forced to admit that there was little evidence against the princess and, in May 1554, she was moved from the Tower to Woodstock. Elizabeth spent a dull and uncomfortable year imprisoned there but, with her release from the Tower, she knew the danger had passed.

The queen believed that she had conceived a child following her marriage to Philip and, on 17 April 1555, Elizabeth received a summons to London to attend Mary in her confinement. She arrived at court on 30 April but her half-sister would not see her for several weeks. The queen was still furious with her half-sister who she, by this stage, entirely disliked. She was also preoccupied in awaiting the birth of her child, with midwives, rockers and nurses engaged to care for the expected prince. Sadly for Mary, her labour pains never began and, as the days turned into weeks, her physicians hastily began to recalculate the estimated due date for the baby. By late May Mary's stomach, which had swelled to give every appearance of pregnancy, had begun to decline. The queen was the last person to continue to believe in the existence of her child, but even she was finally forced to admit defeat. In early August the court abruptly left Hampton Court, something which was a tacit announcement of the failure of Mary's 'pregnancy'; it was probably a phantom pregnancy brought about by her desperate desire for a child. On 29 August Mary's grief was increased with the departure of her husband to Flanders. Her failure to produce a child that summer made Elizabeth's accession a virtual certainty and she returned to her estates, spending her time consolidating support.

Catherine Carey and her husband had troubles of their own following the accession of the Catholic Mary I to the throne. Sir Francis Knollys had staunchly reformist religious beliefs, which he expected his wife to share. This led to him having a particular prominence under the Protestant Edward VI, with Catherine's husband taking part in theological discussions with other dignitaries of the reign.[34] Both Catherine and Francis were dismayed at the accession of Edward's Catholic half-sister, Princess Mary. In the nineteenth century one historian, dating the letter from Princess Elizabeth to Catherine to 1553, considered that the couple were 'compelled to fly from the Marian persecution'.[35] However this would seem unlikely given that, at that stage, Mary was very far from deciding to persecute anyone, even going so far as to send Lady Jane Grey word that she had decided to save her life. There is evidence that Francis Knollys and his eldest son, Henry, visited John Calvin at Geneva late in 1553, when Calvin wrote that two English gentlemen had recently visited him.[36] Calvin was sufficiently pleased with his visitors to heap praise upon them, declaring that both were of good birth, with the son, in particular, meriting 'praise for piety and holy zeal'. It has been suggested, from this, that Francis, due to his wife's relationship with the heir to the throne, may have been chosen by Protestants at court to serve as an emissary to Calvin, particularly since he was certainly back in England in June 1555, something that does not suggest that he was persecuted by the English queen.[37]

In late 1556 he was once again abroad, at the University of Basle. He spent time in the English colony at Strasbourg during 1557, which was a centre of the religious reform movement.[38] The following year he was at Frankfurt, where it was recorded that he was staying in the house of John Welles in June with his wife, five of their children and a maid. His brother Henry was also present in the city, remaining there until early in 1559. The suggestion that Catherine travelled to the Continent with her husband in 1553 rests solely on a dating of Elizabeth's 'farewell' letter to that year, something which is highly debatable. An alternative is that Catherine joined Francis on the Continent later, remaining in England during his visit of 1553–54.[39] While she bore children regularly throughout her marriage, there was no recorded child born between Anne on 19 July 1555 and Thomas at Candlemas 1558. Given that the first reference to Catherine outside England was in June 1557, it does seem plausible that she had remained in England until shortly before that date, perhaps travelling directly to Frankfurt with her maid and some of her children. Since the majority of the children were left behind in England, including, apparently, their eldest son Henry after his first visit, it would appear that the family were under no great threat in England, instead simply choosing to live among their co-religionists. The John Welles with whom they stayed was a merchant from London and a burgher of Frankfurt who had first arrived in 1555 with his wife, sons and servants. As a substantial citizen he would have been able to give Catherine and her family a warm welcome.

Mary I fell ill in August 1558. In early November 1558, she was visited by her husband's ambassador, the Count of Feria, who found her dying.[40] Feria summoned the council and told them that King Philip favoured Elizabeth's succession to the throne. He found the councillors terrified of what Elizabeth would do to them and he resolved to visit her himself to assure her of Philip's support. Elizabeth received Feria but he did not find her as malleable as he had hoped. According to Feria,

> She is a very vain and clever woman. She must have been thoroughly schooled in the manner in which her father conducted his affairs, and I am very much afraid that she

will not be well-disposed in matters of religion, for I see her inclined to govern through men who are believed to be heretics and I am told that all the women around her definitely are.

Elizabeth was indignant at her treatment by Mary and in no mood to give any credit to Philip for helping her win the throne, declaring 'that it was the people who put her in her present position and she will not acknowledge that your majesty or the nobility of this realm had any part in it'. Feria noted that Elizabeth was determined to be ruled by no-one, least of all Philip. The despatch is the first indication of how Elizabeth intended to rule and it is a model which she followed throughout her reign.

On 13 November 1558 the forty-two-year-old queen was given the last rites. She rallied the next day, but it was obvious that her end was near. On 17 November, as her councillors flocked towards Elizabeth at Hatfield, Mary passed quietly away, with bonfires lit and bells rung in some parts of London to celebrate her passing. Catherine Carey and her husband also celebrated Mary's death, glad of the opportunity to return home. For Elizabeth, the effect of the news was even more profound, with a Boleyn woman, only six generations from a prosperous peasant at Salle, succeeding to the throne in her own right. As Elizabeth herself quoted, on hearing of her accession, 'It is the Lord's doing, and it is marvellous in our eyes.'

15

THE LAST BOLEYN WOMAN

Elizabeth was sitting under an oak tree in the grounds of Hatfield House on 17 November 1558 when the earls of Arundel and Pembroke arrived to inform her of her half-sister's death and that she was queen. This news can hardly have been unexpected for Elizabeth, who appeared unable to speak for a moment before giving praise to God. Shortly afterwards a breathless Sir Nicholas Throckmorton arrived bearing Mary's betrothal ring, which she would never willingly remove from her finger, as proof of her death. For Elizabeth and England it was the start of a long and largely prosperous reign. Volumes can be written on the life and reign of Anne Boleyn's daughter.

Elizabeth appointed her household while at Hatfield and set about business requiring her immediate attention. A few days later she set off for London and was met by crowds.[1] Since Catholics considered her to be illegitimate – and, following her accession, her Catholic cousin Mary, Queen of Scots, had been proclaimed Queen of England in France – it was necessary to arrange her Coronation as soon as practicable.[2] According to the historian William Camden, Elizabeth encountered some difficulties with this. Mary's Archbishop of Canterbury, Cardinal Pole, had recently died, and in any event would have been unlikely to have crowned Anne Boleyn's daughter given that he had spent much of his life in exile for opposing Elizabeth's parents' marriage and the changes to religion it had brought. Elizabeth was finally crowned on 15 January 1559 by the Bishop of Carlisle, the only bishop who could be found to crown her:

> For the Archbishop of York and the rest of the Bishops refused to perform the Office, out of a suspicion and jealous fear of the Romish Religion, which both her first breeding up in the Protestant religion had stricken them into, and also for that she had very lately forbidden the Bishop in saying Mass to lift up the Host to be adored, and permitted the litany, with Epistle and Gospel, to be read in the vulgar tongue; which they held for the most heinous sins.[3]

Ignoring this slight, Elizabeth was triumphant and showed her delight to the crowds that lined the route of her Coronation procession, laughing and speaking with those who wished her well.[4] Her cousin Catherine Carey and her husband, Sir Francis Knollys, were also able to be present to wish her well.

Catherine returned to England with her family shortly after Elizabeth's accession. The affection between the cousins was unaffected by their separation, with Elizabeth appointing Catherine as the chief lady of her Privy Chamber on 3 January 1559.[5] On 19 January Francis was appointed to the Privy Council, whose role was to advise the queen, as well as becoming Vice-Chamberlain of the Royal Household. That same month the queen also appointed Catherine's daughter, Lettice, as a gentlewoman of the Privy Chamber, while a younger daughter, Elizabeth, and Catherine's niece and namesake, another Catherine Carey, were made maids of the court.[6] Philadelphia, another daughter of Elizabeth's cousin Henry Carey, also received an appointment as a maid of the queen early in the reign.[7]

On her accession, Elizabeth's England was a Catholic country, something which she found unacceptable. While Elizabeth was no religious fanatic, she was committed to Protestantism, albeit seeking to create a Church that incorporated aspects of both Catholicism and Protestantism, something that would not have pleased the more staunch Sir Francis Knollys and, perhaps, also his wife. Francis's letters display the formality of a puritan; he commonly addressed his children by both their Christian names and surnames, even in letters to his wife, for example, referring to 'Henry Knollys' when discussing his eldest son with Catherine.[8] Elizabeth, on the other hand, was determined to tread a middle way, with her first parliament passing the Act of Supremacy on 29 April 1559, which confirmed the queen as the Supreme Governor of the Church of England.

Religion was not the only item of business in Elizabeth's first parliament. At the time of her accession she was twenty-five years old and unmarried. It was unheard of for a woman to rule alone and it was believed that she would quickly marry, as her sister had done, and, hopefully, settle the succession. In February 1559 Parliament presented the queen with a formal petition, requesting that she choose a husband. To this, Elizabeth responded with a long speech setting out that she had no inclination to marry and that she wished to remain a virgin. She ended this speech saying, 'Lastly, this may be sufficient, both for my memory and honour of my name, if when I have expired my last breath, this may be inscribed upon my tomb: Here lies interred Elizabeth, A virgin pure until her death.'[9] This speech caused very little comment simply because nobody believed it.

Elizabeth's reply to the petition of February 1559 was not, in fact, the first time that she had sworn never to marry. In 1558 she had turned down an offer of marriage from the Prince of Sweden, claiming that she wished to remain a virgin.[10] Throughout her lifetime, Elizabeth flirted with the idea of marriage: she was clearly a woman who liked male company. However, she never wavered in her refusal to marry. There are probably a number of reasons for this. In the sixteenth century, wives were subject to their husbands, a rule that applied even when one spouse was a reigning queen.[11] This was perhaps not the only reason for Elizabeth's refusal to commit herself to marriage. There were few examples of happy marriages in her immediate family, with her own mother, as well as her stepmother, Catherine Howard, being put to death by their husband, while Catherine Parr suffered at the hands of her last husband. In fact, the only really happy examples of marriage in Elizabeth's immediate family were those of her Carey cousins, with Catherine Carey's being the most obvious to her. Elizabeth was prepared to entertain proposals of marriage from foreign suitors when politically necessary, with her brother-in-law, Philip of Spain, proposing in January 1559, for example, something that he saw as his duty given the need to maintain the Catholic religion in his deceased wife's kingdom. Elizabeth was able to keep negotiations open until March 1559, by which time she had concluded a peace with France and Philip's continuing friendship was no longer crucial.

Soon after she rejected Philip, Elizabeth received a proposal from his cousin, the Archduke Ferdinand.[12] This match soon foundered, and Ferdinand's younger brother, the Archduke Charles, proposed marriage himself. Without an empire of his own to inherit, Charles proved considerably more enthusiastic about the English queen than his brother, with his name mentioned in negotiations for over seven years, until he too finally lost patience with Elizabeth.[13] Elizabeth always insisted that she could not marry a man that she had not seen. That this was a delaying tactic is clear from her alarm when she heard, in October 1559, that John of Finland had arrived in England to woo her. Elizabeth was always relieved when marriage negotiations failed, although she professed herself insulted when the Archduke Charles married another woman, after waiting for her for the best part of a decade. Elizabeth persisted with her courtships with foreign princes until well into her fifties.

It was not only foreign princes who sought Elizabeth's hand in marriage. She received proposals from several English candidates, including the elderly Earl of Arundel, who optimistically showered her with gifts.[14] No one but the earl himself took his candidacy seriously. The queen also did not countenance the wealthy Sir William Pickering, who was pleased to offer his hand.[15] Instead, her affection was mostly directed towards Robert Dudley, a close friend of her cousin, Catherine Carey, for whom Catherine's youngest child was named in 1562.[16]

Robert Dudley was almost exactly the same age as Elizabeth and she had known him since childhood. As the son of the Duke of Northumberland, he was a prisoner in the Tower while Elizabeth was there, and this served to forge a common bond between them. On her accession, the queen appointed Dudley as both her master of horse and a Knight of the Garter. Dudley was far from being universally popular and Elizabeth's preference for him mystified her contemporaries, with her biographer, William Camden, summing up the general confusion when he wrote that people asked 'whether this [favour] proceeded from any virtue of his, whereof he gave some shadowed tokens, or from their common conditions of imprisonment under Queen Mary, or from his Nativity, and the hidden consent of the stars at the hour of his birth, and thereby a most strait conjunction of their minds, a man cannot easily say'.[17] Dudley was tall and handsome and Elizabeth found him very attractive. He was not, however, a true suitor in the early years of her reign as he had, by 1558, been married for some years. This unavailability may have been part of his charm for Elizabeth, ensuring that here at least was one man who did not hope to persuade her to marry him. By early 1559 there were rumours that the queen and her handsome master of horse were lovers, something that was dangerous to a queen. Elizabeth's conduct towards Dudley only served to inflame the rumours, with foreign ambassadors openly courting him as a future king, in spite of his wife. Dudley is reputed to have asked the Spanish ambassador to assist him in persuading the queen to marry him, for example.[18]

Dudley's wife, Amy, was not encouraged to come to court by the jealous queen and she stayed with friends near Abingdon during her husband's long absences. On the morning of 8 September 1560, Amy, who was in ill health, insisted that all her servants visit a fair, leaving only her and two other women in the house. When everyone returned that evening, they were horrified to find Amy Dudley dead with a broken neck at the foot of a shallow flight of steps.

When news of Amy Dudley's death was brought to Elizabeth, she was so shocked that she was almost speechless. She immediately ordered Dudley to leave court while the death was investigated. Elizabeth knew that unless she fully investigated the circumstances of the death, both she and Dudley would be tainted with suspicion of murder. The enquiry returned a verdict of accidental death, holding that Amy had fallen down the stairs, but most people believed that Dudley arranged her murder. Amy Dudley's death has never been satisfactorily explained, but the evidence of her ladies and her own conduct points towards suicide. It has also been suggested that she may have suffered a spontaneous fracture due to breast cancer. Whatever the cause, the suspicion under which Dudley was held meant it was impossible for the queen to ever contemplate marrying him, even if she wished to.

Dudley was not Elizabeth's only favourite and she continued to attract male attention until the end of her life. She was never a beauty, but she knew how to make the most of herself and was considered pretty early in the reign, with one contemporary recording that

she was a lady, upon whom nature had bestowed, and well placed, many of her fairest favours; of stature mean, slender, straight, and amiably composed; of such state in her carriage, as ever motion of her seemed to bear majesty; her hair was inclined to pale yellow, her forehead large and fair, a seeming

set for princely grace; her eyes lively and sweet, but short-
sighted, her nose somewhat rising in the midst; the whole
compass of her countenance somewhat long, but yet of
admirable beauty.[19]

In her colouring, Elizabeth resembled her father, but facially she was
her mother's daughter. As she grew older she became acutely aware
of her fading appearance and took to wearing wigs and heavy make-
up in a bid to maintain the appearance of youth. She continued to
enjoy the fiction that her suitors were in love with her well into her
old age.

With her failure to marry, the English succession was uncertain
throughout Elizabeth's reign. Under the terms of Henry VIII's will,
in which he gave priority to the heirs of his younger sister, Mary,
over his eldest, Margaret, Catherine Grey, the younger sister of Lady
Jane Grey, was heir to the throne. Alternatively, by strict heredity,
Mary, Queen of Scots, the only child of Margaret Tudor's only son,
was heir. Since she was born outside of England, there were others
who considered that Mary's Catholic aunt, Lady Margaret Douglas,
who was Queen Margaret's younger, English-born child, should
be Elizabeth's successor. Still others, who sought a male candidate,
looked towards the Earl of Huntingdon, who was descended
from the Plantagenets. Elizabeth's lack of an heir was dangerously
demonstrated in October 1562 when, one evening, she felt unwell
and decided to have a bath.[20] It was soon clear that the queen was
suffering from smallpox and, after falling unconscious, she was
thought to be dying. In a brief moment of lucidity, she begged her
council to make Robert Dudley Protector of England, swearing that,
although she loved him, nothing improper had ever passed between
them. With no clear successor Elizabeth's council were divided, with
some seeking to send for Catherine Grey, who was currently in
disgrace for contracting a secret marriage, while others favoured the
Earl of Huntingdon.

The uncertainty over the succession was further complicated by the return of Mary, Queen of Scots, to Scotland in 1560 following the death of her husband, Francis II of France. Against Elizabeth's wishes, the Scottish queen took Henry, Lord Darnley as her second husband, a teenager who had a strong claim to the throne himself as the eldest son of Lady Margaret Douglas. The marriage proved to be a disaster, with events coming to a head on 9 March 1566 when Darnley accused Mary of having an affair with her secretary, David Rizzio. Darnley and his accomplices then stabbed Rizzio to death in Mary's presence. Mary did not take any action at first and, on 19 June 1566, bore a son whom she named James, news that Elizabeth reacted to in grief, declaring that while the Scottish queen was the mother of a son, she remained barren. The members of Elizabeth's court may have privately thought that it was within the queen's power to do something about this. Elizabeth was, however, soon justified in her wariness to marry. A few months after the birth of her son, Mary and the rest of Edinburgh were awoken by a large explosion. Upon investigation, the house in which Darnley was staying was discovered to have been blown up with gunpowder. Darnley was found in the orchard next to the house, strangled rather than killed by the explosion.

A few days after the murder, Elizabeth wrote to Mary expressing her condolences. Remembering the death of Amy Dudley, she also counselled Mary on how best to protect her reputation, telling her that she must be seen to avenge the murder:

> My ears have been so deafened and my understanding so grieved and my hear so affrighted to hear the dreadful news of the abominable murder of your mad husband and my killed cousin that I scarcely yet have the wits to write about it. And inasmuch as my nature compels me to take his death in the extreme, he being so close in blood, so it is that I will boldly tell you what I think of it. I cannot dissemble that I am

more sorrowful for you than for him. O madame, I would not do the office of faithful cousin or affectionate friend if I studied rather to please your ears than employed myself in preserving your honour. However, I will not at all dissemble what most people are talking about: which is that you will look through your fingers at the revenging of this deed, and that you do not take measures that touch those who have done as you wished, as if the thing had been entrusted in a way that the murderers felt assurance in ding it. Among the thoughts in my heart I beseech you to want no such thought to stick at this point.[21]

Elizabeth's letter contained good advice and genuinely seems to have been full of concern and empathy for her fellow monarch. Mary failed to heed her English cousin's words and, on 15 May 1567, she married the Earl of Bothwell, who was widely reputed to have been responsible for the murder.

Soon after her marriage, Mary was captured by rebel Scottish lords and imprisoned.[22] Elizabeth was furious about this treatment of a fellow queen and sent ambassadors to try to secure Mary's release. The Scottish lords were determined to remove Mary, and she was forced to abdicate in favour of her infant son, who was crowned as James VI of Scotland. Elizabeth refused to recognise the new king and raged at the Scottish lords, but she was not prepared to reinstate Mary by force. She was nonplussed when the Scottish queen, who had escaped from her imprisonment, arrived in England on 17 May 1568. Elizabeth promised her protection, but she refused to meet her while she was suspected of Darnley's murder.[23] Mary was immediately placed under house arrest, with Catherine Carey's husband, Sir Francis Knollys, despatched north to Carlisle to take custody of her, very much against his wishes. The Scottish queen was evidently an irksome burden, with Francis writing to Elizabeth's chief minister, William Cecil, on his arrival with Mary at Bolton that 'since her departure from Carlisle hither unto she hath been very quiet, very tractable, and void of displeasant countenance', something that suggests that this was not usually the case.[24] He also later wrote to Catherine to confess that 'I have been driven to many contentions' with the Queen of Scots, although he considered her bark worse than her bite, uttering the first thing that came to her mind and often later seeking to make amends 'in pleasant sort and manner'.[25] Elizabeth was always suspicious of her royal relatives. For her, part of the continuing attraction of her maternal family must always have been that they were no threat to her throne, unlike her paternal cousins. She was therefore loath to dispense with Francis's services in the North, with him writing plaintively to Catherine that 'I pray you help that I may be revoked and return again, for I have little to do here and I may be spared hence very well'.[26]

Elizabeth remained close to Catherine Carey and Francis Knollys, making use of their services at court. For example, in November 1566 she sent Francis with her answer to parliament when they petitioned her to marry.[27] The couple's daughter, Lettice, in particular flourished at court, marrying Walter Devereux, Viscount Hereford, who would later become the Earl of Essex, when she was aged around nineteen.[28] Lettice, who later married a second earl and survived into her nineties, was the most prominent member of the family until her brother, William, was created Earl of Banbury in 1626. As a result of this she was displayed prominently in ermine and a coronet on the family monument at Rotherfield Greys. Certainly, her mother would have been proud of the marriage her daughter made, although Devereux was not created earl until after his mother-in-law's death.

Catherine was careless in relation to her health, with her friend (and later son-in-law) Robert Dudley writing in August 1568 that 'I fear her diet and order'.[29] Only the month before, Francis had addressed a similar complaint to his wife, worrying that she 'do often forget to prevent sickness by due & precise order'. He felt that his presence was required to ensure that she did what the doctors commanded, declaring that 'I am very sorry to hear that you are fallen into a fever, I would to God I were so dispatched hence that I might only attend and care for your good recovery'.[30] It may be that Catherine was too taken up with her royal duties to take notice of her health, particularly since anyone who had successfully given birth to sixteen children must have been used to a robust constitution. Her husband stated in a letter written during one illness that 'I trust you shall shortly overcome this fever and recover good health again', suggesting usually strong health.[31] She had recovered from her July 1568 fever by the following month, implying that it was of no great consequence, with Robert Dudley writing in August to assure Francis that 'your wife is well again'.[32] It has been suggested that she was someone who refused to listen to medical advice, instead seeking her own remedies, something which suggests that she was as strong-willed as her mother and other Boleyn family members.

The separation of Catherine and Francis that his absence in the North necessitated deeply grieved the couple. A letter survives from Francis to his wife dated 30 December 1568 in which he worried again about her health, having received news from William Cecil that she was again unwell.[33] The relationship between Elizabeth and her favourite cousin had evidently been somewhat strained due to the queen's refusal to allow Francis to return, with Francis complaining to Catherine of 'her majesty's ungrateful denial of my coming to the court this Christmas', as well as her refusal to support the couple in a suit that they had. Francis was further concerned that there had been 'other misconstruings of me and mine' with the queen, something which again suggests that the couple and their royal kinswoman had quarrelled. That the source of this quarrel was their separation is clear from Francis's last letter to Catherine, when he confided 'that in my last letter to the queen's majesty I was about (aft that I had written somewhat plainly to her majesty in her own matters) to have written these words following; that as touching mine own particularity, among all my griefs of mind, it was is not the least to understand that my wife is ready to die in discomfort and in miserable state towards her children even in your majesty's court'. It was only a further letter from Cecil, stating that Catherine was beginning to recover, which stopped her husband writing to Elizabeth in such an accusatory tone. Francis was right to be concerned and he was never able to see his beloved wife again.

Catherine was deeply saddened by her separation from her husband, which did not help her health.[34] While at court late in 1568 she developed a fever which, together with her sorrow, 'did greatly further her end'. The queen was alarmed by Catherine's sickness, ordering that she be well attended and visiting her regularly. Elizabeth stopped short of ordering Francis's return, however, suggesting that she had not believed the sickness to be mortal. In his last letter, written at the end of December, this was also Francis's opinion from the news he had received, ending his letter by saying, 'I trust you have not forgotten to join my New Year's gifts with yours and to deliver it accordingly' – hardly something with which a dying woman would be expected the concern herself.[35] Catherine died suddenly on 15 January 1569 while still at court, to the great grief of her royal kinswoman. There appear to have been some whisperings of blame directed at Elizabeth, with one royal agent, in conversation with Mary, Queen of Scots, mentioning that 'although her Grace [Elizabeth] was not culpable of this accident, yet she was the cause without which their being asunder [Catherine and Francis] had happened'.[36] Catherine was sincerely loved, being grieved for by her husband and children. Elizabeth also grieved deeply for her, arranging a splendid funeral in Westminster Abbey for the woman to whom she was closest. From her own pocket Elizabeth, who was notoriously parsimonious, paid over £640 to ensure that her cousin Catherine, the daughter of a Boleyn, was royally buried. The queen almost shut down for a time with her grief, with Mary, Queen of Scots, being informed that the Queen's Majesty [Elizabeth] (God be praised) did very well, saving that all her felicities gave place to some natural passions of grief, which she conceived for the death of her kinswoman, and good servant the Lady Knollys; and how by that occasion her Highness fell for a while, from a Prince wanting nothing in this world, to private mourning, in which solitary estate being forgetful of her own health, she took cold, wherewith she was much troubled, and whereof she was well delivered.[37]

Elizabeth's grief at Catherine's death was greater than that which she displayed for any other family member: a testament to the cousins' closeness. It may also have been remorse that finally persuaded her to recall Francis Knollys from 'his long and painful service', sending the Earl of Shrewsbury instead to act as the Scottish queen's gaoler on 26 January 1569.[38] She did not entirely dispense with the family's services, however, requesting that Catherine's eldest son, Henry, remain with the Queen of Scots.

With Catherine Carey's death the main Boleyn line was represented mainly by the queen herself. In addition to this, Catherine's six daughters and, later, her granddaughters, could lay some claim to being Boleyn women, as could the daughters of her brother, Henry Carey, who made up some of his twelve children.

Although Sir Francis Knollys was allowed to return south following his wife's death, the problem of Mary, Queen of Scots, remained a very real threat for Elizabeth. The Scottish queen, who was both young and very beautiful, was a romantic figure and attracted interest among the nobility, most notably from Elizabeth's kinsman, Thomas Howard, Duke of Norfolk, the son of the executed Earl of Surrey. In late 1569 a rumour reached court that Norfolk wished to marry Mary in order to become king and return the English church to Catholicism.[39] Elizabeth summoned Norfolk, whom she had always recognised as a kinsman, hoping to encourage him to confess.[40] The peer denied everything, but, failing to heed the danger, became involved in 1571 in a plot to depose Elizabeth and replace her with Mary. While Elizabeth was prepared to sentence Norfolk to death, she could not bring herself to sign the death warrant. She was always squeamish about ordering the deaths of her kin and she spent several weeks wracked with uncertainty. According to a letter from John Lee to Lord Burghley, 'they say on 26 February last, was a warrant directed to the lieutenant for the execution of Norfolk on the following morning, but the queen, after she had signed the warrant, was so greatly disquieted in mind and conscience that she could not rest until she had sent to the lieutenant to return it'.[41] Finally, Elizabeth was prevailed upon to sign and Norfolk was executed on 2 June 1572.[42] This decision caused Elizabeth a great deal of emotional turmoil and many people shared the view of the Earl of Sussex that she needed a husband to keep her safe.[43]

As time went by, Elizabeth came under increasing pressure to marry and settle the succession. In 1571, she received an offer of marriage from the Duke of Anjou, the brother of the King of France. Anjou was over twenty years younger than Elizabeth and a fervent Catholic but the queen, needing a French alliance, informed her council in March that she intended to marry him. Neither Anjou nor Elizabeth were enthusiastic and she employed her usual delaying tactics, insisting that the prince visit her before she would commit herself. Anjou disparagingly called Elizabeth an old woman with a sore leg, and by September negotiations had stalled. The French queen mother, Catherine de Medici, then offered her youngest son, Francis, Duke of Alençon.[44] Elizabeth allowed her ambassadors to open negotiations and, as usual, insisted on meeting him.

Alençon proved a more ardent suitor than Elizabeth's earlier admirers and, on 5 August 1579, he arrived in England. His arrival was a shock to Elizabeth and although she insisted on meeting her suitors she had never imagined that a foreign prince would actually arrive. Elizabeth was charmed by her guest and the couple spent two weeks together, giving every indication that they intended to marry.

That Elizabeth did have genuine feelings for Alençon is clear from the poem, 'On Monsieur's Departure', which she composed when he returned to France:

I grieve and dare not show my discontent;
I love, and yet am forced to seem to hate;
I do, yet dare not say I ever meant;
I seem stark mute, but inwardly do prate
I am, and not, I freeze and yet am scorned,
Since from myself another self I turned

My care is like my shadow in the sun –
Follows me flying, flies when I pursue it,
Stands, and lies by me, doth what I have done;
His too familiar care doth make me rue it.
No means I find to rid him from my breast,
Till by the end of things it be suppressed.

Some gentler passion slide into my mind,
For I am soft, and made of melting snow;
Or be more cruel, Love, and so be kind.
Let me float or sink, be high or low;
Or let me live with some more sweet content,
Or die, and so forget what love e'er meant.[45]

Elizabeth and Alençon corresponded passionately and the attraction between them was genuine. In one letter, Elizabeth wrote, 'For my part, I confess that there is no prince in the world to whom I would more willingly yield to be his, than to yourself.'[46] Alençon's courtship was the most intense that she experienced and he was the man she came closest to marrying. She may, at least in part, have attempted to make Robert Dudley, whom she had created Earl of Leicester, jealous as Alençon's representative had earlier informed her that Dudley had secretly married her cousin, Catherine Carey's daughter, the widowed Lettice Knollys. Elizabeth was devastated at the news and banished Lettice from court, although she was eventually able to forgive Dudley. She never forgave Lettice, who appears to have been as strong-willed as her royal cousin, her mother and their Boleyn women forebears. Lettice bore Dudley a son, who was named for his father, although he died in childhood. She was subject to the queen's anger for the rest of her life, being forbidden from joining her husband in the Netherlands while he was serving there, among other slights.[47] Her two daughters by her first husband, Dorothy and Penelope Devereux, were however welcome at court with their royal cousin.

Alençon returned to England in late 1581. He continued to press Elizabeth for marriage and, finally, while they were walking together, 'discourse carried her so far, that she drew off a ring from her finger, and put it upon the Duke of Anjou's [Alençon], upon certain conditions betwixt the two the standers-by took it, that the marriage was now contracted by promise'. Elizabeth agreed to marry Alençon but she still had doubts, and, that night,

the Queen's gentlewomen, with whom she used to be familiar, lamented and bewailed, and did so terrify and vex her mind, that she spent the night in doubts and cares without sleep amongst those weeping and wailing females. The next day she sent for the Duke of Anjou [Alençon], and they two, all by-standers being removed, had a long discourse together. He at length withdrew himself to his chamber, and throwing the ring from him, a while after took it again, taxing the lightness of women, and the inconsistency of islanders.[48]

Alençon's pursuit of Elizabeth was her last courtship and, when he died only three years after leaving England, she was bereft.

Following Alençon's departure, it was clear that Elizabeth would never bear children to secure the succession. This left the Catholic Mary, Queen of Scots, as her most likely successor, a fact that worried her council. Mary had remained Elizabeth's prisoner since her arrival in England in 1568, with Elizabeth always refusing to meet with her. In May 1586, a young Catholic nobleman called Anthony Babbington was contacted by John Ballad, a Catholic priest, who had obtained Spanish support for a plot to murder Elizabeth.[49] Babbington became involved in the conspiracy and wrote to Mary asking for her support. Mary wrote agreeing to Elizabeth's murder, unaware that the correspondence was monitored.[50] Faced with the proof of her cousin's involvement, Elizabeth ordered that she be tried for treason and Mary was, accordingly, sentenced to death, with Sir Francis Knollys one of the peers sitting in judgement. As with the Duke of Norfolk's earlier condemnation, this sentence sent Elizabeth into turmoil and she pleaded with her council to find a way by which she might spare her cousin and fellow queen. She was angered when everyone insisted that the Scottish queen must die.[51]

Elizabeth prevaricated for several months before finally signing the death warrant and handing it to her secretary, William Davison.[52] Her council acted quickly, fearing that she would recall the warrant on further thought. Elizabeth did indeed send for it to be returned to her the following morning. She was disconcerted to hear that it had already been dispatched to Fotheringay, where Mary was imprisoned. The Queen of Scots was beheaded on the morning of 8 February 1587. According to Camden,

as soon as the report was brought to Queen Elizabeth's ears, who little thought of such a thing, that the Queen of Scots was put to death, she heard it with great indignation, her countenance altered, her speech faltered her, and through excessive sorrow she stood in a manner astonished; insomuch as she gave herself over to passionate grief, putting herself in mourning habit and shedding abundance of tears.[53]

Elizabeth wrote to James VI of Scotland, denying her guilt in the death of his mother.[54] She always maintained that she had signed the warrant only for use in an emergency and that Davison had deliberately disobeyed her orders. In the days following Mary's execution, Elizabeth raged about Davison, threatening to have him hanged. She was restrained by her council but did order that he be fined and imprisoned. The truth of Elizabeth's feelings on the death of Mary, Queen of Scots, cannot be known. The fact remains, however, that she did sign the warrant and that Davison provided a useful scapegoat in mitigating her guilt.

Mary's fellow Catholic monarch, Philip of Spain, was not convinced by Elizabeth's protestations of innocence. He had grown increasingly angry at her promotion of Protestantism and had begun building an invasion fleet even before Mary's execution. Elizabeth anxiously monitored progress in Spain and began preparing for war, placing the English fleet under the control of Lord Howard of Effingham and Francis Drake.[55] On 29 May 1588, 130 ships holding 20,000 troops set sail to invade England. The Spanish Armada made slow progress but, on 19 June, it was sighted off Cornwall and warning beacons were lit along the coast of England. Howard and Drake had assembled a large fleet and they engaged the Spanish in the Channel. These encounters made little impact on the Armada and it anchored off Calais, waiting for further troops from the Netherlands. The English fleet seized their chance by sending in fire ships during the night.[56] This caused panic and the Spanish ships cut their anchors and sailed out to sea to escape the flames. On 29 July they were attacked by the English again and the weakened Armada was scattered, the remnant of the fleet being chased as far north as the Firth of Forth.

This proved to be the final defeat of the Armada but news of the scale of the English victory did not reach Elizabeth for some time. The Armada was merely the fleet that conveyed Spanish troops to England and Elizabeth expected a land-based invasion. She was determined to play a part in the defence of her kingdom and, on 9 August 1588, she reviewed her troops at Tilbury, making one of the most famous speeches of her reign. Elizabeth's speech was stirring and she declared, 'I know I have the body but of a weak and feeble woman, but I have the heart and stomach of a king and of a king of England too – and take foul scorn that Parma [the Armada's commander] or any other prince of Europe should dare to invade the borders of my realm.'[57] Elizabeth was overjoyed to hear the news of the Armada's defeat and she ordered public thanksgiving across England and went in procession through London in a chariot.[58] For the queen, the celebrations ended with the death of Robert Dudley on 4 September 1588.

Elizabeth grieved deeply for Dudley, who had been the love of her life, and, on hearing the news, shut herself in her chamber, refusing to see anyone or come out. Finally, her council ordered her door to be broken open. Dudley's widow, Lettice Knollys, also grieved for him, although she did find consolation in his master of horse not long after his death.

Lettice Knollys was indirectly responsible for further grief to her royal cousin towards the end of the queen's long reign. Following Robert Dudley's death in 1588 she did what many aristocratic widows did and married a young member of her household, Christopher Blount of Kidderminster, who was thirteen years her junior.[59] Blount had distant royal connections as a second cousin of Henry VIII's long-dead mistress, Bessie Blount. He was distantly related to the Dudley family through Robert's mother, Jane Guildford.[60] He was also well educated, having studied at Oxford before being tutored by a Jesuit priest, and future cardinal, on the Continent. He was devoutly Catholic and had been involved with

Mary, Queen of Scots, when he was discovered sending letters to her agents confirming his readiness to espouse her cause. He appears, however, to have served as a double agent, although this failed to save him when he next became involved in treason against the queen. Blount served Robert Dudley as his master of horse, something that brought him to Lettice's attention. He was tall and handsome and the couple made a love match, with Blount soon prospering in the service of his stepson, the Earl of Essex, who instigated a quarrel with Elizabeth when she refused to allow Blount to join her Privy Council.

Elizabeth never had as close a relationship with any man as she did with Robert Dudley. She did however find some consolation in his stepson, the Earl of Essex, who had first come to court in 1585. Essex was young and handsome and Elizabeth adored him, talking of him continually when he was away from court.[61] She ignored the fact that he was also vain, arrogant and ambitious and appointed him to prominent posts, such as placing him in command of her army in Ireland.

As the years went by, the favourite's behaviour became increasingly outrageous. On 28 September 1598, Essex, who had returned to England from Ireland without Elizabeth's permission, arrived at court and burst into her chamber as she was dressing.[62] Essex's intrusion shattered the myth that the passage of time had not touched Elizabeth and he saw her wrinkled face and thin grey hair. She kept her composure and had a private interview with him, but was furious and never forgave him for his insolence.

Essex's behaviour continued to be erratic and he gathered a party of disaffected lords around him. He and his followers conceived a plot to imprison Elizabeth, with Essex to rule in her place as lord protector. By February 1601, the conspirators, who included Christopher Blount, were ready and Essex imprisoned several of Elizabeth's council in his house in London.[63] The earl and 150 armed men then left his house, hoping to gain support from the people of

London.[64] He had badly overestimated his own popularity, and was unable to persuade the Mayor of London or the people to join his coup. This lack of support finally showed him the folly of his actions and his followers returned to Essex House to plan their next move.

On hearing of Essex's conduct, Elizabeth was furious and, according to reports, 'the queen was so far from fear that she would have gone out in person to see what any rebel of them all durst do against her, had not the councillors with much ado stayed her'.[65] She refused to sleep until Essex and his supporters had been arrested and ordered that cannon be brought from the Tower to force him from his house.[66] Essex, fearing that his house would be blown up, surrendered and was sent to the Tower. He was tried and sentenced to death and Elizabeth showed him no mercy, ordering his execution on 25 February 1601.[67] His stepfather, Christopher Blount, who had been wounded during the rebellion and, by all accounts, fought bravely, was also executed. The loss of her third husband and son must have been devastating for Lettice, who survived them by more than thirty years. Essex's treachery was also a great blow to the queen, who suddenly began to feel her age.

By the early 1600s Elizabeth's health was failing and nobody in England expected her to live much longer. On 30 November 1601, she addressed Parliament for the last time, declaring,

> There will never queen sit in my seat with more zeal to my country, care to my subjects, and that will soon with willingness venture her life for your good and safety, than myself. For it is not my desire to live nor reign longer than my life and reign shall be for your good. And though you have had and may have many princes more mighty and wise sitting in this seat, yet you never had or shall have any that will be more careful and loving.[68]

Elizabeth's speech was recognised as the passing of an era and few could really remember a time before she had been queen.

Elizabeth had first appointed Henry Carey's daughter, another Catherine Carey, as a maid of the court back in January 1559 when the girl was aged twelve. The queen remained close to Mary Boleyn's granddaughter throughout her reign, regularly visiting her and her husband, who was created Earl of Nottingham. In early 1603, Catherine Carey, Countess of Nottingham, died, causing the queen to become depressed.[69] Elizabeth seemed suddenly to age and her memory deteriorated, meaning that she could no longer concentrate on political affairs. By March 1603, she was very ill and unable to either eat or sleep.[70] She remained lucid to the end, dying on 24 March 1603 after finally falling asleep. As soon as she died, Lady Scrope took a ring from Elizabeth's finger and threw it out of the window to Robert Carey, who was waiting on horseback below. Carey rode to Scotland and, later that same day, James VI of Scotland was proclaimed King of England.

The death of Elizabeth I was the end of an era in England. It was also the end of a line that can be stretched back into the fourteenth century: the Boleyn women. The Boleyn family rose from humble origins to become one of the grandest in the land, counting two queens among its members. While the Boleyn men rose steadily through society and often found themselves in positions of trust and honour, it was the women of the family who were often the driving force behind their advancement. Never has there been a family as ambitious as the Boleyns, or who have achieved so much. The story of the Boleyn women is a story of family loyalty and of ambition. They were rarely simply wives and mothers; sometimes they made history.

NOTES

The spelling in the sources used has been modernised in all cases where appropriate.

Part 1 The Earliest Boleyn Women: The Thirteenth to the Fifteenth Centuries

1 Norfolk Origins

1. Parsons 1935, p. 387.
2. Parsons 1935, p. 387 and Armstrong 1781, p. 69.
3. Gurney 1858, p. 828.
4. Parsons 1935, p. 387.
5. *Ibid.* p. 389.
6. *Calendar of the Close Rolls Richard II Vol. III*, p. 140.
7. Badham 2011.
8. The de Banco Rolls (quoted from Parsons 1935, p. 393).
9. Will of Sir William Boleyn (*Testamenta Vetusta II*, p. 465).
10. Parsons 1937, p. 19.
11. *Ibid.*, p. 4.
12. Duffy 2004, p. 325.
13. Parsons 1935, p. 389.
14. *Ibid.*, p. 390.

15. *Ibid.*, p. 390.

16. Saul 2009, p. 256.

17. The Visitation of the Archdeacon of Norwich 1368–1420 (Parsons 1935, p. 391).

18. Blomefield and Parkin 1769, p. 626 both state that Alice was the daughter of Sir John Bracton, a claim that Parsons 1935 was suspicious about. It appears that Blomefield and Parkin took their information from the Visitations of Norfolk in the sixteenth and seventeenth centuries which referred to the mother of Geoffrey II (but the wife of Thomas I) as Jane, the daughter and co-heiress of Sir John Bracton. The visitation contains a number of errors but the detail given for Alice's lineage may be accurate. The identification should be treated with caution. It is not impossible that one of Thomas Boleyn I's wives may in fact have been the Bracton heiress.

19. Parsons 1935, p. 391.

20. *Ibid.*, p. 398.

21. *Visitation of Norfolk*, p. 51.

22. *Visitation of Kent*, p. 181.

23. Parsons 1935, p. 392.

24. Venn 1897, p. 18.

25. Cooper 1860, p. 283.

26. Geoffrey Boleyn's will (printed in Gurney 1858, p. 832).

27. Loades 2011, p. 12.

28. Parsons 1935, p. 396 discusses Thomas's will.

29. Cooper 1860, p. 298.

2   Anne Hoo Boleyn & Her Daughters

1. Orridge 1867, p. 181.

2. The Wardens' Account Book 1435 for the Mercers of London, p. 477.

3. The Wardens' Account Book 1435–6, p. 485.

4. The Wardens' Account Book for those years, pp. 517, 527 and 545.

5. *Calendar of the Patent Rolls 1461–1467*, p. 42 for the 1461 grant.

The 1458 grant is contained in *Calendar of the Patent Rolls VI* for 25 October 1458.

6. Sums received for the admission of apprentices during their term of office (Mercers of London Account Books, p. 565).

7. *Calendar of the Fine Rolls* XVIII, p. 130.

8. Parsons 1935, p. 395.

9. Acts of the Mercer's Company 1461 (Lyell and Watney 1936, p. 51).

10. Acts of the Mercer's Company 1461 (Lyell and Watney 1936, p. 54).

11. Election of Wardens 1452 in Acts of the Mercer's Company (Lyell and Watney 1936, p. 42).

12. *Calendar of the Fine Rolls* XIX, p. 195.

13. Warnicke 1995, p. 35.

14. *Calendar of the Patent Rolls* VI for 28 November 1457, p. 416.

15. *Ibid.* for 23 August 1458, p. 444.

16. Mate 1998, pp. 32, 35.

17. *Gentleman's Magazine* 1855, p. 183 notes that Lord Hoo's second daughter, also called Anne, was seven at the time of his death in 1455.

18. *Testamenta Vetusta I*, p. 272. Anne was thirty at the death of her father in 1455.

19. 'Antiquarian Researches', *Gentlemen's Magazine* 1855, p. 182 and Cooper 1856.

20. *Gentleman's Magazine* 1855, p. 183.

21. *Registrum Thome Bourgchier* for 7 December 1455, p. 173.

22. Mate 1998, p. 32.

23. Geoffrey Boleyn's will, p. 839.

24. Margaret Paston to John Paston, 5 November 1452? (Gairdner, ed., Paston Letters 182).

25. Geoffrey Boleyn to John Paston Squire, *c.* 5 December 1460 (Paston Letters 366).

26. Parsons 1935, p. 395.

27. Geoffrey Boleyn's will, p. 832.

28. Agnes Paston to John Paston, 16 November 1452 (Paston Letters 183).

29. Thomas Howes to John Paston, 13 November 1454 (Paston Letters 223).

30. A Remembrance of the Worshipful Kin and Ancestry of Paston, Born in Paston in Genyngham Soken (Paston Letters vol. I, p. xxi).

31. Sir John Paston to John Paston, March 1467 (Paston Letters, 570).

32. Will of Sir William Boleyn (*Testamenta Vetusta II*).

33. Anne Heydon's will (Gurney 1858, p. 827).

34. Parsons 1937, p. 150.

35. John Paston to Sir John Paston, April 1467 (Paston Letters, 573).

36. Geoffrey Boleyn's will.

37. Blomefield and Parkin 1769, p. 626, the confusion appears to come from PRO C1/254/16: Thomas Fenys, knight, Anne, his wife, and Richard, son and heir of Roger Copley *v.* William Fayrefax.

38. Visitation of Norfolk 1563 and 1613.

39. Margaret Paston to John Paston, 5 November 1452? (Paston Letters 182).

40. Anne Heydon's will (Gurney 1858, p. 823).

41. Pedigrees showing the relationship between many of the nobility and gentry, and the blood royal; compiled about the year 1505, p. 314 (Harleian MS 1074) (printed in *Collectanea Topographica et Genealogica vol. I*, London:1834).

42. *Select Cases before the king's council of the Star Chamber*, p. 27.

43. *Ibid.*, p. 27.

44. Blomefield and Parkin 1767, p. 627.

45. Writ of *diem clausit extremum* issued for 'Anne Bolane, widow' in 1485 (*Calendar of the Fine Rolls XXI* no. 833).

3 The Ormond Inheritance

1. This date is calculated by reference to the date of birth of the

couple's eldest known child, a daughter, Anne, who is commemorated in a memorial brass at Blickling.

2. Richardson 2005, p. 163 states that Margaret's mother was born in 1430. Watney 1906, p. 48 claims that Thomas Butler's father's first wife only died on 3 August 1430 and that he was the third son of the second marriage. However this must be an error as Thomas Butler's grandmother, who made her will in 1434, referred to him and his two brothers and one sister fondly. Thomas Butler himself, when he made his will in 1515 also referred affectionately to his long-deceased grandmother, indicating that he remembered her. He was therefore most likely born in the mid-1420s.

3. Loades 2011, p. 12 and 31.

4. Butler in his notes to Grace's *Annales Hiberniae*, p. 163.

5. TNA PROB 11/18 Earl of Ormond's will.

6. Grace's *Annales Hiberniae*, p. 161.

7. Burke 1866, p. 94.

8. Hunter 1819, p. 147 and *Some account of the family of the Butlers*, p. 20.

9. Richardson 2005, p. 163.

10. Richardson 2005, p. 163. Lora's second husband died in January 1495 and she is first recorded as Ormond's wife in November the following year.

11. Elizabeth was commemorated in a memorial brass at Sheffield church, this is the only reference to her existence (Hunter 1819, p. 147).

12. Will of Joanne, Lady Bergavenny (*Testamenta Vetusta I*, pp. 224–30).

13. TNA PROB 11/18 Earl of Ormond's will.

14. Richardson 2005, p. 164.

15. Fenlon 2000, p. 138.

16. TNA PROB 11/18 Earl of Ormond's will.

17. Bradley and Pevsner 2002, p. 396.

18. Will of Sir William Boleyn (*Testamenta Vetusta II*, p. 465).

19. Blomefield 1769, p. 627.

20. Warnicke 1995, p. 35.

21. Blomefield 1769, p. 628.

22. Inscription to Anthony Boleyn in Blickling church, transcribed by the author: 'Here lies Antony Boleyn son of William Boleyn, Knight who died 30 September, 1493 on whose soul God have mercy.'

23. Blomefield 1769, p. 627.

24. *Ibid.*

25. Warnicke 1995, p. 36.

26. *Calendar of the Fine Rolls XXII*, p. 324.

27. *Calendar of the Patent Rolls 1476–1485*, p. 567.

28. *Calendar of the Patent Rolls 1476–1485*, p. 345.

29. Carte 1851, p. lxxxiii.

30. Will of Sir William Boleyn (*Testamenta Vetusta II*, p. 465).

31. Carte 1851, p. lxxxiv.

32. *Some account of the family of the Butlers*, p. 20.

33. BL Harleain MSS 433 f.100b (Horrox and Hammond 1974, p. 274) contains a pardon given to the seventh earl concerning the manor and demonstrates its importance to him.

34. Carte 1851, p. lxxxiv.

35. Will of Thomas, Earl of Ormond TNA PROB 11/18.

36. Thomas Boleyn's Accounts November–December 1526 (L&P IV, App. 99).

37. Round 1881, p. 85.

38. *Some account of the family of the Butlers*, p. 21.

39. Carte 1851, p. lxxxiv.

40. Barnard 2000, p. 3.

41. Fenlon 2000, p. 138.

42. Round 1881.

43. Round 1881, p. 87.

44. Margaret Butler to Thomas Boleyn, 1515 (L&P I 5784).

45. L&P III 160.

46. VCH Cambridgeshire, p. 382.

47. Round 1881, p. 87.

48. State Papers II, p. 58 and Norton 2011a, p. 26.

49. State Papers II, pp. 49–50 and Norton 2011a, pp. 26–7.

50. State Papers II, p. 57 and Norton 2011a, p. 27.

51. Wilkinson 2009, p. 46.

52. Round 1881, p. 87.

53. Round 1881, p. 87.

54. Round 1881, p. 88.

55. Calendar of Carew Manuscripts, p. 107.

56. Calendar of Carew Manuscripts, p. 105.

57. Lord Hunsdon's petition is taken from Round 1886, p. 18.

58. Calendar of Carew Manuscripts, p. 106.

59. Henry Monk to Lady Lisle, 19 July 1538 (Lisle Letters 184).

60. Worcestershire Record Office 705:349/12946/498729.

61. L&P XIV pt I 609.

62. L&P XIV pt I 854.

Part 2   Courtiers: 1485–1526

4   Lusty to Look On, Pleasant, Demure, & Sage

1. *A Brief Account of the Noble Family of the Howards* in Harleian Miscellany IX, p. 136.

2. Grant 1972, p. 7.

3. Tucker 1964, p. 15.

4. Casady 1975, p. 11.

5. Crawford 2010.

6. *A Brief Account of the Descent of the Dukes of Norfolk* in Harleian Miscellany IX, p. 136.

7. Crawford 2010.

8. Tucker 1964, p. 16.

9. John Howard's Accounts in Botfield 1841, p. 149.

10. *Ibid.*, p. 162.

11. *Ibid.*, p. 165.

12. *Ibid.*, p. 168.

13. Wardrobe Accounts of Edward IV, p. 156.

14. Botfield 1841, p. 184.

15. Collier 1844, p. 135.

16. *Ibid.*, p. 352.

17. *Ibid.*, pp. 115 and 146.

18. *Ibid.*, pp. 225 and 514.

19. Botfield 1841, p. 225.

20. *Ibid.*, p. 260.

21. Collier 1844, pp. 275–76.

22. *Ibid.*, p. 275.

23. Crawford 2010.

24. Volkes 1988, p. 7.

25. *Ibid.*, p. 7.

26. L&P VI, App. 2.

27. Collier 1844, p. 147.

28. *Ibid.*, p. 218.

29. Botfield 1841, p. 285.

30. *Ibid.*, p. 503.

31. Tucker 1964, p. 26.

32. *Ibid.*, p. 26.

33. Volkes 1988, p. 12.

34. *Ibid.*, p. 15.

35. *Ibid.*, p. 16.

36. *Ibid.*, p. 16.

37. Tucker 1964, p. 14.

38. Volkes 1988, p. 20.

39. *Privy Purse Expenses of Elizabeth of* York, p. 99.

40. *Ibid.*, p. 9.

41. *Ibid.*, pp. 79 and 94.

42. Volkes 1988, p. 29.

43. *Ibid.*, p. 30.

44. *Ibid.*, p. 30.

45. Tucker 1969, p. 333.

46. *Ibid.*, p. 335.

47. *Ibid.*, p. 343.

48. Skelton 1931, pp. 424–25.

49. *Ibid.*, p. 426.

50. *Ibid.*, p. 426.

51. John Husee to Lady Lisle, 23 June 1537 (Lisle Letters IV 856).

52. John Husee to Lady Lisle, 29 June 1537 (Lisle Letters IV 884).

53. Thomas Warley to Lady Lisle, 14 April 1536 (Lisle Letters III 673).

54. Loades 2011, p. 14.

55. *Calendar of the Close Rolls Henry VII Vol. II*, p. 179.

56. L&P XI 17.

57. L&P I 3196, 3370 and 3460 for example give details of the embassy.

58. L&P I 3370.

59. L&P I 3402.

60. L&P I 4237 and 4307.

61. Volkes 1988, p. 40.

62. Samman 1988 Appendix IV lists a number of members of the Boleyn family as participating in court masques and tournaments.

63. Blomfield 1893, p. 18.

64. L&P XI 17.

65. Weir 2011, p. 12 claims that the memorial at Penshurst to Thomas Boleyn includes the date '1520'. In fact no date is marked and it is simply implausible that the eldest son of Sir Thomas Boleyn could have survived to adulthood with no mention at all being made of him in contemporary records.

66. Cavendish's Metrical Visions in Norton 2011a, p. 227.

67. Anne Boleyn to her father (Norton 2011a, p. 25).

68. L&P X 838, 947 and 956.

69. L&P VI 180.

70. L&P VI 584.

71. L&P VI 1468.

5   Three Lady Boleyns at Court

1. Harris 2001, p. 257.

2. Weir 2011, p. 29.

3. Examination of Thomas Smyth, July 1536 (L&P XI 48).

4. Blomefield, pp. 54–5.

5. Oosterwijk 2000, p. 64.

6. James is referred to only as James Boleyn in a number of documents from early in Henry VIII's reign, such as commissions of the peace from 1511 (L&P I 1714) and 1512 (L&P I 3426).

7. Loades 2011, p. 17 states that James was knighted in 1520. This appears to be taken from James's entry in Bindoff 1982. However, Bindoff took the date from Leonard 1970, p. 309. Upon reviewing Leonard's work there is no source given for the actual date of the knighthood, merely a source showing him as a knight in November 1520. However, as set out below, he was actually already referred to as a knight in December 1516.

8. L&P II 1204.

9. L&P II 2735.

10. L&P X 912.

11. L&P II 3489.

12. L&P III 491.

13. Lincolnshire Pedigrees III, p. 952.

14. Banks 1844, p. 452.

15. Tempest 1937, p. 173.

16. *Ibid.*, p. 172 and Lincolnshire Pedigrees III, p. 954.

17. Tempest 1937, p. 173.

18. *Ibid.*, p. 173.

19. Norton 2011b.

20. Lincolnshire Pedigrees III, p. 954.

21. Blomfield, p. 627.

22. L&P I 82.

23. For example, Ives 2005, p. 14 in his definitive biography of Anne Boleyn and Somerset 1984, p. 13 in her still highly useful

study of ladies-in-waiting.

24. L&P I 1549.

25. Harris 2001, p. 257.

26. Lestrange Accounts, p. 430.

27. Lestrange Accounts, p. 483.

28. Harris 2001, p. 257.

29. Casady 1975, p. 14.

30. Casady 1975, p. 16.

31. *The Field of the Cloth of Gold: List of Noble Persons who Accompanied Henry VIII in June 1520* (Rutland Papers, p. 37).

32. L&P VI 923.

33. The Reeds of Oatlands and their relationship to the Blount and Amadas families are discussed in Norton 2013a (forthcoming).

34. Norton 2011b.

35. Elton 1976.

36. Sander 1877, p. 24.

37. Samman 1988 App. IV.

38. Weir 2011.

39. 'The Justes of the Moneths of May and June' in Hazlitt 1866.

40. Norton 2011.

41. 'The Countess of Wiltshire, Died 1538 – by W.M.L.' in *Miscellanea Genealogica et Heraldica* vol. II fourth series 1908, pp. 246–47.

42. Margaret of Austria to Thomas Boleyn (Norton 2011a, p. 25).

43. L&P I 5483 and 5484.

6 Mary Boleyn, Royal Mistress

1. *Hall's Chronicle*, pp. 567–69.

2. L&P I 3348.

3. Brantôme, p. 368.

4. Wilkinson 2009, p. 39.

5. Brantôme, pp. 9, 102 and 169.

6. L&P X 181.

7. Weir 2011, p. 85.

8. Sander, p. 24.

9. Russell 1969 contains a contemporary account of the Field of the Cloth of Gold.

10. Norton 2011b.

11. Hoskins 1997.

12. Weir 2011, p. 114.

13. L&P III 2074 no. 5.

14. L&P III 2297.

15. Norton 2011b sets out the evidence for Elizabeth Tailboys's paternity, which is strongly in favour of the assertion that Elizabeth Blount's daughter was also the king's child.

16. Bundesen 2008, p. 76.

17. *Ibid.*, p. 77.

18. Varlow 2007.

19. Bundesen 2008, p. 73.

20. Naunton, p. 10.

21. Deuteronomy 33:22.

22. Genesis 49:17 and 49:9.

23. Bundesen 2008, p. 76.

24. Hoskins 1997.

25. *Ibid.*

26. Norton 2011b.

27. Hoskins 1997.

28. Rowley-Williams 1998, pp. 154–55.

29. BL Add. MSS. 12060.

30. Cavendish's Metrical Visions (Norton 2011a, pp. 253–4).

31. Rowley-Williams 1998, p. 162.

32. 'The parcels of stuff here being written being the Lady Rochford's. And they do remain a chest being in the chamber over the kitchen' transcribed in Rowley-Williams 1998, p. 298.

33. L&P X 1251 (William Foster to Cromwell, 1536).

34. Dedication to *A New Year's Angelical Salutation by Thomas Aquine* quoted from Madden, p. cxxviii.

35. Fox 2007, pp. 36 and 39.
36. L&P IV App. 99 Thomas Boleyn's Accounts (Nov.–Dec. 1526).
37. Lady Rochford to Thomas Cromwell (Norton 2011a, p. 253).
38. Thomas Boleyn to Cromwell (Rowley-Williams 1998, p. 163).
39. Rowley-Williams 1998, p. 156.
40. Sander, pp. 32–3.

Part 3   Queen Anne Boleyn: 1526–1536

7   The King's New Love

1. Wyatt 1825, pp. 182–83.
2. Sander 1877, p. 25.
3. Wyatt 1825, p. 183.
4. Anne's relationship with Henry Percy is described in Cavendish 1825.
5. Printed in Singer 1825, p. 250.
6. Wriothesley's Chronicle, p. 41.
7. Wyatt 1825, p. 184.
8. Wyatt 1975, p. 90.
9. Wyatt 1825, p. 185.
10. Wyatt 1975, p. 7.
11. The quotes from Henry's letters are all taken from Norton 2011a.
12. L&P IV App. 206 (Du Bellay to Montmorency, 6 October 1528).
13. L&P IV App. 99 (Thomas Boleyn's Accounts Nov.–Dec. 1526).
14. L&P IV 1939.
15. Wyatt 1825, p. 188.
16. Wyatt 1825, p. 187.
17. Wood vol. II letter 7.

8   Anne Boleyn & the King's Great Matter

1. Herbert 1649, p. 226.
2. Wyatt 1825, p. 188.
3. Chapuys to Charles V, 1 January 1530 (Norton 2011a, p. 110–11).

4. Chapuys to Charles V, 10 May 1530 (Norton 2011a, p. 105).

5. Chapuys to Charles V, 1 October 1532 (Norton 2011a, pp. 124–25).

6. Anne Boleyn to Stephen Gardiner, 4 April 1529 (Norton 2011a, pp. 77–8).

7. L&P IV 187.

8. Thomas Heneage to Cardinal Wolsey, 3 March 1528 (Ellis 1846, pp. 132–33).

9. L&P VI 1468 (Depositions of Elizabeth Barton).

10. Wood II, p. 75.

11. L&P IV App. 9.

12. Chapuys to Charles V, 31 January 1530, 6 February 1530 and 14 May 1530 (all Norton 2011a).

13. Chapuys to Granville, 11 July 1532.

14. Chapuys to Charles V, 13 November 1530 (Norton 2011a, p. 109).

15. For example in her letter to Lady Wingfield.

16. Rowley-Williams 1998, p. 157.

17. Lady Rochford's 1536 inventory (Rowley-Williams 1998, p. 298).

18. *List of plate, apparel and jewels which were Lady Rochford's* (Rowley-Williams 1998, p. 299).

19. *Items received into the Royal Wardrobe after Lady Rochford's death* (Rowley-Williams 1998, p. 300).

20. Cardinal du Bellay, 18 June 1528 (Norton 2011a, p. 78).

21. Cardinal du Bellay, 18 June 1528 and 30 June 1528 (Norton 2011a, pp. 78–9).

22. Henry's letters are all printed in Norton 2011a.

23. Letter 9 (Norton 2011a, p. 43).

24. Henry's correspondence with Wolsey regarding Wilton is printed in St Clare Byrne 1968, pp. 77 and 79).

25. Anne's letters to Wolsey are printed in Norton 2011a.

26. Wyatt 1825, p. 203.

27. Letter 13 Norton 2011a, p. 45.

28. L&P IV 2207.

29. Herbert 1649, p. 231.

30. Campeggio to Salviarti, 28 October 1528 (St Clare Byrne 1968, p. 86).

31. L&P IV 2577.

32. Cavendish records Catherine's speech and conduct. He also recounts Wolsey's fall.

33. *Life of Fisher*, pp. 65–6.

34. L&P IV 2177.

35. L&P V 591.

36. Cranmer to Archdeacon Hawkins, 17 June 1533 (Williams 1967, p. 722).

37. Harpsfield 1878, p. 234.

9   Anne the Queen

1. Chapuys to Charles V, 22 March 1531 (Norton 2011a).

2. Latymer 1990 recounts Anne's religious beliefs.

3. Dowling 1984, p. 36.

4. Guy 1982 and Chapuys to Charles V, 14 February 1531.

5. Chapuys to Charles V, 31 March 1533 (Norton 2011a).

6. Bray 1994, p. 79.

7. Cranmer to Archdeacon Hawkins, 17 June 1533 (Williams 1967, p. 720).

8. Chapuys to Charles V, 16 April 1533.

9. Chapuys to Charles V, 29 May 1533.

10. Wynkyn de Worde 1903, p. 11.

11. Chapuys to Charles V, 29 May 1533.

12. L&P VI 584.

13. L&P VI 613 Sir Edward Baynton to Lord Rochford, 9 June 1533.

14. The Coronation pageants are from Udall 1903.

15. L&P VI 266.

16. L&P VI 613.

17. Chapuys to Charles V, 30 July 1533.

18. Chapuys to Charles V, 3 September 1533.

19. Chapuys to Charles V, 10 September 1533.

20. Chapuys to Charles V, 10 September 1533.

21. Latymer 1990, p. 63 and Chronicle of Henry VIII, p. 42.

22. George Taylor to Lady Lisle, 27 April 1534.

23. L&P VII 366.

24. Norton 2011a, pp. 150–51.

25. L&P X 450.

26. L&P IX 566.

27. Rowley-Williams 1998, p. 1592.

28. *Privy Purse Expenses of Princess Mary*, pp. 7, 51, 82 and 97.

29. *Ibid.*, p. 143.

30. *Ibid.*, p. 49.

31. *Ibid.*, p. 11.

32. *Ibid.*, p. 13.

33. *Ibid.*, pp. 17 and 25.

10   Princess Mary & the Queen's Aunts

1. Remley 1994, p. 43.

2. Whitaker 1929, p. 206.

3. Blomefield 1806, pp. 264–5.

4. *Ibid.*, p. 266.

5. Remley 1994, p. 43.

6. Blomefield 1806, p. 26.

7. Norfolk Visitation (see Shelton). Thomas Shelton was still serving at the Tower at the time of his death in 1595 (Whitaker 1929, p. 207).

8. Burke 1832, p. 118.

9. Armstrong 1781, p. 77.

10. Harris 2002, p. 133.

11. The East Anglian I, pp. 126 and 141.

12. Will of Dame Alice Clere TNA PROB 11/27.

13. Harris 2002, p. 133.

14. *Chronicle of Henry VIII.*

15. William Kingston to Lord Lisle, 18 April 1534.

16. L&P VI 472.

17. Chapuys to Charles V, 15 September 1533.

18. Chapuys to Charles V, 10 October 1533.

19. Chapuys to Charles V, 3 November 1533.

20. Chapuys 16 December 1533.

21. Chapuys 23 December 1533.

22. Chapuys 27 December 1533.

23. Chapuys 11 February 1534.

24. L&P VII 1129 (Dr William Butt to Cromwell, 2 September 1534).

25. L&P VIII 263.

26. *Privy Purse Expenses of Princess Mary*, p. 143.

27. *Ibid*. pp. 7, 8 and 54.

28. *Ibid*. pp. 84 and 73.

29. *Ibid*., p. 184.

30. *Ibid*. pp. 42 and 54.

31. *Ibid*., p. 120.

32. *Ibid*., p. 97.

33. Chapuys 21 February 1534.

34. Chapuys 30 March 1534.

35. Chapuys 22 April 1534.

36. Chapuys 14 May 1534.

37. For example in two recent works on Henry's mistresses, one believed the mistress was Margaret (Jones 2009, p. 241) and the other Mary (Hart 2009, p. 121).

38. Latymer 1990, p. 63.

39. Lisle Letters V 1086.

40. Norton 2011b.

41. Norton 2013b (forthcoming).

42. Wotton 1771, p. 76.

43. Visitation of Norfolk, p. 322.
44. Blomefield 1806, p. 267.
45. Norfolk Lists, p. 12.
46. Norfolk Lists, p. 75.
47. TNA PROB 11/44.
48. L&P XII pt II 1187.
49. Mary's parents married in 1512 and she may have been born as late as 1520 (Remley 1994, p. 43).
50. For example, Hart 2009, p. 122.
51. Latymer 1990, p. 63.
52. Quoted from Heale 1995, p. 301, but with modernised spelling.
53. Hart 2009, p. 127.
54. Kingston to Cromwell, letter 1 (Norton 2011a, p. 246).
55. Chapuys to Charles V, 9 January 1536.
56. Crawford 2002, pp. 179–80.
57. Chapuys 21 January 1536.
58. *Ibid.*
59. *Ibid.*
60. Chapuys 29 January 1536.

11 The Fall of the Boleyns

1. Chapuys to Charles V, 10 February 1536.
2. Chapuys to Charles V, 29 January 1536.
3. Chapuys to Charles V, 10 February 1536.
4. Wyatt 1825, p. 208.
5. Chapuys to Charles V, 25 February 1536.
6. Chapuys to Charles V, 1 April 1536.
7. *Ibid.*
8. *Ibid.*
9. L&P X 275.
10. Chapuys to Charles V, 21 April 1536.
11. Constantine 1831.
12. Wriothesley's Chronicle, p. 36.

13. Warnicke 1989, p. 134.

14. Lisle Letters IV 836.

15. L&P X 912.

16. TNA PROB 11/44 Will of Sir James Boleyn.

17. Letter 3 (Norton 2011a, p. 247).

18. Burnet 1865, p. 318.

19. William Kingston to Cromwell letter 1 (Norton 2011a, p. 246).

20. Letter 3 (Norton 2011a, p. 247).

21. Letter 2 (Norton 2011a, p. 246).

22. Fraser 2002.

23. Burnet 1865, p. 316.

24. Burnet 1865, p. 316.

25. Norton 2011a, pp. 253–54.

26. 1536 inventory transcribed in Rowley-Williams 1998, p. 298.

27. *List of plate, apparel and jewels which were Lady Rochford's* (transcribed in Rowley-Williams 1998, p. 299).

28. William Kingston to Cromwell, letter 2 (Norton 2011a, p. 246).

29. Strype 1822, pp. 462–63.

30. Norton 2011a, pp. 227–28.

31. Warnicke 1989, pp. 216–20.

32. Rowley-Williams 1998, p. 161.

33. Lady Rochford to Cromwell (Norton 2011a, pp. 252–53).

34. L&P XI 17.

35. Spelman 1977, p. 71.

36. Walker 2002, p. 17.

37. John Husee to Lady Lisle.

38. Ales.

39. William Kingston to Cromwell, letter 1 in Norton 2011a, p. 246.

40. L&P X 838 (Bishop of Faenza to Mons. Ambrogio, 10 May 1536) and L&P X 947 (Dr Ortiz to the Empress, 23 May 1536).

41. L&P X 956.

42. Manuscript account of Anne's trial (Norton 2011a, p. 249).

43. L&P X 362–63.

44. Chronicle of Calais, p. 46.
45. Constantine 1831.
46. *Hall's Chronicle*, p. 819.
47. Potuguese account of Anne's death (Norton 2011a, p. 265).
48. De Carles (Norton 2011a, p. 264).

Part 4   The Last Boleyn Women: 1536–1603

12   After Anne

1. L&P XI 48.
2. L&P XII pt I 317.
3. Bindoff 1982 for the 1553 settlement.
4. TNA PROB 11/44 Will of Sir James Boleyn.
5. Bindoff 1982.
6. Blomefield, p. 627.
7. PROB 11/27 Will of Alice Clere.
8. Armstrong 1781, p. 77.
9. Blomefield 1806, p. 267.
10. L&P XIV pt I 854.
11. L&P XI 17.
12. L&P XI 926 (Thomas Boleyn to Cromwell, 31 October 1536).
13. L&P XI 41.
14. Lisle Letters IV 884.
15. Lisle Letters III 673.
16. L&P XII pt I 580 and 722.
17. Lisle Letters V 1086.
18. Lisle Letters V 1137 (Thomas Warley to Lady Lisle, 7 April 1538).
19. Lisle Letters V 1139 (John Husee to Lady Lisle, 9 April 1538).
20. Lisle Letters V 1086.
21. Lisle Letters V 1194 (Henry Monk to Lady Lisle, 19 July 1538).
22. Lisle Letters V 1408 (John Husee to Lord Lisle, 12 May 1539).
23. Wilkinson 2009, p. 170.

24. Weir 2011, p. 210.

25. L&P XII pt I 822.

26. L&P XIV pt I 854.

27. L&P XV 611 (nos 22 and 23).

28. Wilkinson 2009, p. 173.

29. L&P XVIII pt I 623 no. 66.

30. Weir 2011, p. 229 states that Mary left a will but this is incorrect. Married women could own no property themselves in Tudor England and, thus, had nothing to leave, even if they had been able to make a legally valid testament.

31. Surrey's Epitaph for Thomas Clere (Surrey, pp. 62–3).

32. *Ibid.*

33. Blomefield 1806, p. 266.

34. Heale 1995, p. 301.

35. Quoted from Heale 1995, p. 313. I have modernised the spelling.

36. Remley 1994, p. 47.

37. Remley 1994, p. 54.

38. Remley 1994, p. 57.

39. Remley 1994, p. 45.

40. Blomefield 1806, pp. 92–3.

41. Alexander Ales in Norton 2011a.

42. Colwell 1888, p. 310.

43. Lady Bryan to Cromwell (Falkus 1974, p. 88).

44. The Second Act of Succession is printed in Williams 1967, p. 452–54.

45. Mary to Henry VIII, 21 July 1536 (L&P XI pp. 70–1).

13   The Notorious Lady Rochford

1. Fox 2007, pp. 219–21.

2. Jane's letter to Cromwell in Norton 2011a, p. 253.

3. Rowley-Williams 1998, p. 165.

4. Cromwell to Lord William Howard and Stephen Gardiner, October 1537 (Merriman 1902, p. 96).

5. Hall 1904, p. 313.

6 The deposition is printed in Strype vol. I pt II 1822, pp. 462–63.

7. Hall 1904, p. 313.

8. Wriothesley's Chronicle, pp. 121–22.

9. Richard Hilles to Henry Bullinger, 10 May 1542 (Robinson 1846, p. 227).

10. Examination of Queen Katherine Howard, p. 10.

11. Catherine Howard to Thomas Culpepper (Crawford 2002, p. 210).

12. Fox 2007, p. 289.

13. Cavendish's Metrical Visions (Norton 2011a, p. 254).

14. Examination of Queen Katherine Howard, p. 10.

15. Examination of Queen Katherine Howard, 12 November 1542 (Bath Manuscripts, pp. 9–10).

16. Examination of Queen Katherine Howard, p. 9.

17. Examination of Queen Katherine Howard, p. 9.

18. Richard Hilles to Henry Bullinger, 10 May 1542 (Robinson 1846, p. 226).

19. Examination of Queen Katherine Howard, p. 10.

20. The details that emerged of Catherine's childhood came from the later examinations of members of the duchess's household, which have been calendared in L&Ps.

21. 'The Confession of the Queen Katherine Howard', November 1541 (in Bath Manuscripts, pp. 8–9).

22. Wriothesley's Chronicle, p. 131.

23. Examination of Queen Katherine Howard, p. 9.

24. Fox 2007, p. 299.

25. Richard Hilles to Henry Bullinger, 10 May 1542 (Robinson 1846, p. 226).

26. CSP VI pt I 207.

27. Rowley-Williams 1998, p. 179.

28. CSP VI pt I 209.

29. Rowley-Williams 1998, p. 182.

30. CSP VI pt I 209.

31. CSP VI pt I 232.

32. CSP VI pt I 209.

33. Hall 1904, p. 314.

34. Minutes of the Privy Council, 11 December 1541 (Nicolas 1837, p. 282).

35. L&P XVII 34.

36. The Bill of Attainder of Queen Katherine Howard (in Williams 1967, p. 488).

37. Wriothesley's Chronicle, p. 133.

38. L&P XVII 100.

39. Wriothesley's Chronicle, p. 134.

40. CSP VI pt I 232.

41. Hall 1904, p. 314.

42. L&P XVII 100.

43. CSP VI pt I 232.

44. Letter 147 (Ellis vol. II).

14   Boleyn Daughters

1. Bundesen 2008, p. 82.

2. Household Expenses of Princess Elizabeth, p. 35.

3. *Ibid.*, p. 39.

4. *Ibid.*, p. 39.

5. Princess Elizabeth to Catherine, Lady Knollys, 1553 (Wood vol. II 1846, p. 280).

6. Household expenses of Princess Elizabeth, p. 35.

7. Burke and Burke 1841, p. 292.

8. Bundesen 2008, p. 77.

9. L&P 18 pt I 832.

10 Bundesen 2008, p. 78.

11. Papers Relating to Mary, Queen of Scots, letter 3.

12. Varlow 2007.

13. *Ibid.*

14. L&P XVIII pt I 483.

15. L&P XVIII pt II 269.

16. Wood vol. II 1846, pp. 176–77.

17. Williams 1967, pp. 452–56 prints the third Act of Succession.

18. Catherine's earlier relationship with Seymour is noted in a letter to him written by her in 1547 (printed in Crawford 2002, p. 222).

19. CSP 9 123–4.

20. John Fowler's Deposition (in Nichols 1862, pp. cxv–cxvi).

21. Quoted from Seymour 1972, p. 216.

22. Wood 1846, pp. 191–92.

23. APC II 238.

24. APC II 2511.

25. Thomas Seymour's conduct with Elizabeth is taken from the Examination of Katherine Ashley on 2 February 1549 and Katherine Ashley's final Handwritten Deposition, late February 1549 (in Marcus, Mueller and Rose 2002, pp. 25–6 and 29–30) and The Confession of Katherine Ashley (Haynes 1740, pp. 99–100).

26. Life of Jane Dormer, pp. 86–7.

27. Gordon, p. 44.

28. Lady Tyrwhit's Deposition from Strickland 1844, pp. 112–13.

29. CSP 9 332 and APC II, 22 and 24 February 1549.

30. Proctor 1902, p. 239.

31. *Vita Mariae Angliae Reginae.*

32. Printed in Marcus, Mueller and Rose, p. 41.

33. Chronicle of Queen Jane, pp. 70–1.

34. Garrett 1966, p. 211.

35. Wood 1846, p. 279.

36. Garrett 1966, p. 211.

37. Garrett 1966, p. 211.

38. Peck 1941, pp. 163, 167 and 174.

39. Varlow 2007.

40. Rodriguez-Salgado and Adams 1984.

15   The Last Boleyn Woman

1. Hayward 1840, p. 6.

2. Camden 1970, p. 24.

3. *Ibid.*, p. 17.

4. Richard Mulcaster's account of Elizabeth's Coronation (Loades 2002, p. 102).

5. Bundesen 2008, p. 86.

6. *Ibid.*, p. 98.

7. Wilson 1923, p. 10.

8. Bundesen 2008.

9. Elizabeth's first speech before Parliament, 10 February 1559 (Marcus, Mueller and Rose 2002, pp. 58–60).

10. Report by Thomas Pope of Elizabeth's answer to a Marriage Proposal from the King of Sweden (Paper 753) (Knighton 1998, p. 331).

11. Somerset 1991, p. 96.

12. Count of Feria to Philip II, 18 April 1559 (Loades 2002, p. 124).

13. Williams 1992, p. 80.

14. Camden 1970, p. 52.

15. *Ibid.*, p. 52.

16. Dudley Knollys, who died in infancy.

17. Camden 1970, p. 53.

18. Count of Feria to Philip II, 18 April 1559 (Loades 2002, p. 125) and Alvarez de Quadra, Bishop of Aquila to Philip II, 31 January 1562 (Loades 2002, p. 125).

19. Hayward 1840, p. 7.

20. Alvarez de Quadra, Bishop of Aquila, to Philip II, 25 October 1562 (Loades 2002, p. 126).

21. Elizabeth to Mary, Queen of Scots, 24 February 1567 (Marcus, Mueller and Rose 2002, p. 116).

22. Camden 1970, p. 68.

23. *Ibid.*, p. 89.

24. Papers Relating to Mary, Queen of Scots, letter 2, 16 July 1568.

25. Papers Relating to Mary, Queen of Scots, letter 3.

26. *Ibid.*

27. Levien 1863, p. 43.

28. *Ibid.*, p. 44.

29. Papers Relating to Mary, Queen of Scots, letter 5.

30. *Ibid.*, letter 3.

31. *Ibid.*, letter 3.

32. *Ibid.*, letter 5.

33. *Ibid.*, letter 17.

34. Mr White to Sir William Cecil, 26 February 1568 [1569 under modern dating] (Haynes 1740, p. 510).

35. Papers Relating to Mary, Queen of Scots, letter 17.

36. *Ibid.*, p. 510.

37. Haynes, p. 509.

38. Papers Relating to Mary, Queen of Scots, letter 19.

39. Sir Thomas Gargrave to the Council, 2 November 1569 (Green 1871, p. 94).

40. Camden 1970, p. 115.

41. John Lee to Lord Burghley, 2 April 1572 (Green 1871, p. 391).

42. Account of the execution of Thomas Howard, Duke of Norfolk, 2 June 1572 (Green 1871, p. 396).

43. Thomas, Earl of Sussex to Lord Burghley, 10 April 1571 (Green 1871, p. 343).

44. Dispatch of Sir Thomas Smith and Sir Henry Killigrew, 8 January 1572 (Loades 2002, p. 163).

45. 'On Monsieur's Departure' by Elizabeth I (Marcus, Mueller and Rose 2002, p. 302).

46. Elizabeth to Alençon, *c.* December 1579 – January 1580 (Marcus, Mueller and Rose 2002, p. 243).

47. Wilson 1923, p. 124.

48. Camden 1970, p. 136.

49. Somerset 1991, p. 127.

50. *Ibid.*, p. 129.

51. Camden 1970, p. 263.

52. *Ibid.*, p. 283.

53. *Ibid.*, p. 290.

54. Elizabeth to James VI, 14 February 1587 (Marcus, Mueller and Rose 2002, p. 296).

55. Camden 1970, p. 312.

56. *Ibid.*, p. 320.

57. Elizabeth's Armada speech to troops at Tilbury, 9 August 1588 (Marcus, Mueller and Rose 2002, p. 326).

58. Camden 1970, p. 328.

59. Perrett 1942, p. 14.

60. Norton 2011b.

61. Secretary Cecil to Essex, 26 July 1597 (Green 1869, p. 473).

62. Somerset 1991, p. 534.

63. Examination of Sir John Davies, 10 February 1601 (Green 1869, p. 548).

64. Letter to Vincent Hussey, 11 February 1601 (Green 1869, p. 550).

65. Speech by the Lord Keeper in the Star Chamber, 13 February 1601 (Green 1869, p. 554).

66. Letter by Vincent Hussey, 11 February 1601 (Green 1869, p. 550).

67. Account of the execution of the Earl of Essex at 8 a.m. in the Tower, 25 February 1601 (Green 1869, p. 594).

68. Elizabeth's Golden Speech, 30 November 1601 (Marcus, Mueller and Rose 2002, p. 340).

69. Anthony Rivers to Giacomo Creleto, Venice, 9 March 1603 (Green 1870, p. 298).

70. Henry Garney to Thomas Lancaster, 9 March 1603 (Green 1870, p. 298).

BIBLIOGRAPHY

Place of publication is London unless otherwise stated.

Manuscript Sources
British Library Add MS 12060: A Book of Miracles and Examples of Virtue for the Guidance of a Ruler, Dedicated to Queen Mary by Henry Parker, Lord Morley.
The National Archives E150/87/6: Inquisition Post Mortem for Margaret Boleyn, Cambridgeshire.
The National Archives PROB 11/18: Will of Thomas Butler, Earl of Ormond.
The National Archives PROB 11/27: Will of Dame Alice Clere.
The National Archives PROB 11/44: Will of Sir James Boleyn.
Worcestershire Record Office 705:349/12946/498729. Bargain of Sale, 12 October 1538.

Primary Printed Sources
Acts of the Privy Council of England, New Series, vol. II, Dasent, J. R. (ed.) (1893) (APC).
Bayne, R. (ed.), *The Life of Fisher* (1921).
Botfield, B. (ed.), 'Accounts and Memoranda of Sir John Howard, First Duke of Norfolk, AD 1462, to AD 1471' in *Manners and Household*

Expenses of England in the Thirteenth and Fifteenth Centuries Illustrated by Original Records (1841).

Brantôme, Seigneur de, *Lives of Fair and Gallant Ladies.*

Bray, G. (ed.), *Documents of the English Reformation* (Cambridge, 1994).

Calendar of State Papers Domestic Series of the Reign of Edward VI 1547–1553, Knighton, C. S. (ed.) (1992).

Calendar of State Papers Domestic Series, Elizabeth, 5 vols and Addenda, Green, M. A. E. and R. Lemon (eds) (1865–71).

Calendar of State Papers, Spanish, vol. IX, Gayangos, P. de., M. A. S. Hume and R. Tyler (eds) (1949).

Calendar of the Carew Manuscripts Preserved in the Archiepiscopal Library at Lambeth 1515–1574, Brewer, J. S. and W. Bullen (eds) (1867).

Calendar of the Close Rolls Preserved in the Public Record Office, Henry VII Volume II 1500–1509 (1963).

Calendar of the Close Rolls Preserved in the Public Record Office, Richard II Volume III 1385–1389 (1921).

Calendar of the Fine Rolls Preserved in the Public Record Office, vols XVIII–XXII (1939–1962).

Calendar of the Patent Rolls Preserved in the Public Record Office, Edward IV 1461–1467 (1897).

Calendar of the Patent Rolls Preserved in the Public Record Office, Edward IV, Edward V, Richard III 1476–1485 (1901).

Calendar of the Patent Rolls Preserved in the Public Record Office, Henry VI Volume VI 1452–1461 (1910).

Camden, W., *The History of the Most Renowned and Virtuous Princess Elizabeth, Late Queen of England*, MacCaffrey, W. T. (ed.) (Chicago, 1970).

Cavendish, W., *The Life of Cardinal Wolsey*, Singer, S. W. (ed.) (1825).

Clifford, H., *The Life of Jane Dormer Duchess of Feria*, Estcourt, E. E. and J. Stevenson (eds) (1887).

Collier, J. P. (ed.), *Household Books of John Duke of Norfolk and Thomas Earl of Surrey Temp. 1481–1490* (1844).

Colwell, T. in *Historical Manuscripts Commission, Twelfth Report, Appendix, Part IV: The Manuscripts of his Grace the Duke of Rutland, vol. I* (1888).

Constantine, G., 'Transcript of an Original Manuscript, Containing a Memorial from George Constantyne to Thomas Lord Cromwell', Amyot, T. (ed.), *Archaeologia*, 23 (1831).

Crawford, A., *Letters of the Queens of England* (Stroud, 2002).

Ellis, H., *Original Letters Illustrative of English History, First Series vol. II and Third Series vol. II* (London, 1824 and 1846).

Falkus, C. (ed.), *The Private Lives of the Tudor Monarchs* (1974).

Grace, J., *Jacobi Grace, Kilkenniensis, Annales Hiberniae*, Butler, R. (ed.) (Dublin, 1842).

Gurney, D. (ed.), 'Extracts from the Household and Privy Purse Accounts of the Lestranges of Hunstanton, From AD 1519 to AD 1578', *Archaeologia*, 25 (1833).

Hall, E., *Hall's Chronicle Containing the History of England During the Reigne of Henry IV and Succeeding Monarchs to the End of the Reign of Henry VIII* (1809).

Hall, E., *The Triumphant Reign of King Henry the VIII, vol. II*, Whibley, C. (ed.) (1904).

Harpsfield, N., *A Treatise on the Pretended Divorce Between Henry VIII and Catherine of Aragon* (1878).

Haynes, S. (ed.), *Collection of State Papers Relating to Affairs in the Reigne of King Henry VIII, Edward VI, Queen Mary and Queen Elizabeth (from the year 1542 to 1570 Transcribed from the Original Letters and Other Authentick Memorials left by William Cecil* (1740).

Hayward, J., *Annals of the First Four Years of the Reign of Queen Elizabeth*, Bruce, J. (ed.) (1840).

Hazlitt, W. C. (ed.), *Remains of the Early Popular Poetry of England, vol. II* (London, 1866).

Hervey, W. and J. Raven, *The Visitation of Norfolk Made and Taken in 1563 and 1613*, Rye, W. (ed.) (London, 1891).

Historical Manuscripts Commission: Calendar of the Manuscripts of the Marquis of Bath, vol. II (Dublin, 1907).

Horrox, R. and P. W. Hammond (eds), *British Library Harleian Manuscript 433, vol. I* (Gloucester, 1974).

Household Expenses of the Princess Elizabeth During her Residence at Hatfield October, 1, 1551, to September 30, 1552, Strangford, Viscount (ed.) (1853).

Jefferson, L. (ed.), *The Medieval Account Books of the Mercers of London, vol. I and II* (Farnham, 2009).

Latymer, W., 'William Latymer's Cronickille of Anne Bulleyne', Dowling, M. (ed.), *Camden Miscellany*, 30.

Letters and Papers, Foreign and Domestic, of the Reign of Henry VIII, vols I–XXI, Brewer, J., J. Gairdner and R. H. Brodie (eds) (1876–1932).

Lincolnshire Pedigrees, vol. III, Maddison, A. R. (ed.) (1904).

Loades, D. (ed.), *The Chronicles of the Tudor Queens* (Stroud, 2002).

Lyell, L. and F. D. Watney (eds), *Acts of the Mercers' Company* (Cambridge, 1936).

Marcus, L. S., J. Mueller and L. B. Rose (eds), *Elizabeth I, Collected Works* (Chicago, 2002).

Merriman, R. B. (ed.), *Life and Letters of Thomas Cromwell, vol. II* (Oxford, 1902).

Naunton, R., *Fragmenta Regalia: Memoirs of Elizabeth, Her Court and Favourites* (1824).

Nicolas, H. (ed.), *Proceedings and Ordinances of the Privy Council of England, vol. VII 1540–1542* (1837).

Nicolas, J. G. (ed.), *Literary Remains of King Edward the Sixth* (1862).

Norfolk Lists from the Reformation to the Present Time (Norwich, 1837).

Norton, E., *Anne Boleyn in Her Own Words and the Words of Those Who Knew Her* (Stroud, 2011a).

'Papers Relating to Mary, Queen of Scots, Mostly Addressed to or Written by Sir Francis Knollys', *Philobilon Society Miscellanies*, 14 (1872).

Philipot, J., *The Visitation of Kent, Taken in the Years 1619–1621*, Hoveden, R. (ed.) (London, 1898).

Privy Purse Expenses of Elizabeth of York and Wardrobe Accounts of Edward the Fourth, Nicholas, N. H. (ed.) (1830).

Privy Purse Expenses of the Princess Mary, Madden, F., (ed.)

Proctor, J., 'The History of Wyatt's Rebellion' in Pollard, A. F. (ed.), *Tudor Tracts* (1903).

Registrum Thome Bourgchier Cantuariensis Archiepiscopi 1454–1486, Boulay, F. R. H. (ed.) (Oxford, 1957).

Robinson, H. (ed.), *Original Letters Relative to the English Reformation, vol. I* (Cambridge, 1846).

Rodriguez-Salgado, M. J. and S. Adams (eds), 'Count of Feria's Despatch to Philip II of 14 November 1558', *Camden Miscellany*, fourth series, 28 (1984).

Rutland Papers: Original Documents Illustrative of the Life and Times of Henry VII and Henry VIII Selected from the Private Archives of his Grace the Duke of Rutland, Jerdan, W. (ed.) (1842).

Sander, N., *The Rise and Growth of the Anglican Schism*, Lewis, D. (ed.) (1877).

'Select Cases before the king's council of the Star Chamber commonly called the court of the Star Chamber 1477–1509', L. S. Leadam (ed.), *Selden Society*, XVI (1903).

Skelton, J., *The Complete Poems of John Skelton*, Henderson, P. (ed.) (1931).

Spelman, J., *The Reports of Sir John Spelman*, Baker, J. H. (1977).

St Clare Byrne, M. (ed.), *The Letters of King Henry VIII* (1968).

Strype, J. (ed.), *Ecclesiastical Memorials, vol. I pt II* (London, 1822).

Surrey, Henry Howard, Earl of, *The Poems of Henry Howard, Earl of Surrey* (1831).

Testamenta Vetusta, 2 vols, Nicolas, N. H. (ed.) (London, 1826).

The Chronicle of Calais, Nichols, J. G. (ed.) (1846).

The Chronicle of Queen Jane, and of Two Years of Queen Mary, Nichols, J. G. (ed.) (1849).

The Lisle Letters, 5 vols, St Clair Byrne, M. (ed.) (1981).

The Paston Letters, 3 vols, Gairdner, J. (ed.) (Westminster, 1896).

Udall, N., 'English Verses and Ditties at the Coronation Procession of Queen Anne Boleyn' in Pollard, A. F. (ed.), *Tudor Tracts* (1903).

Williams, C. H. (ed.), *English Historical Documents, vol. V* (1967).

Wills from Doctors' Commons, Nichols, J. G. and J. Bruce (eds) (1863).

Wingfield, R., 'The Vita Mariae Angliae Reginae of Robert Wingfield', MacCulloch, D. (ed.), *Camden Miscellany*, fourth series, 28 (1984).

Wood, M. A. E. (ed.), *Letters of Royal and Illustrious Ladies, vols II and III* (1846).

Worde, W. de, 'The Noble and Triumphant Coronation of Queen Anne' in Pollard, A. F. (ed.), *Tudor Tracts* (1903).

Wriothesley, C., *A Chronicle of England During the Reigns of the Tudors, vol. I*, Hamilton, W. D. (ed.) (1875).

Wyatt, G., 'Extracts from the Life of the Virtuous Christian and Renowned Queen Anne Boleigne' in Singer, S. W. (ed.), *The Life of Cardinal Wolsey* (1825).

Wyatt, T., *Collected Poems*, Daalder, J. (ed.) (1975).

Secondary Sources

'Antiquarian Researches – Sussex Archaeological Society', *The Gentleman's Magazine*, new series, XLIV (1855).

Armstrong, M. J., *History and Antiquities of the County of Norfolk, vol. III* (Norwich, 1781).

Badham, S., 'Brass of the Month, May 2011 – Geoffrey Boleyn, 1440, and Wife Alice, Salle, Norfolk' (Monumental Brass Society, www.mbs-brasses.co.uk).

Banks, T. C., *Baronia Anglica Concentrata, vol. I* (1844).

Bannerman, W. B. (ed.), *Miscellanea Genealogica Et Heraldica, vol. II* (4th series, 1908).

Bindoff, S. T. (ed.), *The History of Parliament: The House of Commons 1509–1558* (1982).

Blomefield, F. and C. Parkin, *An Essay Towards a Topographical History of the County of Norfolk, vol. III* (Lynn).

Blomefield, F., *An Essay Towards A Topographical History of Norfolk, vol. V* (1806).

Blomfield, J. C., *Deanery of Bicester Part VII: History of Fritwell and Souldern* (1893).

Bradley, S. and N. Pevsner, *The Buildings of England: London I: The City of London* (2002).

Burke, B., *A Genealogical History of the Dormant, Abeyant, Forfeited, and Extinct Peerages of the British Empire* (1866).

Burke, J. and J. B., *A Genealogical and Heraldic History of the Extinct and Dormant Baronetcies of England, Ireland and Scotland* (1841).

Burke, J., *A Genealogical and Heraldic History of the Extinct and Dormant Baronetcies of England* (1832).

Burnet, G., *The History of the Reformation of the Church of England, vol. I*, Pocock, N. (ed.) (Oxford, 1865).

Carte, T., *The Life of James Duke of Ormond, vol. I* (Oxford, 1851).

Casady, E., *Henry Howard, Earl of Surrey* (New York, 1975).

Cooper, C. H., *Memorials of Cambridge, vol. I* (Cambridge, 1860).

Cooper, W. D., 'The Families of Braose of Chesworth, and Hoo', *Sussex Archaeological Collections*, 8 (1856).

Crawford, A., *Yorkist Lord: John Howard, Duke of Norfolk c. 1425–1485* (2010).

Dowling, M., 'Anne Boleyn and Reform', *Journal of Ecclesiastical History*, 35 (1984).

Duffy, E., 'Salle Church and the Reformation' in Tracy, J. D. and M. Ragnow (eds), *Religion and the Early Modern State: Views from China, Russia, and the West* (Cambridge, 2004).

Elton, G. R., 'Presidential Address: The Tudor Government: The Points of Contact. III. The Court', *Transactions of the Royal Historical Society*, fifth series, 26 (1976).

Fenlon, J., 'Episodes of Magnificence: The Material Worlds of the Dukes of Ormonde' in Barnard, T. and J. Fenlon (eds), *The Dukes of Ormonde, 1610–1745* (Woodbridge, 2000).

Fox, J., *Jane Boleyn* (2007).

Fraser, A., *The Six Wives of Henry VIII* (1992).

Garrett, C. H., *The Marian Exiles* (Cambridge, 1966).

Gordon, M. A., *Life of Queen Katharine Parr* (Kendal).

Grant, N., *The Howards of Norfolk* (1972).

Gurney, D., *Supplement to the Record of the House of Gournay* (King's Lynn, 1858).

Guy, J. A., 'Henry VIII and the Praemunire Manoeuvres of 1530–1531', *English Historical Review*, 97 (1982).

Harris, B. J., *English Aristocratic Women 1450–1550* (Oxford, 2002).

Harris. B. J., 'Space, Time, and the Power of Aristocratic Wives in Yorkist and Early Tudor England, 1450–1550' in Schutte, A. J., T. Kuehn and S. Menchi (eds), *Time, Space, and Women's Lives in Early Modern Europe* (Kirksville, 2001).

Hart, K., *The Mistresses of Henry VIII* (Stroud, 2009).

Heale, E., 'Women and the Courtly Love Lyric: The Devonshire MS (BL Additional 17492)', *Modern Language Review*, 90 (1995), pp. 296–313.

Herbert, E., *The Life and Raigne of King Henry the Eighth* (1649).

Hoskins, A., 'Mary Boleyn's Carey Children: Offspring of King Henry VIII?', *Genealogists' Magazine*, 25 (1997).

Hunter, J., *Hallamshire: The History and Topography of the Parish of Sheffield in the County of York* (1819).

Ives, E., *The Life and Death of Anne Boleyn* (Oxford, 2005).

Jones, P., *The Other Tudors* (2009).

Loades, D., *The Boleyns* (Stroud, 2011).

Mate, M. E., *Daughters, Wives and Widows After the Black Death: Women in Sussex, 1350–1535* (Woodbridge, 1998).

Norton, E., *Bessie Blount* (Stroud, 2011b).

Norton, E., *Margaret Skipwith of Ormesby: A Lincolnshire Mistress to Henry VIII* (Lincolnshire History and Archaeology, 2013b forthcoming).

Norton, E., *The Reeds of Oatlands: A Tudor Marriage Settlement* (Surrey History, 2013a forthcoming).

Oosterwijk, S., 'Chrysoms, Shrouds and Infants: A Question of Terminology', *Church Monuments*, XV (2000).

Orridge, B. B., *Some Account of the Citizens of London and their Rulers, from 1060–1867* (1867).

Parsons, W. L. E., 'Some Notes on the Boleyn Family', *Norfolk Archaeology*, 25 (1935).

Parsons, W. L. E., *Salle: The Story of a Norfolk Parish and Its Church, Manors and People* (Norwich, 1937).

Peck, G. T., 'John Hales and the Puritans During the Marian Exile', *Church History*, 10 (1941).

Perrett, A. J., 'The Blounts of Kidderminster', *Transactions of the Worcestershire Archaeological Society*, 19 (1942).

Polinaeus, 'London Arms on Clere Brass' in Tymms, S. (ed.), *The East Anglian; or, Notes and Queries on Subjects Connected with the Counties of Suffolk, Cambridge, Essex & Norfolk, vol. I* (Lowestoft, 1864).

Remley, P. G., 'Mary Sheton and her Tudor Literary Milieu' in Herman, P. C. (ed.), *Rethinking the Henrician Era* (1994, Illinois).

Richardson, D., *Magna Carta Ancestry* (Baltimore, 2005).

Round, J. H., 'The Earldom of Ormond in Ireland' in Foster, J. (ed.), *Collectanea Genealogica* (1881).

Russell, J. G., *The Field of the Cloth of Gold* (1969).

Saul, N., *English Church Monuments in the Middle Ages* (Oxford, 2009).

Some Account of the Family of the Butlers, But Most Particularly of the Late Duke of Ormond, the Earl of Ossory his Father, and James Duke of Ormond his Grandfather (1716).

Somerset, A., *Elizabeth I* (1991).

Somerset, A., *Ladies in Waiting* (1984).

Tempest, E. B., 'The Manor of Great Houghton', *The Yorkshire Archaeological Society Record Series*, 94, Miscellanea IV (1937).

The Harleian Miscellany IX (1810).

Tucker, M. J., 'The Ladies in Skelton's "Garland of Laurel"', *Renaissance Quarterly*, 22(4) (1969).

Tucker, M. J., *The Life of Thomas Howard Earl of Surrey and Second Duke of Norfolk 1443–1524* (1964).

Varlow, S., 'Sir Francis Knolly's Latin Dictionary: New Evidence for Katherine Carey', *Historical Research*, 80 (2007).

Venn, J., *Biographical History of Gonville and Caius College* (1897).

Victoria County History: A History of the County of Cambridge and the Isle of Ely, vol. 9, Wright, A. P. M. and C. P. Lewis (eds). (1989).

Walker, G., 'Rethinking the Fall of Anne Boleyn', *The Historical Journal*, 45 (2002).

Warnicke, R., 'Family and Kinship Relations at the Henrician Court: The Boleyns and Howards' in Hoak, D. (ed.), *Tudor Political Culture* (Cambridge, 1995).

Warnicke, R., *The Rise and Fall of Anne Boleyn* (Cambridge, 1989).

Watney, J., *Some Account of the Hospital of St. Thomas of Acon, in the Cheap, London, and of the Plate of the Mercers' Company* (1906).

Weir, A., *Mary Boleyn* (2011).

Whitaker, A. E., 'The Shelton Family', *The William and Mary Quarterly*, second series, 9(3) (July 1929).

Wilkinson, J., *Mary Boleyn* (Stroud, 2009).

Williams, N., *The Life and Times of Elizabeth I* (1992).

Wilson, V. A., *Queen Elizabeth's Maids of Honour* (1923).

Wotton, T., *The Baronetage of England, vol. I* (1771).

Unpublished PhD Theses

Bundesen, K., '"No Other Faction But My Own": Dynastic Politics and Elizabeth I's Carey Cousins' (University of Nottingham, 2008).

Leonard, H., 'Knights and Knighthood in Tudor England' (University of London, 1970).

Rowley-Williams, J. A., 'Image and Reality: The Lives of Aristocratic Women in Early Tudor England' (University of Wales, 1998).

Samman, N., 'The Henrician Court During Cardinal Wolsey's Ascendancy *c.* 1514–1529' (University of Wales, 1988).

Vokes, S. E., 'The Early Career of Thomas, Lord Howard, Earl of Surrey and Third Duke of Norfolk, 1474 – *c.* 1525' (University of Wales, 1988).

LIST OF ILLUSTRATIONS

1. The Boleyn women genealogical table.
2. Blickling Hall, Norfolk. Blickling became the seat of the Boleyns in the fifteenth century. A later house now stands on the site of the Boleyn family residence. (© Elizabeth Norton)
3. Blickling church. The parish church, sited next to the manor, would have been familiar to the early Boleyn women. (© Elizabeth Norton)
4. The Boleyn chantry chapel in Norwich Cathedral. William Boleyn asked to be buried here, close to his mother, Anne Hoo Boleyn. (© Elizabeth Norton)
5. Isabel Cheyne Boleyn from her memorial brass at Blickling church. Isabel, who was the daughter of William Boleyn and Anne Hoo, was buried at her family home following her early death. (© Elizabeth Norton)
6. Anne Boleyn, eldest daughter of William Boleyn and Margaret Butler, from her memorial brass at Blickling church. Anne died in childhood and a younger sister, Anne Boleyn, Lady Shelton, was later named after her. (© Elizabeth Norton)
7. The remains of the funeral monument to Anne Hoo Boleyn in Norwich Cathedral. Sadly, the memorial brass for the first Anne Boleyn has long since disappeared. (© Elizabeth Norton)
8. Cecily Boleyn from her memorial brass at Blickling church. The sister of Geoffrey Boleyn, Lord Mayor of London, joined him at Blickling following his purchase of the manor. (© Elizabeth Norton)
9. Hever Castle, Kent. Margaret Butler Boleyn spent her last years at Hever, which was also the family home of her son, Sir Thomas Boleyn. (© Elizabeth Norton)
10, 11, 12, 13, 14. Anne Boleyn, Lady Shelton, and her husband, Sir John Shelton, depicted at various stages of their lives in stained glass at Shelton church, Norfolk. (© Elizabeth Norton)

from Hampton Court. Henry tried to erase all memory of his second wife, Anne Boleyn. (© Elizabeth Norton)

32. A romantic depiction of the execution of Anne Boleyn. The queen was beheaded with a sword – a kinder death than a clumsy axe. (© Jonathan Reeve, JR965b20p921 15001600)

33. Princess Mary. Anne Boleyn, Lady Shelton, found her young charge a troublesome burden when she was appointed as her governess. (© Elizabeth Norton)

34. Catherine Howard, the queen whose indiscretions led Jane Boleyn to the block. (© Elizabeth Norton & the Amberley Archive)

35. Traitor's Gate. Anne Boleyn was taken to the Tower of London by water and reputedly passed through this gate. (© Elizabeth Norton)

36. The Tower of London. Anne Boleyn, her sister-in-law, Jane Boleyn, and daughter, Princess Elizabeth, were all imprisoned in the ancient fortress. (© Elizabeth Norton)

37. A memorial marking the supposed site of the scaffold on Tower Green where both Anne and Jane Boleyn died. (© Elizabeth Norton)

38. The Bishop's Palace at Lincoln, where Jane Boleyn led Thomas Culpepper to a secret nocturnal meeting with the queen. (Elizabeth Norton)

39. Mary Shelton. The daughter of Lady Shelton was a poet with remarkably modern views about love, becoming a mistress of Henry VIII in her youth. (© Elizabeth Norton & the Amberley Archive)

40. Henry Howard, Earl of Surrey, who was reputed to have been romantically involved with his friend, Mary Shelton. (© Elizabeth Norton)

41. Catherine Carey and her husband, Sir Francis Knollys, from their memorial at Rotherfield Greys in Oxfordshire. (© Elizabeth Norton)

42. The six daughters of Catherine Carey (and one daughter-in-law). Lettice Knollys, the second daughter, is first in the line depicted at Rotherfield Greys. (© Elizabeth Norton)

43. Robert Dudley, Earl of Leicester, from his tomb in Warwick. Dudley was Elizabeth I's greatest favourite, with speculation that the pair would marry. (© Elizabeth Norton)

44. Lettice Knollys from her tomb in Warwick. Lettice's royal cousin never forgave her for secretly marrying Robert Dudley. (© Elizabeth Norton)

45. Robert Dudley, the only child of Lettice Knollys' second marriage, who died young. (© Elizabeth Norton)

46. Hatfield House. Elizabeth I was resident at the palace when she discovered that she had become queen. (© Elizabeth Norton)

47. Princess Elizabeth as a child. (© Jonathan Reeve, JR997b66fp40 15001600)

48. Elizabeth I as queen. Anne Boleyn's daughter was the greatest, and the last, of the Boleyn women. (© Jonathan Reeve, JR1168b4fp747 15501600)

INDEX

Tudor History from Amberley Publishing

THE TUDORS
Richard Rex

'The best introduction to England's most important dynasty'
DAVID STARKEY

'Gripping and told with enviable narrative skill... a delight'
THES

'Vivid, entertaining and carrying its learning lightly'
EAMON DUFFY

'A lively overview' **THE GUARDIAN**

£9.99   978-1-4456-0700-9   256 pages PB 143 illus., 66 col

CATHERINE HOWARD
Lacey Baldwin Smith

'A brilliant, compelling account' **ALISON WEIR**

'A faultless book' **THE SPECTATOR**

'Lacey Baldwin Smith has so excellently caught the
atmosphere of the Tudor age' **THE OBSERVER**

£9.99   978-1-84868-521-5   256 pages PB 25 col illus

MARGARET OF YORK
Christine Weightman

'A pioneering biography of the Tudor dynasty's most
dangerous enemy'
PROFESSOR MICHAEL HICKS

'Christine Weightman brings Margaret alive once more'
THE YORKSHIRE POST

'A fascinating account of a remarkable woman'
THE BIRMINGHAM POST

£10.99   978-1-4456-0819-8   256 pages PB 51 illus

THE SIX WIVES OF HENRY VIII
David Loades

'Neither Starkey nor Weir has the assurance and command
of Loades' **SIMON HEFFER, LITERARY REVIEW**

'Incisive and profound. I warmly recommend this book'
ALISON WEIR

£9.99   978-1-4456-0049-9   256 pages PB 55 illus, 31 col

MARY ROSE
David Loades

£20.00 978-1-4456-0622-4
272 pages HB 17 col illus

MARY BOLEYN
Josephine Wilkinson

£9.99 978-1-84868-525-3
208 pages PB 22 illus, 10 col

JANE SEYMOUR
Elizabeth Norton

£9.99 978-1-84868-527-7
224 pages PB 53 illus, 26 col

HENRY VIII
Richard Rex

£9.99 978-1-84868-098-2
192 pages PB 81 illus, 48 col

THOMAS CROMWELL
Patrick Coby

£20.00 978-1-4456-0775-7
272 pages HB 30 illus (20 col)

ANNE BOLEYN THE YOUNG QUEEN TO BE
Josephine Wilkinson

£9.99 978-1-4456-0395-7
208 pages PB 34 illus (19 col)

ELIZABETH I
Richard Rex

£9.99 978-1-84868-423-2
192 pages PB 75 illus

ANNE OF CLEVES
Elizabeth Norton

£9.99 978-1-4456-0183-0
224 pages HB 54 illus, 27 col

Available from all good bookshops or to order direct
Please call **01453-847-800 www.amberleybooks.com**